THE CLEVELAND 200

The Most Noted, Notable & Notorious in the First 200 Years of A Great American City

by

THOMAS KELLY

With Contributing Authors

GEORGE CONDON
CHUCK HEATON
MARC JAFFE
CRISFIELD JOHNSON
MARY ANNE SHARKEY

Introduction by **DICK FEAGLER**

ARCHIVES PRESS

PRINTED IN THE U.S.A.

ISBN #0-9644509-2-5

Library of Congress Catalogue-In-Publication Data

The Cleveland 200.

1. Cleveland (Ohio)—History—Biographies.
2. Cuyahoga County, Ohio—History—Biographies.

    I. Kelly, Thomas.
    II. Condon, George.
    III. Heaton, Chuck (Charles).
    IV. Jaffe, Marc.
    V. Sharkey, Mary Anne.

FIRST EDITION PRINTING: JULY, 1996

ACKNOWLEDGMENTS

The Cleveland 200 is overloaded with testosterone. Sorry. Historic injustice precluded women's participation in most public arenas over the past two centuries and remains a deterrent today. It may be small consolation, but at least the acknowledgments in this book can offer a token of compensation by excluding all males solely on the basis of sexual discrimination. Call it the *Cleveland 200 Affirmative Action Plan*.

Many sincere thanks to Wendy Lewis, Jan Leitch, Dr. Karen Jaffe, Sharon Coughlin, Maggie Rogers, Helga Sandburg Crile, Cathy Kraft, Terri DeChant, Dorothy Grim, Charlotte Auroux, Mary Conway Sullivan, Madison Mars, Susan Unik, Jane Walborn, Helen Moise, Anne Comptois, Catherine Boyle, Christine Burke, Angel Joseph, Susan Pollock, Kim Van Valkenberg, Beth Lucas, Eleanor Fanslau, Maureen Pergola, Christine Burke, Mary Beth Barabas, Karen Climaco, Sandra Sullivan, Courtney Maroon, Sarah Rego, Dorothy Sheehan, Susie Kirby, Ann Phifer, Elizabeth Dotson, Elaine Simmons, Colleen Yanatchko. Special thanks to Hannah, Emma, Dana, Paula, Melissa, Tara, Lori, Kathy, Susie Q, Bernadine & Marietta. And Anne Sheehan Kelly, #1 on another list.

Photo Consultant: **William Becker**
Photo Credits: **CSU Archives, *Press* Collection**
Content Editing: **Nancy Walters**
Format Editing: **Joseph Lake**

Cover & Interior Design
by
ANNE COWIN NEW YORK

DEDICATION

To The Unknown Clevelanders

Burdened by the weight of life, shorn of illusion, bruised by defeat, tempered by tragedy, they have toiled through the longest days, kept watch through the darkest nights, built our homes, paved our roads, stoked our fires and raised our children.

Never knowing wealth or power, never asking for glory or fame, they have given comfort to the sick, aid to the poor, counsel to the troubled and example to the young.

They have kept calm in times of crisis, kept strong when others wavered, kept hope when others despaired, kept faith when all was lost.

Mothers and fathers, sisters and brothers, friends and neighbors, they gave Cleveland everything they had and left with nothing but their shining souls.

Cleveland is their monument.

CONTENTS

FORWARD

The world's richest man. The most decorated civilian on earth. An American President. The most powerful politician the nation has ever known. So many billionaires and Nobel prize winners that some of them didn't make the cut. Famous senators and congressmen, Supreme Court justices, world renowned statesmen.

A cardinal, two bishops, the first woman rabbi, courageous missionaries and inspiring religious orators. Legendary pioneers and frontiersmen.

America's best architect. America's favorite leading man. The most honored female writer. The most popular composer. The best conductor. The father of TV talk shows, two great actresses, the foremost female television journalist, a lovable kids' show host and a goofy ghoulmeister. The most popular superhero, the funniest cartoon character.

The first black author in America, the first black talk show host, the first black resident of the Western Reserve, the black woman whose fight for freedom made history, the first black mayor in America, the greatest black inventor, the most famous black poet.

The foremost American Indian spokesman, the last great Indian chief.

The first newspaper columnist, the best newspaper editor, the patriarch of modern media and the first communications mogul in the world. Award-winning journalists. Famously tragic poets.

The inventor of the generator and the modern electric light, the gas mask, oil refining, auto manufacturing, global communication, the VCR, the Black Box, audio tape, hair straightener, high performance engines, video tape, the rotary bobbin, prepared food, modern x-ray technology and the clothes pin.

The first neurosurgeon, the best heart surgeon, the leading pediatrician, the dean of pharmacology. Founder of the world's pre-eminent hospital. Esteemed medical researchers and authors.

The finest athlete in professional sports, the winningest coach ever, the greatest pitcher, the wildest owner, the first black player, the greatest black pitcher, the most successful female athlete. The fastest man in the world.

Civil War heroes, Spanish-American War heroes, World War I leaders, World War II Medal of Honor winners, honored military strategists.

The first serial killer, the world's leading pornographer, foremost art swindler, the leader of the Communist party, the Mafia chieftain, the numbers kingpin and the most notorious murder case in the nation for 40 years. And, maybe, the most famous war criminal since Eichmann.

The first woman lawyer, woman judge, female power broker, leaders of the WCTU, suffragettes, the most famous female photographer, the greatest philanthropist, most honored educator, most celebrated black performer and the most influential women in Cleveland's civic and social history.

The founder of rock and roll, the man who made Elvis, the ruler of sports marketing, the father of modern advertising, the mastermind of the federal banking system, the man who ended polio, the most powerful union boss, the man who gave us Medicare and the most respected political crusader.

They can't all be from one place, can they? Sure they can. But only if it's Cleveland. Why do you think they call it the Best Location in the Nation? Not because of the natural beauty, nice as it is. Not because of the prime location, even though its handy for travel and commerce. And certainly not because of the weather.

It's the people. People of Cleveland. A melting pot of iron ore, crude oil, forged steel, pulp wood, muddy water...and gold.

INTRODUCTION

by

Dick Feagler

Author Thomas Kelly assures me that this book was written mainly for the fun of it. It is full of history but does not claim to be a grave historical work. It is chock full of small biographies but they deal with zany antics as much as gallant deeds. It is a book about characters, for characters are what gives a city its character.

As a lifelong Clevelander, I have always been troubled by a certain deceptive blandness that is misleading about our town. Our public square is named Public Square, our public auditorium is called Public Auditorium, and sometimes Public Hall. The old stadium on the lakefront was called, alternatively, Lakefront Stadium or Municipal Stadium.There is no romance in any of these names. No allure. No poetry.

The unfortunate exception is Terminal Tower, so called because it is a tower erected over what was once the train terminal. This name, Terminal Tower, which natives find unremarkable, falls gruesomely upon the ears of visitors to our town. To them it speaks of fatal illness and living wills. Some of them shudder when they hear it. They don't realize that it is just another lifeless name for an inanimate landmark.

But the people who wrote the story of our city were far from lackluster. Some of them were visionaries, some were scoundrels, some were half nuts and some were a mixture of all these elements.

The Van Sweringen Brothers, Orris and Mantis, built the Terminal Tower. Their ambitions as developers made Donald Trump look like a kid playing with Lego blocks. An office building wasn't enough for them. They added a residential bedroom community (Shaker Heights) and a rail line (the Shaker Rapid). In the end, their dreams turned on them and they went broke. But they left a civic symbol as a legacy. Their story is in this book.

As is the story of Albert "Starlight" Boyd, an African American who came north toward the end of the last century and made his mark in Cleveland politics. He loved diamonds, and the twinkling stones on the fingers of both his hands gave him his nickname.

Starlight Boyd was once a political power broker with the clout to deliver thousands of votes in any election. But his star flickered and fell and his deeds slept in darkness until they were awakened within these pages.

Kelly assures me that the selection process used to assemble the cast of characters herein was precisely arbitrary. He included people who struck his fancy and omitted some significant achievers who did not. It was that simple. There were, however, a set of flexible guidelines. Fame was an admission ticket, but so was notoriety, which is the gaudy and unsavory brother of fame. Money helped but was not necessary. A lifetime of Cleveland service was a plus. If a character committed the sin of moving out, he had to make a substantial contribution to the world to compensate enough to warrant inclusion.

Are the very best Clevelanders of all time on this list? In a word, no. Some of them are in here and some of them are not. The best of humanity is not often found in headlines, motorcades or history books. This is, in many ways, a book of unusual people; some of them noble, some driven, some lucky, some ornery and some just plain ridiculous.

But all of them are, or were, Clevelanders. And in this monumental birthday year---the Big Two-Oh-Oh---their little stories remind us of the great, unchronicled treasure trove of humanity that lived here and schemed here and won here and sinned here, and then exited the stage.

For our town is a stage. Its drama has run for two centuries and is nowhere near closing. The plot was shaped by greed and grit and smoke and smell and molten metal and immigrants and lust and self-sacrifice. As the pages of our history turned, the characters herein moved from the wings on cue, did their little specialty numbers to mixed applause, then vanished.

They were anything but bland. This book welcomes them back for a curtain call.

THE CLEVELAND 200

ROLL CALL

1. *John D. Rockefeller*
2. *Lorenzo Carter*
3. *Alfred Kelley & Family*
4. *Cyrus Eaton*
5. *Tom L. Johnson*
6. *Marc Hanna*
7. *Bob Hope*
8. *Charles Brush*
9. *Henry Flagler*
10. *Frederick Crawford*
11. *The Van Sweringens*
12. *Superman*
13. *Eliot Ness*
14. *Jeptha Wade*
15. *Newton D. Baker*
16. *Leonard Case & Family*
17. *George Crile & Family*
18. *Louis Seltzer*
19. *Jared Potter Kirtland*
20. *The Stokes Brothers*
21. *The Severance Family*
22. *Garrett Morgan*
23. *Andrew Squire*
24. *Paul Newman*
25. *Charles Thompson*
26. *The Payne Family*
27. *The Mather Family*
28. *Toni Morrison*
29. *Alexander Winton*
30. *George Peake*
31. *Edward W. Scripps*
32. *Seneca*
33. *Frances Payne Bolton*
34. *Alva Bradley & Family*
35. *Henry Chisholm*
36. *Charles Otis & Family*
37. *Florence E. Allen*
38. *Henry Mancini*
39. *Edwin Cowles*
40. *James Garfield*
41. *Philip Johnson*
42. *Langston Hughes*
43. *Thomas White*
44. *Dorothy Fuldheim*
45. *Charles Chestnutt*
46. *Paul Brown*
47. *Amadeus Rappe*
48. *The Lincoln Brothers*
49. *Jim Brown*
50. *George Hulett*
51. *Oghema Niagara*
52. *Harold Burton*
53. *Artemus Ward*
54. *William Hopkins*
55. *Abba Hillel Silver*
56. *Bill Randle*
57. *Ned Jordan*
58. *Sam Sheppard*
59. *Anthony Celebrezze*
60. *Semi Begun*
61. *Charles Whittlesey*
62. *George Gund & Family*
63. *William Howard Day*
64. *Bob Feller*
65. *Luther Day & Family*
66. *Henry Sherwin*
67. *Joseph Gray*
68. *Theodore Burton*
69. *George Szell*
70. *William W. Armstrong*
71. *Fred Kohler*
72. *Reuben Wood*
73. *The Humphrey Family*
74. *Mike Douglas*
75. *Hector Boiardi*
76. *Leon Csolgosz*
77. *Linda Eastman*
78. *Don Shula*
79. *The Baldwin Families*
80. *Irene & Joel Scranton*
81. *The Mad Butcher*
82. *John Patterson Green*
83. *Mary Grossman*
84. *Sam Miller*
85. *Ernest Ball*
86. *The Halle Family*
87. *Eunice Kingsbury*
88. *Ralph Russell*
89. *Hart Crane*
90. *Caesar Grasselli*
91. *Theo Moll*
92. *Noble Sissle*
93. *Menobsy*
94. *George Humphrey*
95. *Starlight Boyd*
96. *John O'Mic*
97. *Phil Donahue*
98. *Dick Jacobs*
99. *Horace Ackley*
100. *Anton Grdina*

101. Jesse Owens
102. Johnny Kilbane
103. William Stinchcomb
104. Myra King Merrick
105. Dorothy Dandridge
106. Jane Scott
107. Samuel Andrews
108. John Krol
109. Amasa Stone
110. Chief Wahoo
111. Allan Freed
112. Bert McDonald
113. Liberty Holden
114. The Herrick Family
115. The Flemings
116. The Vail Family
117. Harold T. Clark
118. Charles Ruthenberg
119. Mark McCormack
120. Anthony Pilla
121. Herman Baehr
122. Shondor Birns
123. Harvey Cushing
124. Larry Doby
125. Bill Veeck
126. James Van Dorn
127. Cy Young
128. Samuel Huntington
129. John Heisman
130. Joseph Badger
131. Rocky Colavito
132. Margaret Hamilton
133. Napoleon Lajoie
134. Lucy Bagby Johnson
135. Don King
136. Cassie Chadwick
137. Otto Graham
138. Zenas King
139. John Demjanjuk
140. Vernon Stouffer
141. Maurice Maschke
142. Isaac Kidd
143. Harry Bernstein
144. Al Sutphin
145. David Ingalls
146. Tris Speaker
147. Archibald Willard
148. George Voinovich
149. Roger Penske
150. The Doan Family
151. Alfred Benesch
152. Edwin Beeman
153. John Butler
154. Dennis Kucinich
155. John Ellser
156. Herman Finkle
157. Ray Chapman
158. The Ratner Family
159. Bernie Kosar
160. Darryl Alan Levy
161. George Worthington
162. George Steinbrenner III
163. Margaret Bourke-White
164. Arsenio Hall
165. Harry F. Payer
166. Lottie Pearl Mitchell
167. Eva Kaber
168. Dudley Blossom
169. Will Cook
170. Mary Bigelow Ingham
171. George Forbes
172. Adella Prentiss Hughes
173. Edward Morley
174. Theodatus Garlick
175. Jeremiah Sullivan
176. Mike White
177. Hamilton Biggar
178. Laura Mae Corrigan
179. William White
180. Jackie Presser
181. William Masters
182. Dayton Miller
183. Alonzo Wright
184. Nick Mileti
185. William Creighton
186. Ernie Anderson
187. Albert Belle
188. Robert Jr. Lockwood
189. Ross Hunter
190. Barnaby & Friends
191. Reuben Sturman
192. Cornell Gabos
193. Donald Glaser
194. Jack Graney
195. Addie Joss
196. Stella Walsh
197. Moses Cleaveland
198. Ziggy & Friends
199. Drew Carey
200. Art Modell

Anderson
Ball
Bourke-White
Carey
Chestnutt
Cook
Crane
Dandridge
Ellser
Hamilton
Hope
Hughes
Hunter
Lockwood
levy
Mancini
Morrison
Newman
Sissle
Superman
Szell
Willard
Ziggy

Art & Entertainment

186 Ernie Anderson

(1934- , Cleveland)

The Blob. No, Ernie Anderson wasn't the Blob, it was just one of the classic films he brought to us during his incarnation as the original and outrageous Ghoulardi. With his button-festooned vest, fright wig and goatee, Anderson created a lasting character for Cleveland's children of the early 60s.

He started out in television with a local "F Troop" of zany and talented characters, all headed for bigger things, including comic Tim Conway, sitcom sideshow Jack Riley and radio great Smoochie Gordon. The Ghoulardi bit started as a joke, the cheapest possible weekend fill-in: Anderson with a flashlight on a blank stage with low rent horror movies. But the Ghoul caught fire (along with the beard, some props and an occasional rodent). Ernie used his fifteen minutes of fame as a stairway to Hollywood. After struggling for a few years as an actor and comedian, he found his calling in the sound studio. His timbrous *basso profundo* led to hundreds of commercials and ultimately to a lifetime contract as the voice of ABC and the highest paid voice-over vocalist in television.

Back home, he left his Friday night horror show in the able hands of Camera #3 hunk, Chuck Schodowsky. Now a local TV institution, it remains on the air over thirty years later, hosted at first by Hoolihan & Big Chuck, then Big Chuck & Little John, always popular but never more outlandish than in the days of the great ghoulmeister .

Knif ghoul! Turn Blue! Hey, Dorothy! Get Bent!
The Luuuuuuuuuv Boat.

85 Ernest Ball

(1878-1927, Cleveland)

Cleveland's best known and most celebrated composer-lyricist (at least until Trent Resnor of Nine Inch Nails), Ernest Ball created or collaborated on several of the most enduring popular tunes of the early 20th century, including the St. Patrick's Day standards, "When Irish Eyes are Smiling" and "Mother Machree." Among dozens of other memorable ballads, he wrote the well known theme song for celebrated New York mayor, Jimmy Walker, "Will You Love Me in December As You Do In May?"

Ball's initial success was as a vaudeville pianist, then composer. He started adding his own lyrics and produced a series of hit tunes that opened the door to Broadway. He wrote the musical scores for hit shows like *Barry of Ballymore* and *The Isle of Dreams*. Ernest Ball was so highly regarded that contemporaries like George M. Cohen and the Gershwin brothers cited him as the model popular composer. His style was emulated by many of the hopeful young talents who flocked to Tin Pan Alley. Ernest Ball was a charter member of ASCAP in 1914.

He added another success to his résumé when he began touring as a singer of his own songs. Critically acclaimed everywhere and wildly popular with Irish fans, Ball was performing on tour in California when he was struck down by a heart attack. He died at 46. A huge display of flowers from New York included an anonymous note that expressed the mournful sentiments of his fellow entertainers: "How many words unwritten? How many songs unsung?"

163 Margaret Bourke-White

(1904-1971, New York, New York)

She was only here for a few short years, but it was the beginning of a magical career with a camera, one that left an enduring legacy in photography and classic images of the city where she "learned to see." Margaret Bourke-White came to Cleveland to live with her mother in 1927, after graduating with a degree in biology from Cornell University. She had become interested in picture-making in college and scoured the area for suitable subject matter, hoping to earn a living as a freelancer.

She found the Flats---the monumental structures, harsh textures and the endless varieties of light that contrasted shafts of sun with the glint of steel and the blazing fires of the mills. Using a 35 mm Leica, the new precision camera from Germany, Margaret experimented with angles and exposures. The result was her first great series of images, haunting in their evocative power. She seemed capable of expressing the monolithic might and the humanity of the industrial age in a single flash of black & white.

Quickly recognized for her unmistakable talent, Margaret's works fetched high prices. She was commissioned to shoot the mills for Otis Steel, then photographed the rising Terminal Tower for the Van Sweringens. It wasn't long before the publishing barons in New York heard about the Cleveland phenomenon. Trendy Henry Luce, founder of the Time-Life empire, hired her as the ace shooter for his latest magazine venture, *Fortune*. Later, he named her one of the four original photographers for *Life Magazine*. Margaret provided *Life*'s first cover in 1936, a majestic portrait of Fort Peck Dam.

Her career soared. She went on to live a life of glamour and achievement, traveling the world for *Life*, married briefly to author Erskine Caldwell, winner of countless photography awards, author of several books. She was a fixture at the sensational Lindbergh kidnapping trial, a decorated war correspondent in World War II and the first woman to fly with the Air Force in combat. She charged through Germany with George Patton and took some of the first and most horrifying photographs of liberated concentration camps. She recorded the last formal pictures of Mahatma Gandhi, a few hours before his assassination. Bourke-White was the rarest of combinations, a supremely talented artist and a bold journalist, first hand witness to great moments in history.

Through it all, she never forgot where she started. In books and lectures, she harked back to Cleveland, fondly citing the city as the inspiration for her art.

199 Drew Carey

(1957- , Cleveland)

Ingratiating and self-effacing, Drew Carey parlayed a Fifties look with a Nineties sense of timing into the first Cleveland prime time network comedy. "The Drew Carey Show" debuted in the fall of 1995 and climbed steadily into the TV ratings. Set in Cleveland, with an array of real Cleveland props and references, the Carey sitcom has contributed to the rehabilitation of the city's image, besmirched for decades by below-the-rust-belt references to burning rivers and flaming mayors.

Carey himself remains an enigma. A deadpan straight man, he flashes barbs of wit and pearls of wisdom, sometimes incongruous bon mots coming from the mouth of a man with the look of a wide-eyed tourist for life. His paradoxical persona is nothing short of Full Cleveland.

Carey's show continues to rise in popularity and Drew does, too, a welcome guest on the talk shows, recognized now as that affable fellow in the huge horn-rims who always has a good word about Cleveland.

True, he hasn't been around that long and most of his career story is yet to be told. As usual, he stands patiently at the end of the line, barely making the cut for the *Cleveland 200*. But Drew can take consolation in the fact that, if nothing else, he beat the heck out of Art Modell.

45 Charles Chestnutt

(1858-1932, Cleveland)

Oldest son in a slave family freed by the Civil War, Charles Chestnutt was so obviously bright and talented from his youngest days that his parents struggled mightily to send him to Howard School when the family moved to North Carolina. The financial hardships were too much, and his father told Charles he must quit school for a job he had lined up for him in a local saloon. The principal at Howard came to the rescue, granting him employment as the school's youngest teaching assistant so he could continue his education.

In the classroom and on his own, he was a voracious student, mastering philosophy, literature, mathematics, religion, Latin, German and French and classical music. He went on to become principal at Howard School himself in 1881, at the tender age of 23. Determined to advance the cause of the Negro, he resigned to move back to Cleveland in 1884. Charles worked at the Nickel Plate

Railroad, then found employ with a local judge because of his proficiency at stenography. Judge Williamson encouraged him to study law. Chestnutt followed his advice, passing the bar exam in 1887 with class honors. Instead of practicing law, he opened a company that provided legal stenography services to Cleveland firms. It provided more than enough income to enable Charles Chestnutt to focus, at long last, on the career of his dreams.

From the time he learned to read, Charles was determined to be an author himself, creating the words that filled the precious pages of books. After receiving glowing reviews for two short stories, Chestnutt published his first book in 1899, *The Wife of His Youth and Other Stories of the Color Line*, followed quickly by two widely praised novels, *Conjure Woman* and *The House Behind the Cedars*. Within a year, he added a biography of Frederick Douglass. Embraced as one of the most important authors of his day, Chestnutt was welcomed to the upper echelons of literary society. He became a member of the exclusive Rowfant Club. In 1905, he was the only Clevelander invited to attend the famous 70th birthday extravaganza for Mark Twain at Delmonico's in New York City.

Chestnutt became one of the most active and respected voices for equal rights. Many of his works were satirical attacks on the hypocrisy of discrimination in the land of freedom and democracy. In 1928, he received the prestigious Springarn Medal from the NAACP for his contributions to racial equality.

It was Chestnutt himself who often cited one factor in his rise to prominence never mentioned by others. His fair skin and Caucasian features provided a personal exemption from the prevalent bigotry.

An African American, he would not have secured employment, admittance to the bar or acceptance as an author if others even suspected his heritage. In spite of the subject matter of his books, many readers long believed he was a white man writing about Negroes. His publisher, aware of his race from the beginning, withheld the information for ten years before finally releasing it to the public, at the author's insistence.

Cleveland born Charles W. Chestnutt was the first black man to achieve recognition as a professional writer in America.

169 Will Marion Cook

(1871-1944, Cleveland)

Without Will Cook, John Coltrane might have been a famous clarinetist and Bill Clinton would have played the tuba at his inaugural party. The saxophone had languished as a novelty instrument since its invention in 1840, rarely employed in any format. That changed in 1905 when Clevelander Will Cook put it to use in his local dance band. It was the introduction of the saxophone to popular music.

Cook studied music at Oberlin and later became the first Negro to play with the Boston Symphony Orchestra. He wrote a Broadway musical and composed "Mammy," made famous by Al Jolson. He not only resurrected the sax, but he had a keen sense of who could play it best. Cook hired young Sidney Bechet to play in his band, handed him the odd-looking instrument and told him to get to work. Cook watched with pride as Bechet became the world's first master saxophonist.

In the late 1920s, Will Cook made his last major contribution to music. He helped a raw but promising young piano player learn the fundamentals of composing and the subtleties of musical arrangement. In his autobiography more than fifty years later, the kid gave credit to Cook as the most important influence in his early career. Will was gone by then, but he would have appreciated those kind words of thanks from Duke Ellington.

89 Hart Crane

(1899-1932, Garrettsville, Ohio)

He suffered as a child, sole witness to the ugly disintegration of the marriage of his father, C. A. Crane, a titan in the candy business and a tyrant at home, and his mother, the lovely but fragile Grace Hart. He found solace in words, first the classics, then the galaxy of grand romantic poets that course across the literary heavens---Marlowe, Blake, Edgar Allan Poe, Walt Whitman, then his own.

Hart Crane began writing poetry in elementary school while living in Cleveland. Crane was published before he was 16. He gained national recognition in his early 20's and continued to grow, in both talent and fame, culminating with his masterpiece, *The Bridge*, in 1930. An eclectic collection in style and verse, *The Bridge* encompassed a powerful array of poems that each embraced the Brooklyn Bridge as symbolic of man's hopes or fears, strengths or burdens, dreams or shadows. This landmark work earned him a place in the inner circle of the New York literati.

With a Guggenheim fellowship in 1931, Hart Crane, at 32, should have been basking in the summer of a stellar career. The arbiters of literary taste had already recognized his spirited compositions as the bright future of American verse. He was described by reigning American poet laureate Robert Lowell as "the greatest voice of his generation."

It was not to be. The demons that plagued him since youth overcame him in 1932. Plagued for years by alcoholism and a manic-depressive lifestyle that left his health and his spirit in ruins, Crane spent a year in self-exile in Mexico, wrestling with whiskey and an ambitious epic poem on Montezuma. He never overcame the bottle, and never completed the work.

Depressed and exhausted, he set sail back to America. While other passengers lounged on the sunny deck, Hart Crane quietly slipped over the rail and leapt into the sea, no words spoken. His body was never recovered. He was 32 years old.

105 Dorothy Dandridge

(1923-1965, Cleveland)

Star of stage and screen, Dorothy Dandridge rose from her Cleveland roots to become the most famous black female performer of her day and, in a career cut tragically short, left a legacy of powerful performances.

Dorothy's mother, Ruby, was a noted performer herself, with many film and radio drama credits, later appearing on the *Beulah* television series. Inspired by Momma, Ruby's two daughters left high school to seek careers in entertainment. Dorothy, Vivian and cousin Etta Jones formed a singing trio that quickly found success, first on the Big Band circuit, then at the legendary Cotton Club in New York. Dorothy met and married Harry Nicholas, already a star with a famous black dance duo.

Her big break came when she appeared with Desi Arnaz at the Mocambo in the early 1950s. Critical raves led to a starring role opposite Harry Belafonte in the Broadway musical, *Carmen Jones*. She reprised her role in the hit film version and became the first black woman nominated for an Academy Award as best actress. Through the 50s, she ranked among Hollywood's female performers, culminating with her stellar performance in *Porgy and Bess*.

A second marriage to a Las Vegas nightclub owner led to a bitter divorce and a string of personal setbacks. She became reclusive, her health suffered and her career declined. In 1963, she filed for bankruptcy. Friends rallied to her aid and Dandridge was on the brink of a comeback in 1965 when she broke her foot in a minor accident. A rare infection followed the injury, claiming her life in 1965.

155 John Adam Ellser

(1821-1903, Philadelphia, Pennsylvania)

One of Cleveland's proudest assets is Playhouse Square, the sparkling performing arts complex unrivaled beyond Broadway. Almost lost in the 1960s, it was salvaged in the 70s, rehabilitated in the 80s and revitalized in the 90s. So much for recent history, but where did it all start? How did Cleveland come to be one of the grand theatrical centers in America? Because of one man. John Ellser.

Involved in the theater from an early age, Ellser was an actor, director and producer with various repertory companies in the east. He married noted actress Euphemia Meyers. Performing in road shows, the couple came to Cleveland in 1854 and stayed on after an extended run at Cleveland Theater. Ellser took over the Academy of Music in 1856 and elevated the fledgling institution into one of the foremost drama schools in the nation. Famous performers like Edwin and John Wilkes Booth and James O'Neill (father of Eugene) were featured in the Academy's first rate productions.

In 1873, Ellser the impresario reached higher, undertaking his most ambitious project. The Euclid Avenue Opera House was designed to surpass the finest edifices in New York and San Francisco, with impeccable acoustics, a spectacular stage and opulent architectural details and accessories. The grand opening on September 6, 1875 is still considered the most lavish affairs in Cleveland history. Beautifully appointed carriages rolled up to the entrance as the cream of Millionaire's Row turned out in most fashionable attire. Rockefellers, Hannas, Paynes, Chisholms, Wicks, Mathers and Wades flocked to their seats, swaddled in silks and furs, glittering with diamonds and gold. It was Ellser's finest hour, but the joy was short lived. Delays and cost overruns had cost him dearly. A nationwide financial panic cost him more. Ellser's showcase theater was hardly complete before his personal finances were wiped out. Three years later, his pride and joy was on the auction block. Marc Hanna bought the place at sheriff's sale---lock, stock and footlights. The broken-hearted Ellser stayed on in Cleveland a few more years. He managed the Park Theater while trying to gather financing to repurchase his dream. All of his efforts failed. He finally gave up and returned to New York. He and his wife resumed their acting careers, appearing in supporting roles in many Broadway productions. He left his heart and his heritage in Cleveland. The Opera House was torn down in 1922, replaced by the Hanna Theater, the modern cornerstone of Playhouse Square.

132 Margaret Hamilton

(1902-1985, Cleveland)

Hey Scarecrow, want to play ball?

Daughter of a prominent Cleveland attorney, Margaret graduated from Hathaway Brown School in 1921 and attended Wheelock School in Boston. It was there that she was first smitten by acting, performing in a local production of *Little Women.* Returning to Cleveland, she taught at Hough Elementary School briefly in 1927, but her real love was the stage. She took lessons and joined the company at the Cleveland Playhouse. Her outstanding talent as an actress soon became evident. She starred in several local productions, then was tapped for the lead in *Another Language* on Broadway in 1932. The play was a smash hit and Margaret was soon on her way to Hollywood to star in the film version with Helen Hayes.

Director Victor Fleming remembered the film in 1938 while casting *The Wizard of Oz*. Although the part of the Wicked Witch of the West called for an elderly woman, Fleming thought Margaret, only 35, would be perfect, with her distinctive profile and memorable cackle. So did she.

The success of *The Wizard of Oz* not only made Margaret Hamilton a star, it typecast her forever as the ultimate witch. From that time on, it was impossible for her to get a meaningful part unless there was an opening for an evil-minded crone. Her magnificent performance in one of the world's most popular films ruined her career.

She took the twist of fate with aplomb, continuing to appear in small film roles, touring with theater companies and appearing in guest roles on television. A series of commercials for Maxwell House coffee returned her to the public eye in the late 1970s. She looked the same as she had forty years before, when she was surrounded by flying monkeys, pointing a menacing green fingernail at Dorothy.

Margaret Hamilton often returned to her Cleveland home for speaking engagements or special guest turns at the Cleveland Play House. More than a half century after her showcase performance with cape and broom, her title remains undisputed: the finest witch the screen has ever known.

7 Bob Hope

(1903- , Eltham, England)

Well, lemmetellya...

Born Lesley Towne Hope in Eltham, England, his family came to Cleveland in 1908 after father Harry received word that there were good prospects for stonemason work. As a young newsie on an east side street corner, Hope sold a paper to John D. Rockefeller more than once. Years later, he reminisced about wanting to be as rich and famous as the old tycoon. As time would tell, he came pretty close on the money side and made Rocky look like a pauper when it came to international acclaim.

In 1915, he scored his first success in show business, winning a Charlie Chaplin contest at Luna Park, but he showed no real interest in performing except as a pool hustler and would-be boxer. With Johnny Kilbane's championship reign the biggest local boy-makes-good story of the day, thousands of city kids were inspired to visions of a title. Gyms were filled in the Old Angle. Fight nicknames were all the rage as well. Hope's older brother signed on for bouts under the meaningless name of "Packy West." It was only pretzel logic for Leslie to be "Packy East."

Little Packy was quick with his mitts and light on his feet, out-pointing his first six opponents to take a perfect record into the local amateur finals. He ran into Happy Walsh, a well known local thug who earned his moniker for beating people senseless with a sadistic grin on his face. It turned out he was aptly named. Hope was pummeled, losing badly, and Packy East was sent packing. He never stepped in the ring again.

He lost interest in boxing, but he acquired a taste for enthusiastic crowds. He plunged headlong into another dangerous spectator sport---comedy. Vaudeville was all the rage and Leslie's talents were nicely suited to the fast-paced song-and-dance shows. He could dance and tell jokes but his voice would never be mistaken for Caruso's, so he hooked up with a nightingale named Mildred Rosequist, his first show business partner and steady date in the early 1920s.

Mildred and Bob (Leslie was left behind in Cleveland) were a modest hit on the vaudeville circuit. They even got engaged. But Millie took umbrage at the ever-escalating portion of the act that featured Hope's chatter instead of her lovely warbling. They broke up in 1924. Other partnerships followed. Durbin & Hope. Hope & Byrne. Bob moved up the comic ladder, traveled the country, honed his sharp wit.

His biggest break came in 1927. Agent Charles Hogan gave him a job as substitute master of ceremonies at one of the best theaters, the Stratford in Chicago. He was a smash his first night, hired immediately as permanent MC. It was a role he was made for. Bob Hope never looked back.

Already a star in the late 1920s, he toured with famous comedienne Grace Louise to standing room crowds. He returned often to Cleveland, staying at the spacious house on Yorkshire Road he purchased for his parents. In the 1930s, he conquered the two new giants of entertainment, radio and film, starring on his own radio show and in a series of "Road" movies with Bing Crosby and Dorothy Lamour.

His Midwestern roots served him in good stead as time passed. He lived well, but not as lavishly as his Hollywood peers, preferring to put his money in common sense investments like real estate and basic stocks. The market recovery and California boom made him rich beyond his wildest expectations. By the 1950s, he was one of the largest landowners in California. By the 60s, he found himself ranked not only among the funniest individuals in the country, but also one of the wealthiest. The money didn't diminish his humor or his patriotism. He added television to his list of conquests, enduring as one of TV's most popular performers for decades. At the same time, he became a symbol of American good will as surely as Mom and apple pie with his annual overseas tours to visit the troops. For more than forty years, he took his show to the front lines, offering a few welcome hours of relief to the boys in uniform. He covered hundreds of thousands of miles and performed in front of millions of smiling faces, always without compensation, often at risk of his life.

A friend of thirteen presidents (a golf partner to 10), Bob Hope has always been just as at ease as host of the Academy Awards, at a formal dinner White House dinner or making small talk in a trench with a couple of GI's. Controversial for his unwavering support of the armed forces even through the darkest days of Vietnam, Hope shrugged off the criticism and emerged as America's most beloved ambassador abroad and a living national treasure at home. With Bob Hope, America laughed through the 20th century. God knows, we needed him.

His legacy was a smile. A list of the awards, honorary degrees, medals and testimonials bestowed on him for distinguished service to many nations, institutions and charities would fill a book larger than this one.

Bob Hope is listed in the *Guinness Book of World Records* as the Most Decorated Civilian in the World.

42 Langston Hughes

(1902-1967, Joplin, Missouri)

He was swept into Cleveland with the great migration that replaced immigrant labor with the first generations of blacks born free in the South, welcomed to the industrial northern states as World War I reduced the flow from Europe to a trickle.

It was here that the century's most influential black poet studied the works of Carl Sandburg at Central High School. It was here that the rich pen of Langston Hughes first touched paper. One of his earliest recorded works was a tribute to his literary mentor:

Carl Sandburg's poems
Fall on the white pages of his books
Like blood-clots of song
From the wounds of humanity...

A popular student in the all too brief age before racism seized the northern cities like a chronic disease, Hughes counted Germans, Poles, Irish and Jewish youths among his close friends. It broadened his horizons and heightened his sense of excitement about the world. He attended Columbia on a scholarship, then left school abruptly at 22 for the peripatetic life of a poet.

He prowled the night spots in Harlem, the Cotton Club and Leroy's, then grabbed a chance to sail to Africa in 1923 as a mess boy on the *S. S. Malone*. Hughes spent a year abroad, returning to write some of his most celebrated poems, including his bittersweet paean to his native land. "I, too, sing America," declared the bold spokesman of an emerging race of newcomers groping for a place in a newcomer nation.

In 1925, he published the prize-winning book of essays, *The New Negro.* His national tour the following year was an enormous success, including an historic night in Cleveland on April 16, 1926, when a vast and varied crowd turned out to celebrate him home.

Hughes continued to produce fine work at a prodigious pace. By the 1940s, he was the most famous black poet in the western world, yet still growing as an artist and a man. His accomplishments as poet, playwright, novelist, lyricist, essayist, social activist, historian and columnist were hailed worldwide. Hughes was honored by the Library of Congress, the BBC, the NAACP and numerous universities, including Howard and Western Reserve.

In the 1950s, Langston Hughes became a political target. Adamantly opposed to all war, he had still been unwavering in his support of U. S. troops, writing patriotic songs during World War II. But his social idealism left him vulnerable to the likes of Roy Cohn, who grilled him mercilessly during the McCarthy Hearings in the Senate.

Hughes was unbowed and articulate in his own defense. The changing tides of politics turned his way a decade later. He was an honored guest at the Kennedy White House. Gushing praise from Jackie thrust him back into the limelight. Rediscovered by a new generation, he spent his last years in great demand, feted as one of America's great poets and inspiration to a chorus of African American literary voices that followed his lead, including James Baldwin, Arthur Haley and Toni Morrison.

189 Ross Hunter

(1920-1996, Cleveland)

Martin Fuss was born and raised on Cleveland's east side, then left the city in his late teens to pursue a career in Hollywood. Changing his name to the Tinseltown generic, "Ross Hunter," he met with some success as a B-movie actor, then struck gold on the other side of the camera. One of the industry's most consistently successful producers, Ross Hunter had a sense for combining star power with tear-jerker scripts that won few accolades from critics but plenty where it counted, at the box office.

Rock Hudson, Lana Turner, Doris Day, Debbie Reynolds, Julie Andrews and a gaggle of other Hollywood luminaries can thank Hunter for finding them the right vehicle in pictures like *Magnificent Obsession, Pillow Talk, Back Street, Flower Drum Song* and *Thoroughly Modern Millie*. He had already posted one of the best track records in box office history when he taxied down the runway in a brand new movie vehicle---the blockbuster. In 1970, he introduced the over-the-top action-thriller with an all-star cast. *Airport* started a Hollywood stampede that hasn't slowed yet. His movie-making peers, never shy when it came to mimicry, paid Hunter his greatest tribute by generating countless imitations and permutations: a fleet of *Airport* sequels, then the *Airplane!* comedy versions. *Airport* went to sea with the *Poseidon Adventure* and its spin-offs; to land with the *Cassandra Crossing* and *Runaway Train*; to the highways with *Speed*; outer space with *Marooned* and *Apollo 13*. Directly or indirectly, Cleveland's Ross Hunter put more people to work than the WPA.

41 Philip Johnson

(1906- , Cleveland)

Generally regarded as the most renowned American architect of the second half of this century, Philip Johnson has put so much glass into the urban landscape that he is worshipped by the Windex company.

Johnson grew up on Overlook Road in Cleveland Heights. He attended New York's Hackley School, graduating as valedictorian and picked as most likely to succeed. It didn't take long. Thanks to his father's gift of rapidly appreciating stock in ALCOA, Philip became a millionaire while still at Harvard.

With no financial worries, Johnson was free to meander while pondering a suitable career for his brilliance. Traveling in Europe, he was introduced to Walter Gropius, Mies van der Rohe and the Bauhaus architecture that inspired them all. He returned to the states and became a curator at the Museum of Modern Art in New York where he helped stage the International Exhibition of Modern Architecture in 1932, the event that firmly established architecture as art and Johnson as one of its leading practitioners.

At 26, he co-authored *The International Style: Architecture Since 1922*, the work that predicted and defined the re-building of the world's metropolises with clustered glass towers of commerce. He developed a distinctive style that conceded all to the functionality of the monumental glass and metal skyscraper, then drew his strong aesthetics from the form itself. After several personal successes, he returned to MOMA for another six-year stint, then joined forces with Van Der Rohe to design the Seagram's Building in New York, still recognized as a turning point in modern design.

Johnson spent a strange interlude engrossed in politics in the 1930s. He became a disciple of demagogue Huey Long, and even ran for office himself. His radical views were culled from the mouthings of Long, outspoken radio crusader, Father Coughlin, and even the mesmerizing young leader of the National Socialist Party in Germany, Adolph Hitler. Johnson soon saw the light, recanted the extremist philosophy and apologized for his indiscretions in both word and deed. Later in life, he made a point of designing synagogues and public projects in Israel.

In the 1960s, Philip Johnson returned to major commercial work, leading the firm of Johnson & Burghee, responsible for more than 200 notable structures around the world, from London to Singapore, Mexico City to Tokyo. His most conspicuous work in his hometown is the Cleveland Playhouse. Among the enduring testaments to his skill are the PPG world headquarters, the AT&T building and his own residence, the Glass House (don't throw stones, please). He remains active at 90 years of age. Only recently he revealed plans for a magnificent, monolithic sculpture ensemble intended for permanent display in the perfect environment for the latest design of the world's best architect. It's coming to Cleveland. It will probably be mentioned in the next book like this, two hundred years from now.

160 d. a. levy

(1942-1968, Cleveland)

Already a respected poet in his early twenties, d. a. levy's fame arose more from his defiance of social mores than his literary skill. He was instrumental in Cleveland's rude awakening to the 60s, a local hybrid of Allan Ginsberg and Lenny Bruce.

In 1964, levy edited and published Cleveland's first underground paper, the *Buddhist Third Class Junk Mail Oracle* along with a poetry journal, *The Marijuana Quarterly.*

In Cleveland, this was pretty heady stuff. levy garnered praise in literary circles and condemnation from law enforcement officials. Police launched a campaign of harassment that culminated with levy's arrest on obscenity charges in 1966. Terrorized into submission, he finally plea bargained his way out, admitting guilt for "contributing to the delinquency of a minor" for reading his poetry aloud in the presence of teenagers. It enabled him to avoid jail time, but the hounding by authorities didn't cease. In 1968, bitter and despondent, levy burned his works in progress and committed suicide.

In retrospect, his poems were good but not great and the legal squabbles seem insignificant compared to the tidal wave of drugs and obscenity that followed. But don't overlook the fact that d. a. levy shares with e. e. cummings and k. d. laing the distinction of being the only members in that tiny, quirky club of famous people in Western civilization who have no capital letters in their legal names.

188 Robert Jr. Lockwood

(1915 - , Marvel, Arkansas)

When Robert Lockwood's mother married the man known as the father of the blues guitar, Robert Johnson, the "Junior" was slipped into young Robert's name. Johnson taught Lockwood to play guitar and a legacy was passed across a generation. Lockwood became the living link to Johnson's blues. He was his one and only student.

After the lessons ended, Robert Jr. Lockwood set out to play his music around the Mississippi Delta, in tandem with blues man Sonny Boy Williamson. He followed the blues migration to Chicago, but didn't stay, returning south to Memphis for a regular gig and regular money on the "King Biscuit Time" radio show. Broadcast across the South, the King Biscuit program influenced a generation of black blues, jazz and rock musicians. Years later, B. B. King recalled listening to King Biscuit on his lunch break from the cotton fields in Mississippi. Robert Jr. performed with Muddy Waters and other legends. From an early age, he was respected among his peers as a superb guitarist and innovator, musically wise beyond his years. He played in hundreds of studio sessions for historic Chess Records.

In 1961, with the popularity of blues overshadowed by its wild child, rock 'n' roll, Lockwood made the painful decision to abandon the career he loved for the sake of his wife and children. He moved to Cleveland, where a day job had been secured through friends, playing only rarely in local night spots. Two decades later, interest in blues music and history was re-awakened. Robert, Jr. was re-discovered, first for his singular connection to Robert Johnson, then for his own masterful guitar. His popularity soared. Long overdue recognition was forthcoming at last.

At 80, he continues to play regularly at clubs and festivals in the United States and abroad. He returns to play the King Biscuit Festival held each October in Helena, Arkansas. In 1995, he was honored with a National Heritage Fellowship Award.

38 Henry Mancini

(1924-1994, Cleveland)

Winner of 4 Academy Awards and 20 Grammys, Henry Mancini wrote and recorded more music heard more often by more people worldwide than any other contemporary composer.

His father was a Cleveland steelworker. His mother was a music lover. She saved the money and forced little Hank to take piano lessons. He remembered being angry with Mom for forcing him to toil at the keyboard while his pals were out playing ball. All was forgiven a few years later.

The jazzy progression of the TV theme for *Peter Gunn* vaulted him to the status of designated composer for a horde of television shows, then movie scores spanning five decades. His signature song is only one of the many perennial standards Henry Mancini churned out in one of music's most prolific careers, but it wouldn't be right to profile Henry without singing a few bars. You know the words. Okay, all together now, "Moon River, wider than a mile, I'm crossing you in style some day...."

28 Toni Morrison

(1931- Lorain, Ohio)

She was born Chloe Anthony Wofford and grew up in a working class family in Lorain. There was little in her childhood to indicate the splendid career awaiting her. Working nights as a copy editor to help finance her studies at Howard and Cornell, Morrison somehow found time to write her first novel, *The Bluest Eye*, a coming of age story set in Northeast Ohio. Quickly recognized as a talented writer, she won the respect of important New York publishers who supported Morrison in her determination to produce works of literature that rarely achieved the kind of commercial success enjoyed by lightweight contemporaries like Jackie Collins or Danielle Steele. After her marriage to Harold Morrison, she chose Toni Morrison as her author's signature.

She continued to mix her erudite craftsmanship with subtle and complex commentary on American society. Her Ohio roots played a significant role in her increasingly rich body of work. She painted the Ohio seasons in *Beloved* as "...a prima donna, convinced its performance is the reason the world has people in it....Summer had been hooted offstage and autumn with its bottles of blood and gold had everybody's attention." *Beloved* earned her a Pulitzer Prize in 1987.

In 1993, Toni Morrison reached the pinnacle of her profession, winning the Nobel Prize for Literature. She was only the eighth woman and the first African American to win this most coveted award in its 92-year history.

Still in her prime as a writer, with the most impressive credentials in American and world literature already secured, Toni Morrison continues to write while teaching as a guest professor at Princeton. In 1996, President Clinton singled her out as a shining example of someone who rose above the "twin burdens of sexism and racism" during Black History Month.

24 Paul Newman

(1925- , Cleveland Heights)

The son of a Jewish father and Catholic mother, Paul Newman and his brother Art were raised as Christian Scientists after Mom converted, accounting for his cavalier attitude toward religion. His father's family owned Newman-Stern, a retail sporting goods company. Dad wanted him to enter the business, but mother Teresa pushed him into children's theater at Cleveland Playhouse, where he debuted as the Court Jester in *The Travails of Robin Hood* in 1930.

He was a good athlete and a fair student at Shaker Heights High. He started college at Ohio University, but quit to join the Navy Air Corps in 1943, soon after he turned 18. Those famous blue eyes are colorblind from Paul's side. To his dismay, that meant he was washed out as a pilot, ending up a radio man and tail gunner in the South Pacific.

After the war, Newman enrolled at Kenyon College. Bigger and stronger, he played football while majoring in economics. A rowdy, fun-loving jock, he was kicked off the football team after he and his buddies were caught in a brawl wild enough to make the front page of the *Cleveland Plain Dealer*.

It was a blessing in disguise. He turned to acting as an alternate to sports. Paul was soon enamored with the stage, signing up for summer theater, acting in a dozen productions over two years. After school, he tried to make it with a stock theater group, but the pay was meager. By 1950, he was married, with an infant son, and unable to pay the bills. When his father took ill, he responded to his mother's call to return home and help run the family business. Newman-Stern thrived with Paul running the shop, but he stayed less than two years, setting off again in 1952 as soon as he had enough savings to finance another year trying to make it as an actor.

In 1956, he was appearing in a stage production of *Picnic* when he was smitten by the sultry Southern girl playing understudy for the female lead. Paul Newman, meet Joanne Woodward. Forty years later, in the twilight of parallel careers of extraordinary success in film, they remain one of Hollywood's most admired couples.

Paul Newman has starred in over fifty major motion pictures, earned 7 Oscar nominations, a Best Actor award and a special Academy Award for film achievement. He fulfilled his dream while giving millions of women something to dream about. For the better part of three decades he topped the charts as the most popular leading man since Clark Gable.

The Sting, *Hud*, *The Hustler*, Hombre, *Butch Cassidy & The Sundance Kid*, *The Verdict*, *Absence of Malice*, *The Color of Money*---everyone has a favorite Paul Newman film, but it could be any of more than dozen.

At the recommendation of activist friends, he cashed in on his world-famous name in the 1980s, dusted off his business skills and returned to sales. This time it was not for Newman-Stern, but Newman's Own, a line of pricey salad dressings with Paul's pleasing visage on the label, better-looking than any logo. The catch was that all of the profits were earmarked for charities that fought drug abuse, helped kids and aided the environment. A modest venture at first, Newman's Own has grown into an international food conglomerate, with products ranging from popcorn to peanut butter and a charity windfall of millions every year.

Distinguished actor, award-winning director, movie idol, businessman mogul, political activist, philanthropist---he's Cleveland's Own, Paul Newman.

92 Noble Sissle

(1889-1975, Indianapolis, Indiana)

The most important extracurricular at fabled Central High School was the Glee Club, and its most renowned alumnus was Noble Sissle, the velvet-voiced warbler who graduated to the big leagues, performing on national tours with black quartets and vocal groups while still a teen-ager.

Eubie Blake & Noble Sissle

Already a star performer in 1915, he hooked up songwriter Eubie Blake. Inspired by his new partner, he found composing came as naturally as singing. Their most successful collaboration produced a string of hits, including standards like "Love Will Find a Way" and "I'm Just Wild About Harry" (a tune that President Truman was most grateful for thirty years later).

Sissle served with a regimental band in World War I, then returned to an even greater success at home, first with Blake, then on his own as bandleader, solo performer, lyricist, music publisher, columnist and nightclub owner.

In the 1930's, he formed the Noble Sissle Orchestra, touring the country to rave reviews for another twenty years. An icon among black performers, Noble was a co-founder of the Negro Actors Guild and its first president.

12 Superman

(1933- , Cleveland)

The comic books say he came from the distant planet Krypton, but the truth is the greatest superhero of pop literature was a native Clevelander, born in the fertile minds of two high school kids in Glenville, Jerry Siegel and Joe Schuster. Siegel came up with the name and Schuster drew the first pictures of the muscular, dark-haired sole survivor of the cataclysm that destroyed Krypton and gave earth its most beloved personification of "truth, justice and the American way."

It was certainly helpful that the peculiar yellow sun of the local planetary system endowed the former Kal-el with extraordinary abilities, far beyond those of mortal man. Before they were finished with their creative input, Siegel and Schuster's prodigy could "fly faster than a speeding bullet and leap tall buildings in a single bound." X-ray vision, super-hearing, invulnerability and an abiding compassion for the puny residents of his adopted home made Superman not only the most admired and imitated superhero to come along, but an awfully nice guy as well. He fit snugly into the inflated sense of self-admiration assumed by Americans in the latter half of the 20th century---a benevolent hybrid of god and man.

Siegel and Schuster couldn't find a publisher smart enough to appreciate their creation, so they featured him in their own science-fiction publications, beginning in 1936. In 1938, the rights to Superman were finally sold, for the un-super sum of $135. From his debut in *Action Comics* in June of that year, it was a short flight to superstardom for the Man of Steel. A comic book staple ever since, Superman proved just as durable on radio, television, in feature films and even on Broadway.

While Superman was winging his way to fame and riches, Siegel and Schuster earned little more than a one-way ticket to Palookaville. Stripped of their ownership and all residual rights by the 1938 agreement, they were both mired in poverty when a national cartoonists group rallied to their cause. Finally, in 1975, the modern corporate owner of all Superman rights responded. Warner Brothers granted both men a $20,000 annual lifetime royalty and restored their name to future comic book and film credits.

It wasn't much, considering the billions of dollars of revenue generated by the godfather of superheroes, but a lot better than getting hit over the head with a piece of kryptonite.

69 George Szell

(1897-1970, Budapest, Hungary)

Not merely the conductor, Szell was the Cleveland Orchestra from 1946 until his death in 1968. He had only one stipulation in coming to Cleveland, that he be given absolute control. The leaders of the orchestra wisely did so. Under his guidance, the orchestra went from being a solid, well respected regional group to a world renowned ensemble.

Szell was a European musical thoroughbred who found himself marooned in the United States when war broke out in Europe in 1940. He guest conducted for several years and listened to various overtures (not to be confused with the William Tell) before the Cleveland opportunity arose. With an icy glare and uncompromising demand for precision, he achieved his vision of an orchestra that played like a string quartet.

In 1957 he took his musicians on a European tour that drew ecstatic reviews and enhanced the orchestra's reputation. His most impressive success came in 1962, when he led the orchestra at the opening of Philharmonic Hall in Lincoln Center. Szell's band easily outperformed the New York, Boston and Philadelphia Orchestras in the first big time "battle of the bands," winning the unofficial title as the best orchestra in the world. *Time Magazine* put Szell on it's cover.

Jack Benny auditions for Goeorge Szell

Over 25 years after his death, the Szell influence endures. There are still some 30 musicians who remain from Szell's era. They pass along the master's rule of perfectionism to newer members, including the use of even Szell's famous stare when one of the rookies slips on a discordant note.

The magic still works. Through two more conductor eras, the city's most illustrious living institution continues to live up to the sterling reputation it first achieved under the steely baton of George Szell. In 1995, after another spectacularly successful world tour, *Time Magazine* again declared the Cleveland Orchestra "The Best Band in the Land."

147 Archibald Willard

(1836-1918, Bedford, Ohio)

Quick---what's the most famous painting in American history? *Whistler's Mother*? *American Gothic*? Something by Norman Rockwell or Andrew Wyeth?

Think hard. For instant recognition, emotion and pure patriotism, how about the *Spirit of '76*? That ragged, wounded trio carrying fife, drum and flag is as ingrained in the American memory as the Statue of Liberty. It was painted by self-taught Archibald Willard in 1876, the same year he moved his studio to Cleveland, an inspirational city.

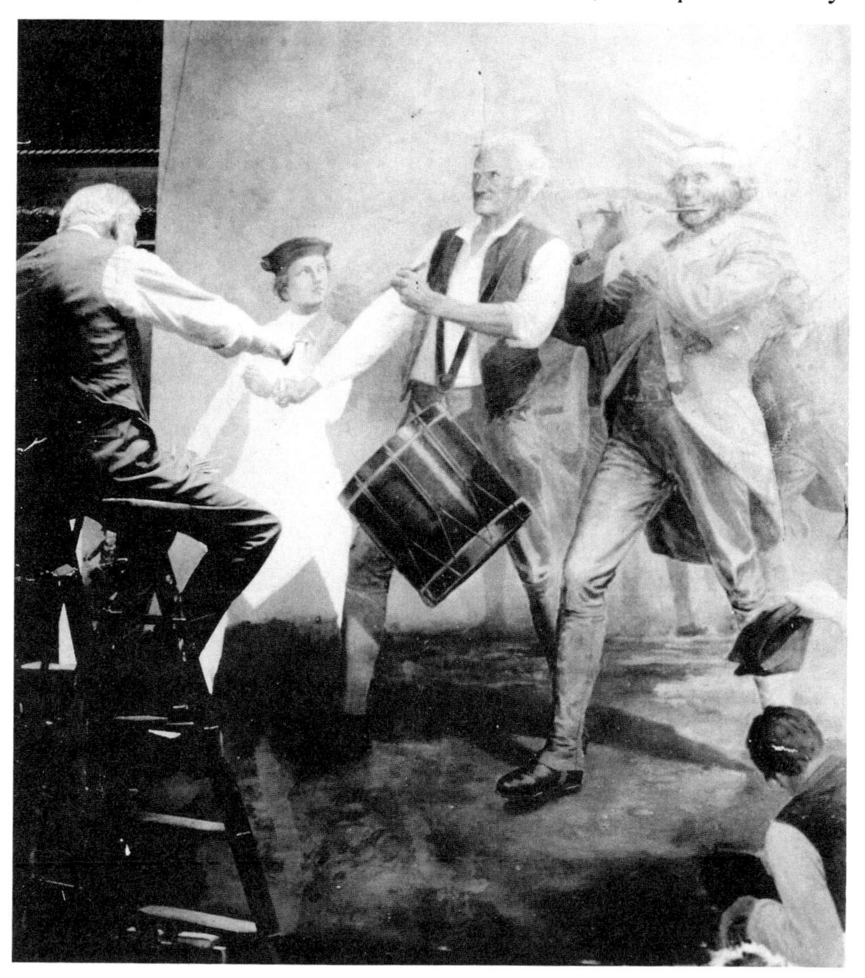

Willard painted designs on wagons and carriages before the Civil War interrupted his career. He served with the 86th Ohio Infantry and the 176th Ohio Volunteers, returning home in 1865. A whimsical portrait of his family called *Pluck* launched his career as an artist. He was commissioned to produce a series of comical scenes for the nation's bicentennial in 1876, but abruptly changed to more serious subject matter after his father's death. The result was the magnificent *Spirit of '76*.

198 Ziggy & Friends

(1962 - , Cleveland)

You want cartoons? We got 'em.

Led by Tom Wilson's inimitable *Ziggy*, a Cleveland character if ever there was one, locals have covered the newsprint of the nation with several of the most memorable paper personalities in existence.

Ziggy is as Cleveland as you get. Things don't always go so well for the little guy, always cursed with more than his share of problems, but he is certainly well respected in journalistic circles, syndicated in over 400 newspapers. Needless to say, he's a very wealthy figure. He may be just a figment of Tom Wilson's imagination, but the money's not.

Ziggy is everywhere, all right, but he's not alone. Among his proud companions are *Calvin & Hobbes*, Bill Watterson's fun-loving duo, the most popular cartoon characters in America for the last five years, at least until Watterson announced he was hanging up his pen for awhile.

Watterson was an editorial cartoonist for his Kenyon newspaper and landed the same position for the *Cincinnati Post* when he graduated. Later, he penned editorial cartoons for the *Sun Newspapers* and submitted strips to syndicators with no success. Among his failures were Spaceman Spiff, a talking groundhog, and another about a newsman. One rejection letter suggested he concentrate on the side characters of a boy and his stuffed tiger. Good advice.

Watterson named them Calvin and Hobbes after 16th century Protestant reformer John Calvin and 17th century political philosopher John Hobbes. The strip outpaced even *Doonesbury* and *The Far Side*. When the first *Calvin and Hobbes* book came out, the publisher asked Watterson to go on the tour to help sell the 50,000 copies printed. The very private Watterson refused. The book sold over 500,000 copies. Watterson shuns publicity, even refuses to have his picture taken. But he does answer all his fan mail, just as Charles Schulz did for him when Watterson wrote to Schulz as a kid in love with *Peanuts* and Charlie Brown.

Tom Batiuk has contributed his share with Funky Winkerbean. Harvey Pekar covers the dark side with his *American Gothic* series. Over at American Greetings, Ziggy is the grand stallion, but he has plenty of company in the stable, including homespun Holly Hobby, sugar sweet Strawberry Shortcake and the hundreds of characters populating the millions of greetings cards churned out each year.

No doubt about it, Cleveland is the cartoon capital of the world. What...you think that's funny?

Boiardi
Bradley
Chisholm
Crawford
Eaton
Flagler
Gund
Grasselli
Humphrey
Jordan
Lincoln
McDonald
Moll
Otis
Payne
Ratner
Rockefeller
Sherwin
Steinbrenner
Stouffer
Sullivan
Thompson
White
White
Wade
Worthington

75 Hector Boiardi

(1897-1985,Italy)

The award for Cleveland's warmest success story goes to Hector Boiardi. Never heard of him? Oh, yes you have. You know him as the "Chef." Chef Boy-Ar-Dee.

Hector came to the United States as part of the second wave of southern Italian immigrants, arriving in New York in 1914. Unlike many of his compatriots, Hector had a special talent. At 17, he was already a master in the kitchen, and quickly found work at no less an establishment than the swanky Ritz Carlton in New York.

Within a year, Hector's spicy, tomato-based Italian cuisine was all the rage in Manhattan, new and exquisite flavors to a continent full of people who had been eating the world's blandest diet for more than century.

From the time the Mayflower landed until the middle of the nineteenth century, the basic American diet was meat and bread. That was it until the Irish arrived. They brought potatoes. Everyone had meat, bread and potatoes for another eighty years.

Then Hector showed up.

In 1917, leading Cleveland industrialist Alexander Winton had just completed the luxurious Hotel Winton at East 12th and Euclid. With the appointments worthy of a fine establishment, it still lacked the finishing touch Winton craved---a world class chef for the restaurant. Discussing the problem with fellow auto mogul Fred Chandler over dinner at the Ritz in New York, Winton took time out to remark at the exotically delicious food. Chandler recommended he speak with the chef. Four days later, Boiardi was on a train to Cleveland.

Hector exceeded Winton's wildest hopes. People flocked to the restaurant. The young chef was so successful that he left the hotel in 1924 to open his own eatery, the Giardino d'Italia, a few blocks down East 9th Street. Often, customers who didn't have time for a sit down dinner would knock on the back door and beg Hector for a jar of the scrumptious sauce, along with a handful of homemade pasta.

The demand for the "take-home" dinners soared. Before long, a new building was required to house the operation. Boiardi was changed to the phonetic "Boy-Ar-Dee" to help slow-witted WASPs, and Chef Boy-Ar-Dee products were born. A pre-packaged spaghetti dinner for four cost 35 cents. By the late 1930s, Chef Boy-Ar-Dee was a multi-million dollar industry, selling ready made Italian dinners nationwide.

Regional packaging and manufacturing plants were added. Everybody loved the Chef's spaghetti, but the key was convenience. You didn't have to stand around in the kitchen all day mixing and stirring. Boil water, toss it in, heat it up. Presto! Hector Boiardi was the godfather of convenient food.

You would think that's enough. Penniless young Italian comes to Cleveland and makes a fortune in spaghetti. But Hector wasn't finished yet.

After the war started in 1941, the U. S. government woke up to a disconcerting problem. The standard field rations issued to troops in battle, unchanged since World War I, were unfit for human consumption. A crash program was undertaken to improve the food content. To expedite the process, the army was authorized to offer a reward of one million dollars to the company or individual that submitted the most viable, palatable, cost-effective alternative. Who do you think won? Our hero, Chef Boy-Ar-Dee. And he didn't even take the money, donating the whole, cool million to the war effort.

He received a special commendation from President Roosevelt for his unique contribution. Hector Boiardi may have done more to help win World War II than anyone except Ike, Patton and Audie Murphy, and he never even fired a gun.

After the war, Hector continued to prosper. By the early Fifties, the Chef Boy-Ar-Dee companies were grossing several hundred million dollars a year. Hector sold everything to a food conglomerate and went into semi-retirement. Chef, restaurateur, industrialist, agribusinessman, war hero, philanthropist. He died at 88 in 1985.

Got any recipes?

34 Alva Bradley & Family

(1814-1885, Elington, Connecticut)

Cleveland was custom-made to be a great port city, but it didn't mean much until somebody came along to build ships and get some heavy traffic moving across water.

Alva Bradley's your man. Best damn hand at the helm in Great Lakes history. He spent thirty years sailing those treacherous waters, as a captain for more than twenty, everything from light-rigged schooners to heavy steamers. Bradley never lost a ship. His company, Bradley & Cobb, constructed some of the largest vessels on the lakes. In 1859, Bradley took over sole ownership and moved to Cleveland. For years, Bradley Transportation operated the largest, safest fleet on the Great Lakes, hauling the ore, coal, oil and steel that fed the hungry economy of the industrial revolution.

Old Alva's sea legs were just as sure on dry land. He invested in the one thing he couldn't get on the water---real estate. Cleveland's prosperity throughout the latter part of the 19th century sent property values soaring, augmenting his vast wealth. At the time of his death, Alva Bradley was said to be the area's largest individual landowner. His character and presence were known to inspire respect and loyalty from his crew, his employees and his peers. It must have been evident to others from an early age. As a young sailor, he stayed briefly at a rooming house in Milan, Ohio. The lady proprietor thought enough of Alva to name her son after him. The baby boy was called Thomas. Thomas Alva Edison.

MORRIS BRADLEY succeeded his father as head of Bradley Transportation. The company continued to grow, producing the ships and systems that transformed the raw materials of the region into finished goods and money. His son was ALVA T. BRADLEY, an independent thinker who put the family's money into a new venture. Baseball.

Alva T. bought the Cleveland Indians in 1927, along with blue chip partners that included Newton D. Baker and the Van Sweringen Brothers. Alva ran the show, but, with the Vans involved, you knew something awfully big was going to happen. Sure enough, they unveiled plans for the country's largest sports facility. By 1931, Cleveland Stadium was a reality. The Van Sweringens, wiped out by the market crash and Depression, weren't around to see it through, but Bradley made sure the job was completed. The family name was at stake. Grampa Alva never lost a ship. This one wasn't about to lose a stadium.

35 Henry Chisholm

(1822-1881, Lochgelly, Fifeshire, Scotland)

His father died when he was ten, he quit school and took a carpenter's apprenticeship to help his widowed mother. Three years later, he started his own carpentry business, then emigrated to Canada to seek his fortune in the New World.

He found it. Not in wood, but metal. Not in Canada, but Cleveland. Coming here to work on the new pier, he met the Jones brothers, owners of a small iron mill. Chisholm moved in, invested in the business and took over as chief of operations. An industrial visionary, Chisholm could see the future of steel as the rigid backbone of the age of industry. He implemented the new Bessemer process, diversified operations to include everything from heavy steel to horseshoes, and provided a range of benefits to his workers, a philosophy that facilitated productivity and stable operations.

By the 1870s, Chisholm's conglomerate was producing over 150,000 tons of high grade products annually. Sprawling operations covered thirty acres in the Flats, mines in Minnesota and mills in Illinois and Indiana. It is said that, at the time of his premature death at 59, Henry Chisholm's only peer in the steel business was fellow Scotsman, Andrew Carnegie.

Chisholm's untimely demise was hard on the family and harder on Cleveland. Chisholm's son, William, was not his father's equal in business. Deteriorating labor relations and missed opportunities soon jeopardized the company's future. Major stockholders were relieved when the assets were sold to Pittsburgh interests, incorporated into U. S. Steel. Henry's death altered the history of the business. The loss of this most talented steel man shifted the balance from Cleveland to Pittsburgh. The city down the pike took a lead it never relinquished. The tragedy was that Henry Chisholm's death was no accident. It was the climax of one of the greatest personal feuds that ever darkened the face of the city.

In 1880, Chisholm's son was wrongly identified in the fledgling *Cleveland Press* as the youth involved in a sordid downtown street incident. Enraged, Henry summoned the reporter to his office. Although a fine gentleman with a generous nature, Henry Chisholm was rather sensitive about his family's reputation. The newsman showed up expecting a stern but polite lecture about identification procedures. Instead, he was stripped, beaten, painted black and tossed out on the street. When it came to reporters, Henry Chisholm was worse than Albert Belle.

There was no sense calling the police. Chisholm ranked alongside Rockefeller and Hanna among the city's most elite. No cop in his right mind was about to put the cuffs on Hank. The only one to call was Edward Scripps, owner and editor of the *Press*. Scripps was deeply disturbed by the attack on his employee, but that was good news compared to what happened next.

First, a mob of Chisholm's millworkers showed up to bust up the *Press* and Scripps had to personally disperse them with his revolver and some men of his own. Once again, the police were nowhere to be found that night, but they did show up the next morning to serve an arrest warrant on Scripps for criminal libel. He was hauled off to jail while sheriff's deputies shut down the *Press* to attach and appraise the property pursuant to Chisholm's claim for damages.

Scripps posted bond and returned to his office to find that Chisholm had somehow managed to get two men appointed as appraisers by the court who were unlikely to be much help in Scripps' efforts to resume publication---the rival owner of the *Cleveland Leader* and another man wired to the *Plain Dealer*.

Scripps was in big trouble. He needed another $100,000 bond to regain control of the paper's facilities. He didn't have the money, and none of his wealthy friends dared get involved and face the wrath of Henry. With time running out, he found an ally in Sam Baldwin, a wizened old bail bondsman who made his fortune in the shady streets of the red light district and carried an ancient grudge against Chisholm. Baldwin put up the money and Scripps, armed only with ink and paper, launched his counterattack.

The front page of the *Cleveland Press* trumpeted the story of "The Shame of Chisholm," a harsh rendition of unbridled power, arrogance, violence and abuse. Pleased with his editorial skills, Scripps ran it again on the front page the following day. And the next, and the next after that. The fury of Scripps was every bit of Chisholm's, and the influence of his paper was a match for Chisholm's money.

The standoff continued for weeks. The daily thrashing of his reputation took its toll on Chisholm. He took to bed with fever while his illustrious friends tried to intercede with Scripps. The publisher was unmoved. Finally, a settlement was reached, with Chisholm capitulating, withdrawing all lawsuits and paying a settlement in the matter. Scripps stopped his attacks, but it was too late.

Depressed and debilitated, Henry Chisholm died a few weeks later. The huge monument that stands over his grave at Lake View Cemetery was built entirely through thousands of small contributions from the workers at Cleveland Rolling Mill. Years later, in his autobiography, publishing mogul Scripps did not hesitate to admit his role in a chapter titled, "I killed Henry Chisholm."

10 Frederick Crawford

(1891-1994)

He joined Thompson Products in 1916 as a millwright's helper, and ultimately rose to lead the company into an unprecedented era of expansion after the death of founder Charles Thompson in 1933. Originally formed as the Cleveland Cap Screw Company in 1900, Thompson Products was a crucial contributor to the city's emergence as the nation's machine tool center, manufacturing high quality engine valves and fittings for most of America's automobiles. Controlled at one time by Winton Motor Car, the company was acquired by Thompson in 1908. Thompson's record as president was admirable. Crawford's was astounding.

Host of the spectacular Cleveland Air Races for two decades, Thompson Products not only kept pace with the rapid evolution of the auto industry, transforming itself into the world's leader in replacement parts, it ventured into aviation with dazzling success. With Crawford at the throttle, the grand finale of the races, the Thompson Trophy Race, became the Indy 500 of the air, pitting the world's best fliers against each other in an all-out sprint for the title of Fastest Man in the Air. The leading names in aviation were drawn to Cleveland on Labor Day until 1949, when a souped-up P-51C, piloted by Billy Odom, crashed into a Berea home, killing a woman and her infant son. Cleveland never hosted the event again, opting for the safer Cleveland Air Show, still held Labor Day weekend.

Under Crawford's leadership, the company became a leader in the community as well as an innovator in automotive and aeronautical technology. After unprecedented growth as a defense contractor in World War II, Thompson Products joined forces with rapidly emerging Ramo-Woolridge to create a massive corporation on the cutting edge of electronics and advanced systems engineering.

Even today, few know that the matchmaker of the Thompson-Ramo-Woolridge marriage was not a business broker, but the Pentagon. Military brass, uneasy with the increasingly erratic behavior of eccentric billionaire Howard Hughes, sought to reduce its reliance on Hughes' companies and urged the unification of Thompson in Ohio and Ramo-Woolridge in California into a single, viable alternative. Their efforts, again guided by Fred's steady hand, laid the foundation for one of largest, most diversified and technologically advanced corporations on the international scene. The company simplified its name in 1965, known ever since as TRW.

Frederick Crawford was born before the dawn of flight and lived to see the company he nurtured dominate the aerospace industry, along with a diversified presence in auto parts, engineering, electronics and data systems. Somehow, he also found time to become one of Cleveland's most active civic benefactors. Including points for business and charity, loyalty and longevity, Frederick Crawford can lay serious claim to the title of one of Cleveland's all-time most productive citizens.

4 Cyrus Eaton

(1883-1979, Pugwash, Novia Scotia)

A serendipitous trip to Cleveland in 1901 changed the life of a young Nova Scotia seaman's son with his heart set on a vocation as a minister. The lad came here to visit his uncle, pastor at Euclid Avenue Baptist Church. After Sunday services, he made the acquaintance of a few parishioners, including Mr. and Mrs. Rockefeller, who were both taken by the Canadian lad with the bright smile and formal manners. Within a week, Eaton had a summer job working for the richest couple in America.

That's right. There was a time when one of America's most illustrious billionaire philanthropists was employed as a houseboy by another. Cleveland is the only place in the world that, in a brief and wondrous era, billionaire philanthropists were growing on trees.

Before long, Cyrus was personal secretary to Mr. John, serving as office boy, messenger, social companion and watchman over the private telegraph room into which flowed messages from the money capitals of the world. He sat in the throne room of international finance, the only student in Professor Rockefeller's advanced class on power economics. Many believe that John D. was grooming Eaton as one of his successors, equal to his own sons. He offered him a post at Standard Oil headquarters, already re-located to New York. Amazingly, Eaton turned down the offer.

"I'm sure," Eaton later said, "that if I had gone, I eventually would have become president of Standard Oil. But I didn't want to go to New York City. I wanted to stay in Cleveland, and I did."

He returned to college, then took a modest post as lay minister at Lakewood Baptist Church, but his religious vocation was short-lived. Rockefeller tempted him again, this time with a chance to spearhead a venture into Canada for a syndicate of Standard Oil associates, securing rights for gas and utility franchises throughout the untapped provinces. It was an offer he couldn't refuse.

He was successful in Manitoba, but the Panic of 1907 curtailed his financing. Sanguine and self-assured in spite of the setback, Eaton used his financial skills and connections to secure Canadian loans and continued his efforts, adding franchises across Canada, then down into the Midwestern U. S. Soon, Eaton's Continental Gas & Electric was serving some eight hundred U. S. and Canadian communities. He was a multi-millionaire at 28.

In 1930, after a bitter battle for control of the industry, Eaton apparently surrendered to Charles Insull and Commonwealth Edison of Chicago. He sold his interests for fifty-six million dollars. In the subsequent crush of the Great Depression, the deal proved to be a disaster for Insull and a reprieve for Eaton. Insull's utilities empire collapsed under the crush of debt and the stock market debacle. A broken man, he fled to Greece to avoid prosecution.

Eaton, meanwhile, had deftly shifted to steel, seeing that industry ripe for Rockefeller-style monopolization. He bought Trumbull Steel, the keystone in a design which, if successfully completed, would give him a combine to rival U. S. Steel. In a determined series of transactions, he bought United Alloy, Central Steel and Republic, merging them into Republic Steel Corporation. Finally, in the climactic financial struggle with New York-backed Bethlehem Steel, Eaton won out, gaining control of the last piece in the puzzle, Youngstown Sheet & Tube, with his personal purchase of 51,000 shares of stock only hours before the closing date for transfer of ownership. Infuriated opponents challenged his sly maneuver in court, but Eaton prevailed.

It was a pyrrhic victory for Eaton. The acrimony of the legal give-and-take had lost him some old friends and supporters. The battle had been a distracting influence at a time when the worst economic storm in American history was brewing.

In the process of putting together Republic Steel, Eaton had used a most effective welding instrument called Continental Shares, an investment trust. Riding high, Continental had soared to $300 a share by 1929. A year later, by the time of the court's final decision in the Bethlehem fight, Continental Shares was quoted at $8. When a jesting stockholder offered a hundred shares for a pack of cigarettes, he had no takers. The trust was able to distribute only pennies on the dollar to 18,000 shareholders in 1933. Many of these unfortunate investors were Clevelanders. Eaton's stature in his home city was considerably diminished by the fiasco.

Others suffered, but Eaton was wiped out. He lost control of Republic and most of his vast stock portfolio, retaining only his home and some small properties. For all real purposes, Cyrus Eaton was bankrupt. Easy come, easy go.

At 50, Eaton used his last investment vehicle, the Otis Company, to launch a comeback. He managed to acquire some Canadian real estate in a speculative search for a source of iron ore to supplement the dwindling reserves of the Mesabi Range when World War II broke out and the critical demand for ore opened the door to the gamble of a lifetime.

The precious natural resource was known to exist in abundance in the area of Steep Rock Lake in Ontario, but it was inaccessible, buried under a body of water fifteen miles long and four miles wide. Eaton supported a bold plan. Drain the whole lake. The concept staggered the engineers. It required boring a 3,000-foot tunnel under the lake to its center point, curving upward there to the lake bed. A final blast of dynamite would create a hole into which the waters would descend, to be drained away as a bathtub is emptied. The engineers said the rocks and boulders on the bed would quickly plug any hole. Eaton took the contrary position and proceeded to sell his theory to both the U. S. and Canadian governments. With investments and loans over ten million dollars, the gamble was on.

The tunnel was completed. At the given signal, the plunger was pushed and the dynamite exploded. It was one of the most dramatic moments in industrial history.

The water in the middle of the lake suddenly rose in a great bubble, there was a roaring sound, and boulders shot high into the air. There was a quickening whirlpool, and the waters rushed down through the tunnel. The gamble was won. Steep Rock Basin still stands out as one of the principle sources of high-grade iron ore in North America. Cyrus was back in the saddle. Profits poured in. Over the next decade, Eaton used them wisely.

In partnership with the Krupp dynasty in Germany, he controlled "more iron ore than any other man in the world." At the same time, he re-entered the electric, telephone, coal, banking and real estate businesses with shrewdly timed investments.

At 70, he realized he had overlooked railroads. In 1954, he paid less than four million dollars for controlling interest in the Chesapeake & Ohio, once the Van Sweringens' flagship line, then merged the C & O with the Baltimore & Ohio, the same B & O Railroad immortalized in *Monopoly*, the only game he enjoyed playing. Cyrus Eaton didn't have time for a lot of hobbies.

By the mid-1950s, his colossal fortune and financial influence fully restored, he was, in his own words, "...the last of the tycoons." It was then that he began to focus on greater concerns than world finance. At his own expense, he invited scientists and intellectuals from both sides of the Iron Curtain to an informal conference in Pugwash, Nova

Scotia, the home of his youth. A successful exchange of ideas led to a series of meetings hosted by Eaton. The Pugwash Conferences came to symbolize the first inkling of a thaw in Cold War relations and led to international recognition for Eaton. In Russia, he was regarded as the most progressive of American capitalists and was awarded the Lenin Peace Prize in 1960. Though often criticized at home for his cozy relationship with Soviet leaders, he was ultimately hailed for his groundbreaking efforts on behalf of world peace.

9 Henry Flagler

(1830-1913, Hopewell, New York)

Leaving New York after the 8th grade to follow his half-brother Daniel Harkness to Ohio, Henry Flagler moved up quickly from laborer to clerk at a general store in Republic, earning a respectable salary of $5 a month.

In 1853, he married Mary Harkness, cementing his relationship with that family and its patriarch, Stephen, a successful grain merchant and distillery operator in Bellevue. Stephen Harkness made Henry his sales agent for the large quantities of wheat the company traded on the nearby Cleveland market. It was there that Henry initiated a second fortuitous alliance, this time with a young commissions agent, John Rockefeller. A few years later, Harkness, Flagler and Rockefeller scored a coup in the wheat market and shared the profits.

As time would tell, this incident ultimately spawned several of the great family fortunes of the 20th century and changed the course of world economics. The whole thing was based on inside information.

Months before the Internal Revenue Act of 1862 came to a vote in Congress, Ohio senator John Sherman learned of the impending tax on liquor ingredients. Sherman warned his friend Harkness of the bill's assured passage. Flagler saw this as good news instead of bad, a chance to make a killing by stocking up on distillery grain to avoid the draconian taxes. In a few months, with Rockefeller directing trade traffic, Harkness & Company had reaped a windfall of several hundred thousand dollars. Henry and John each took home a $50,000 bonus.

Rockefeller invested his money in a risky new fuel called "petroleum" while Flagler took his stake and headed north, to the salt boom in Saginaw.Fortunes were won and lost as a flock of entrepreneurs parlayed the discovery of salt reserves in Michigan. Flagler lost. When the Civil War ended, the market collapsed. Henry was wiped out. He returned to Ohio and took work as a commissions merchant, faced with the laborious task of working off his debts.

It was then that Johnny Rockefeller entered his life again. For Henry, this Rockefeller guy was like gum on a shoe. Rockefeller's new venture was going well, but Rocky could see his way to much bigger things. He knew the inchoate oil industry well enough to realize that the company with the best technology could control the market. His partner, Samuel Andrews, was a brilliant technician, but lots of money was required to implement Sam's methods and Johnny's tactics. Money for refineries, pipelines to replace teamster wagons, metal tank-cars instead of wood for shipping.

Rockefeller sought investors to back his plan. The first two turned him down. The third was Henry Flagler. Henry didn't have any cash, but his Harkness relatives did. Stephen Harkness soon agreed to put up the six-figure amount required, as long as Rocky agreed to let trusted Henry handle the money. The firm of Rockefeller, Andrews & Flagler officially opened for business in 1867.

It was Flagler who suggested the acquisition strategy that Rockefeller used to gobble up competitors, Flagler who dealt with the railroads, forcing them to make huge concessions to secure transport contracts, and Flagler who developed the concept of a holding company to control the increasing number of business entities directly or indirectly controlled by the Rockefeller-Andrews-Flagler triumvirate. He even came up with the name: Standard Oil.

In the next ten years, as the world knows, John D. Rockefeller became the wealthiest man in America. And Henry Flagler, the third largest shareholder in Standard Oil, wasn't exactly struggling to make ends meet.

In 1881, his beloved wife Mary died, and a shaken Flagler changed his life. He kept his Standard Oil stock, but walked away from the business. Not quite ready to retire, he soon found something to occupy his time. Act II of Henry Flagler's life was even more amazing than the first. Although he was a few hundred years behind Ponce De Leon, it was really Henry Flagler who discovered Florida.

He remarried in 1883, taking his new wife, Alice, on a honeymoon to St. Augustine. At the time, the sleepy town nestled on the state's northeast coast was the southernmost point of real civilization. Beyond it lay the untouched jungle of central and south Florida.

The Flaglers loved Florida, staying for months, basking in the sun and walking the pristine beaches. Encouraged by Alice, Henry decided to invest in the least populous state in the eastern United States. Never one for halfway measures, he re-created St. Augustine, erecting the elegant Ponce De Leon Hotel, then surrounding it with shops and smaller hotels. He donated millions for new schools and churches in the area and paid good wages for a work force to cater to all the new tourists. The only remaining hurdle was getting there. No problem. Henry built a railroad to St. Augustine from Georgia.

Within a year, northern Florida was bristling with development. Henry realized that the railroad line was the path to prosperity, so he headed south, first to Del Ray, then Deerfield, Ft. Lauderdale, Dania and Hollandale. And Palm Beach. Henry envisioned that magnificent oceanfront property as a vacation mecca. As usual, he was right. Well-to-do northerners filled the hotels and restaurants as fast as he could build them.

Creating modern Florida from scratch was not cheap, but, with cash pouring in from his Standard Oil stock, money was never a problem. Alice was the problem.

Sometime in the mid-90s, his lovely bride went mad. Erratic and confused at first, she deteriorated rapidly, caught in a web of paranoia and hallucination. By 1895, she was spending most of her time at a ouija board, convinced she was corresponding with the Czar of Russia, whom she believed was madly in love with her. The best doctors and alienists were unable to effect any relief. At the unanimous urging of medical consultants, Henry committed her to the Pleasantville Asylum in New York.

Eight months later, she was declared cured and released to a tearful reunion with Henry. At first, the marriage was more blissful than ever. But somehow, in spite of Henry's explicit instructions to the contrary, Alice managed to get her hands on another ouija board. She plunged back into the mental abyss, never to recover. When it came to reality, Alice didn't live there anymore. She returned to the asylum. Two years later, doctors reported to Henry that it was hopeless. She was officially declared incompetent.

Henry carried on. At the urging of Mrs. Julia Tuttle, another former Clevelander and one of the first major landowners in South Florida, Flagler extended his railroad to the Miami River from West Palm Beach. The city of Miami soon sparkled as the crown jewel of Flagler's Florida.

In his seventies, Henry fell in love again, this time with 34-year-old Mary Lily Kenan. He filed for divorce, citing Alice's insanity. But there was no such thing as divorce on the grounds of insanity in turn-of-the-century New York. The courts refused his request.

New York might not cooperate, but if any man owned a whole state in the Union, Henry owned Florida. It didn't take long for a compliant legislature to pass a new law and certify Flagler's divorce. He and Mary Lily were wed later that year. Re-invigorated by his new bride, Henry undertook his last and most difficult task. The only part of Florida still untouched by the Flagler magic was the Keys, 156 miles of islands spiraling off the southern tip of Florida, separated by treacherous stretches of ocean, some as wide as seven miles. Everyone agreed it was impossible to stretch a railroad line across the Keys. Everyone but Henry. Cost overruns ran into the millions. Hurricanes killed dozens of workers. Nothing could stop him. In 1912, the first Flagler locomotive chugged into Key West. He had conquered the Florida jungle from the Georgia border to the last square mile of American soil, 90 miles from Cuba. He had built the great cities of the Southeast and hauled them into the twentieth century like a string of Standard Oil tank cars. His life's work complete, he passed away in 1913 at 83.

90 Caesar Augustin Grasselli

(1850-1927, Cincinnati, Ohio)

The Grasselli family traces its roots back to the medieval alchemists in the European courts of the Borgias and Machiavelli. Eugene Grasselli left Strasbourg early in the nineteenth century, bringing hundreds of years of family experience with him to the new world. He was founder of the Grasselli Chemical Works in America, moving to Cleveland in 1867 to oversee the company's distribution of industrial chemicals to the new businesses sprouting up along the Ohio Canal. His son, Caesar, was raised here, one of fewer than thirty first generation Italian Americans in the city. The name "Caesar" was so bizarre to his Anglo-Saxon peers that young Caesar quickly dropped it in favor of the simple initials, "C.A."

The Grassellis were not just good businessmen, they were exceptional chemists. C. A. received his doctorate in science and spent thousands of hours in the company's laboratories before assuming the presidency in 1885. Many of GCW's most successful compounds and chemical products resulted from his personal efforts.

Grasselli Chemical excelled in two timely areas. They introduced an inexpensive process for providing high quality sulfuric acid, a critical ingredient in the oil refining process. Later, the Grassellis went back to the lab to tinker with combustible compounds, improving power and compression capabilities just in time to take advantage of the coincident explosion of international hostilities. The company grew at exponential rates through the violent years of World War I.

C. A. presided over the company for thirty years and served as Chairman of the Board for a dozen more. His heritage went far beyond business. He imbued his family and employees with his spirit of friendship, loyalty and community service. He was honored internationally as a major contributor to a multitude of civic, academic and scientific institutions and charities.

Grasselli was a co-founder of the Museum of Art and the Institute of Music and the Chamber of Commerce. He supported many charities and endowed several Catholic schools in the area. The tower at John Carroll University is a monument to his generosity.

C. A. Grasselli watched with pride when, after he had lived in Cleveland for 25 years, the first full wave of Italian immigrants joined him. For the next three decades, he was the living patron saint of the crowded Italian enclaves in Big and Little Italy, an inspiration to all, the personification of the American Dream.

A year after C. A.'s death, Grasselli Chemical merged with DuPont to forge the chemical titan of modern times.

62 George Gund & Family

(1888-1966, La Crosse, Wisconsin)

Son of a second-generation German-American who had made his fortune in the beer business, George Gund, Jr. was sent to Harvard, where he edited the *Daily Crimson* and graduated with the first class of the Business School. He returned to assume the presidency of Gund Brewing Company---not a bad start for a kid fresh out of school---until the company closed operations under prohibition.

He hauled in barrels of profits, applying the new Ivy League strategy of heavy marketing. His star brew was the Clevelander, "A Wonderful City---A Wonderful Beer."

Gund switched effortlessly to the coffee business when federal law closed the brewery, acquiring Kaffe Hag, a company that had introduced "de-caffeinated" coffee to the American market. Applying a financial twist widely used decades later but uncommon in the 1920s, Gund scored another coup by selling the company's de-caffeination process to Coca-Cola, then selling the remaining assets and operations to Kellogg.

It was not until 1937, at 49 years of age, George Gund first walked through the doors of the company he would come to embody in action and image---Cleveland Trust. He was hired as a vice-president of Cleveland's largest bank with a directive to expand investment and the customer base. Four years later he became president of the institution and set its course for the next 25 years.

Under his guidance, Cleveland Trust ascended to rank among the ten largest financial institutions in the nation. Gund introduced the concept of "convenient branch banking" and other customer-oriented innovations. Criticized for a tight money policy, Gund's conservative style guided Cleveland Trust through a changing economic climate while more aggressive banks faltered.

He was the Cleveland financial community's most influential voice. It was Gund who determined that the city's Depression wounds were deep and devastating, that recovery would be difficult and prolonged. He was a cautious and patient watchman over a city on the mend.

George Gund was also known for his personal fastidiousness. A Waste Not, Want Not Republican, he drove the same car for fifteen years, carried his brown bag lunch to work in his briefcase and scolded employees for wasting time or facilities. But his civic generosity was unquestionable. Cleveland Trust became the undisputed champion of corporate activism. George personally established the Gund Foundation, responsible for millions in charitable endowments. It remains one of the city's largest and most beneficent.

His sons, GORDON and GEORGE GUND III, own the Cleveland Cavaliers. At first, old George might bridle at the thought of the boys paying abnormally tall young men millions of dollars to throw a pumpkin-sized ball through a metal hoop. But the senior Mr. Gund would relax when he saw the prices they were getting for premium seats, TV rights...and beer.

94 George Humphrey

(1890-1970, Saginaw, Michigan)

A lawyer who came to Cleveland in 1918 to serve as general counsel to the M. A. Hanna Company, George Magoffin Humphrey demonstrated such a knack for understanding the mining business that they made him a partner, an officer, and, in 1929, president of the company. Hanna had been a successful operation since its founding in 1842 by Daniel Rhodes as Rhodes & Co. It didn't hurt any when Marc Hanna and his brothers took over in 1885 and changed the name. By the fourth generation, the privately held partnership was starting to wind down, showing little profit when Humphrey took charge and changed it from a family concern to a conglomerate.

It was his idea to incorporate, and his negotiating and administrative skills that opened the doors to profitable expansion. Within a decade, M. A. Hanna Company owned immense mining tracts in Ohio, Pennsylvania, Michigan, Minnesota and across Canada. After World War II, Humphrey presided over another wave of growth and diversification. A prodigious accomplishment, considering how busy Humphrey had been in public service.

He was chairman of the War Reparations Committee after the war, overseeing Allied control of German industrial and financial operations. His efforts won unanimous praise in both Europe and America. In 1953, he became Secretary of the Treasury, appointed by Ike to promote conservative policies of downsizing the government and restraining inflation. The Eisenhower administration's record for least inflation, least debt, least growth in spending and least increase in taxation in any post-war period confirms Humphrey's ability. He is widely regarded as the most active and most successful Treasury Secretary in modern times. George Humphrey returned to Cleveland in 1957 to devote full-time to his business and charitable interests.

Renewed by George, the Hanna Company (Hanna Mining) kept growing under his son, GILBERT HUMPHREY, through the 60s and 70s. Before Gilbert retired, Hanna ranked among the world leaders in production of iron ore, coal, nickel and silicon.

In similar fashion, the Humphrey family ranked among Cleveland's finest. Foundations established in the names of both father and son continue to contribute millions to local charities.

57 Ned Jordan

(1882-1958, Merrill, Wisconsin)

Coming to Cleveland at the invitation of Newton D. Baker to join the reporting staff of the *Cleveland Press*, Edward Stanlaw Jordan honed his skill as a wordsmith then hired out as a press agent, first with National Cash Register, then a Detroit car manufacturer. The automobile market was already as crowded as Moriarity's on St. Patrick's Day in 1916 when Ned Jordan decided to get into the business, producing an upscale vehicle for the high-toned crowd.

He created the term "luxury car" to describe his elegantly appointed Jordan Roadmaster. In the process of promoting his product as the finest standardized vehicle available on the market, Jordan made up modern advertising. Disdaining his competitors' pre-occupation with mechanics and economics, Jordan went right for the hearts and minds of women. He launched ad campaigns of romance and adventure---let cylinders and spark plugs be damned.

While others sold horsepower, Ned Jordan sold lifestyle. His cars reeked of sex appeal and a spirit of excitement that meshed with the liberated attitudes of the twenties---the Sports Marine and the Playboy delivered style and self-assurance. Sure they were expensive, but with bliss as a standard feature, they were a bargain.

Competitors scoffed at his strategy and his absurd ads with windswept women, angular men and poetic babble about candlelit evenings in faraway places. Ned Jordan shrugged and winked. Jordan Motorcars sales soared, with unheard of profits on every vehicle. By the mid-20s, the rest of the industry was hiring romance novelists to write their brochures and advertising copy.

Jordan withdrew from the business late in the decade, with imitators cutting into his profits and the changing economic winds dampening his enthusiasm. The company closed its doors a few years later. But, to appreciate the lasting impact of Ned Jordan, all you have to do is open a magazine or turn on the television today. Everything from toilet bowl cleaners to dog food is sold as a luxury item, with the promise of a better life or sexual euphoria.

48 The Lincoln Brothers

JOHN LINCOLN *(1866-1959, Painesville, Ohio)*
JAMES LINCOLN *(1883-1965, Painesville, Ohio)*

In more than a few instances, a member of the *Cleveland 200* not only made his own way to the hallowed halls of Cleveland's most exclusive club, but left the door open for others to follow. The Lincoln brothers came hard on the heels of Charles Brush, the human dynamo. John Lincoln learned all he needed to know about electrical engineering in one of Mr. Brush's early generator shops.

In 1895, the last of Cleveland's first hundred years, he opened a little place of his own on Frankfort Street, making electric motors. His only employee was a teen-age boy. It became the Lincoln Electric Company.

John was an excellent engineer and craftsman, and the kid must have been a real hard worker. Early in the new century, a larger building was required to handle all the business. John even had room on the payroll for his little brother, Jimmy, a star athlete at Ohio State who didn't know much about motors yet, but he was a good-looking guy with a winning personality who could sell anything that wasn't nailed down. When he wasn't out with customers, Jim spent time back in the shop, learning about engines and generators. Quick study.

Lincoln Electric quickly moved ahead of the competition because of its advances and improvements in generators, arc-welding and specialized electrodes. Just as important, its progressive philosophy in labor relations and teamwork management was an anomaly in the age of sweat shops and robber barons. The Lincolns treated their employees like close relatives. The result was one big happy family.

James Lincoln

Lincoln Electric's innovations and the explosion of demand precipitated by burgeoning heavy industry and the military needs of two world wars launched the company into the top ranks of Cleveland businesses. The success of the company's employer-employee partnership has been a showcase for worldwide industry. While basic worker compensation approximates average industry rates, Lincoln has paid year-end incentive bonuses to employees every year since 1934, now totaling tens of millions of dollars. Guaranteed employment (no layoffs since 1949), life insurance for employees (since 1918), employee stock options, enhanced retirement plans and a mutual commitment to excellence have been the key to success for Lincoln Electric, now entering its second century of operating on the same principles established by James and John.

112 Bert McDonald

(1892-1974, Cherokee, Iowa)

Old McDonald had a farm. Not Bert, but his father, an immigrant from Scotland who settled in a tiny Iowa town. He didn't have many ducks, geese or chicks, but he did have plenty of little McDonalds running around---13 in all, including little Charles Bertram. In spite of limited resources, the McDonalds believed in education. Every one of the children earned a college degree.

Bert taught school briefly, then enlisted with brothers Tim and Harry in the navy during World War I. Training on the Great Lakes, the young sailors arrived in Cleveland and marveled at the energy and excitement. Bert and Tim made a pact to return after the war.

Tim McDonald became a lawyer, one of Cleveland's brightest, and went on to found the firm of McDonald, Hopkins & Hardy. Bert was hired to play clarinet in the house orchestra at the Statler Hotel. This left his days wide open, so he talked his way into a job with Charles Otis & Company, the ancient investment house that had dominated Cleveland finance for generations. It wasn't a glamour position---chalk boy---but it may have been a better learning environment than the Wharton School of Business. Every day, Bert read the stock ticker and posted the quotes on the huge slate fronting the Otis "war room."

Within months, he knew more about the trends and fluctuations in the market than most of the veterans. Otis hired him as a broker and a legend in local investment circles started trading shares on the floor. Bert established a reputation for integrity and good judgment. In 1924, he scraped up fifty thousand dollars with a partner and opened McDonald & Callahan. Two years later, the firm handled the first public stock offering for a growing welding and parts company. Thompson Products would go a long way in the next seventy years. So would McDonald.

With the market booming, McDonald & Callahan looked to the future with unbridled enthusiasm. Bert was confident enough to finally take his first vacation in the fall of 1929, a belated honeymoon cruise with his wife. He sailed to England, only to learn that the Great Crash had all but wiped out his company. He rushed home to pick up the pieces.

Callihan fell by the wayside, as did other partners through the trying years of the 30s, but McDonald held on. With the help of financial whiz Jim Coolidge, the company survived, primarily as the Cleveland's most astute bank industry advisors, assisting in several area mergers and reorganizations.

Bert's chalk boy days served him well. His personal knack for picking stocks led to major shareholder positions in wholesome local outfits like Central National Bank.

The firm became McDonald & Company in 1944. Bert had learned two lessons very well. First, he rewarded his best employees, adding many partners over the years while decreasing his ownership position. Second, he never took another lengthy vacation and never retired, remaining active until his death at 82.

Bert McDonald had no sons, but he treated his successors in business like family and they responded in kind. Under Tom O'Donnell and Bill Carmel, McDonald & Company converted to a corporation and grew tenfold again from the 60s to the 90s. In 1983, it took honors as the first company traded on the New York Stock Exchange from the first day of its existence as a corporation. Today, McDonald remains the top underwriting firm in Ohio, with more than 1,000 employees and hundreds of millions in annual sales.

91 Theo Moll

(1905-1996, Herborn, Germany)

You probably don't know much about Theo Moll, but if you had to use one man's chronicle of life as the definition of the Cleveland Success Story, Theo's would be as good as any. He was a German immigrant who came to Cleveland at 19 and worked as a tool and die maker at Easy-On Cap Company, one of hundreds of little machine shops that sprouted up in Cleveland like weeds. Cleveland is very good at a lot of things, but we have always been the undisputed national champion of machine tools. Still are.

We know Theo Moll was machine tool man. He and his buddies, Emil and Erwin, opened a shop of their own in Parma. They made the machines that make things, and they used their modern ideas to make them work faster and more efficiently. They called it Modern Tool & Die.

Theo was good at working with tools and working with people. He was down to earth but believed in his vision. Over many years, toiling long hours, he built his business into an industry leader. After the war, the company diversified into garden, landscape and recreational products. They changed the name to MTD in 1968, continued to grow, and now provide machines, tools, vehicles and products for use by millions of people all over the world.

Theo Moll shared his blessings with his family, friends, employees and neighbors. His generosity came back to him as greater prosperity and more good fortune. We know Theo stayed true to his work ethic and never retired. He passed away in 1996 at 91.

From a distance, that was the life of Theodore Moll. And what else is known, up close and personal? Nothing. Nothing at all. Theo Moll was a very private person. You never read about him in the *National Enquirer*. You never saw him on *Hard Copy*. He didn't pop up at events all over town just to get a mention in "Mary, Mary."

Theo Moll thought Greta Garbo spent way too much time in public.

His company, MTD, is said to be a one of the largest privately held companies in America, with sales in the billions, but it's still a family business and they don't like to talk about money. Theo himself was probably a billionaire, but he never mentioned what he was worth. It's believed he donated millions to a number of charities and that institutions like Lutheran Hospital, Lutheran West and Baldwin-Wallace continue to thrive largely because of his generosity. He asked them not to make a big deal out of it, so there aren't any busts of Theo Moll or Moll Towers as a tribute to the man. People all over Northeast Ohio tell stories about how Theo Moll paid for this orphan kid's tuition or paid the mortgage for that unfortunate widow. A pastor might mention how the church replaced its windows or the school built a gymnasium. There seems to be a great number of Theo Moll parables like that out there. How many? Don't know. No one ever wrote them down.

How noble a man was Theo Moll? How honored was Cleveland to have him as a citizen? Don't know. Never will. Theo Moll was good at almost every everything but fame.

36 Charles Otis & Family

(1827-1905, Bloomfield, Ohio)

One of Cleveland's most influential families ever, the Otis clan was dominant in shipping, railroads, highways, industry and finance for more than a century. Patriarch WILLIAM OTIS (1794-1868) was a tavern owner who moved his business here to cater to the thirsty workers on the Ohio & Erie Canal. The most precious commodity in the early 1800s was cash, No one had much, so William often bartered his whiskey for other goods. Before long, he ended up with a barn full of stuff and reluctantly left his bartending for more serious work as a man of commerce. For William, the simplest principles still applied. Pour a drink, get paid. Sell a wagonload of pork, get paid. By the late 1820s, Otis was one of Cleveland's most successful businessmen and industrial pioneers. The father of Cleveland commerce, Otis recognized that Cleveland had a natural abundance of talent and resources. The trick was getting the goods to eager buyers. He built many of the first highways and railroads and helped organize the Board of Trade.

His son, CHARLES A. OTIS (1827-1905), picked up right where Pops left off. He concentrated on the small ironworks William had founded to make railroad tracks and built it into Otis Steel, later to become the massive Cleveland division of Jones & Laughlin. He later added American Wire and American Steel Screw to his credits and constructed Cleveland's first intra-city rail system. Charles was also the only member of the Otis family to venture into politics, elected mayor of Cleveland in 1873. He did a fine job, but did not stand for re-election and never ran for any office again. He just couldn't afford it. Charles estimated that his income declined 98% during his two years in public service.

The third Otis generation maintained the family's standard of excellence in business and branched out even further, this time into the media. CHARLES OTIS, JR. (1868-1963) was the first Clevelander to own a seat on the New York Stock Exchange and a founder of Otis & Hough brokerage firm. In Cleveland's golden age, Otis was its leading financier. He used a few of the family dollars to become a dominant factor in the local news business at the turn of the century. At one time, Charles Otis, Jr. owned or controlled the *Cleveland Leader*, the *Evening Plain Dealer*, the *News & Herald* and the *Cleveland News*.

How did Charles Otis rank among his Cleveland peers, the captains of industry and finance? Suffice to say, for the last 25 years of his life he was known throughout Ohio by the nickname first used to describe him by John D. Rockefeller, Jr., another namesake son of a famous father: "Mr. Cleveland."

26 Oliver Hazard Payne & Family

(1837-1885, Cleveland)

Two of Cleveland's oldest and proudest families were bonded in Oliver Hazard Payne, son of HENRY PAYNE and Mary Perry. Father Henry was a nationally esteemed Clevelander. Senator and congressman, lawyer and business leader, he was even touted for President in 1880. On his mother's side, Oliver was related to Commodore Oliver Hazard Perry, American legend and hero of the Battle of Lake Erie. His older brother, NATHAN PERRY PAYNE, was a Cleveland mayor and commissioner. His sister was married to one of those Whitney boys in New York (perhaps you've heard of Payne-Whitney).

Oliver was a businessman first. Another Cleveland oil baron, he was Rockefeller's largest competitor until his company merged with Standard Oil in 1872. Thereafter, his Standard stock and other investments made him one of the wealthiest men in the country. Oliver Payne became one of Cleveland's leading philanthropists. All of the first rank hospitals, schools, charities and institutions here benefited from his help, as did many others across the nation. Cornell Medical School was built on Payne money, and Hamilton College, and University of Virginia's Science Center.

Oliver Payne died in 1917. He never married and had no heirs. His vast estate was divided among his Perry and Payne nieces and nephews.

Hey, Uncle Oliver! Remember me?

158 The Ratner Family

The Ratowezns emigrated from their home Poland in 1920 and arrived in Cleveland with a new surname: Ratner. LEONARD, the oldest of three boys, started a creamery with his sister, DORA, and younger brother, MAX.

In 1922, brother CHARLES arrived. The dairy was already a little crowded with Ratners, so he looked around for another way to make a living. Charles was a carpenter. When he learned they called Cleveland the Forest City, it seemed only logical to get into wood. He opened the doors of the Buckeye lumberyard. The others said goodbye to the milk and cheese and threw their lot in with him. Charlie made enough in a few short years to retire to Florida. (Little did he know what a precedent he was setting.) Dora married and retired to her home, where she worked 20 hours a day as a homemaker. Leonard and Max changed the company's name to Forest City Materials, rolled up their sleeves and went back to work.

Under their guidance Forest City thrived, even through the Depression years when the Ratners used their stockpile of profits to acquire large tracts of land at bargain prices. In the 1940s, they diversified into construction and real estate. At the same time, the core company expanded to become one of the leading manufacturers of pre-fabricated houses, the hot post-war fad.

In 1960, operations were consolidated into Forest City Enterprises and the family launched more new ventures with similar success. Retail stores, apartment buildings and commercial development were added to the Ratner portfolio. Today, Forest City remains a major presence in the Cleveland business community, owner/developer of landmarks like Tower City.

For the Ratners, business success was only half the story. A commitment to the Jewish community, in Cleveland and across the world, was coupled with the heritage of "tzedakah," the duty of giving unto others according to the ancient guidelines of Judaism. The National Conference of Christians and Jews and the United Jewish Appeal are among the national institutions that have benefited from the Ratner philosophy. In Israel, Hebrew University, the Weizman Institute and the Jewish Theological Seminary are grateful recipients of Ratner Halls, Ratner Wings and Ratner Towers. The Jewish Welfare Federation, Park Synagogue and Mt. Sinai Hospital are a few of their favorites, but their generosity hasn't been limited to strictly kosher causes. For generations, just about anyone with a good cause and a good story could trek out to the modest Forest City headquarters on Brookpark Road and leave with a hefty check.

They're all gone now. Max, the last of the original Ratners and a fixture in the local community for more than 70 years, died in 1996. Forest City is still a local company with extensive local interests, with lots of second- and third-generation Ratners in the board room, renown as a leading developer, with billions invested in real estate and retail operations nationwide. But Leonard, Charles, Dora and Max would be proudest of their heritage in philanthropy. The Cleveland Jewish community provides more per capita support to Israel than any other city in the world. Tzedakah.

1 John D. Rockefeller

(1839-1937, Richfield, New York)

Could it have happened anywhere but Cleveland? The introverted son of an itinerant flim-flam man works hard and pinches pennies to become the richest man in the world, patriarch of the family whose very name came to be synonymous with unfathomable wealth.

John D. Rockefeller is proof positive of the vagaries of genetics. Poppa Wild Bill Rockefeller could have been the poster boy for Attention Deficit Disorder, a medicine man always one step ahead of irate customers and the law. By the turn of the century, his son was the world's first official billionaire. Later historians estimated his real net worth in 1900 at over 2 billion. By today's standards, that would be the combined net worth of Bill Gates, all the DuPonts, Oprah Winfrey and Michael Jordan. A lot of authors, economists and historians have tried to reconstruct exactly how he did it, but no one really knows. And if they did, do you think they'd write it down in a book so everyone could be a billionaire for the price of a paperback?

If business were religion (and maybe it is now), the faithful would kneel at the shrine of John Davison Rockefeller

He was 14 when the family moved to the Cleveland area. John and brother William enrolled at Central High. They found themselves among some interesting classmates, including Laura Celestia Spelman and Marcus Hanna. Laura would marry John one day, while Marc would become, with the help of his high school chums, the nation's most powerful politician.

John dropped out of high school (so much for the importance of a good education), then took a few courses at Folsom's (not the prison, the mercantile college) to prepare himself for a business career. In 1855, he found work at the wholesale commission house of Hewitt & Tuttle at a salary of $25 a month. He proved to be a reliable bookkeeper. The company offered him a raise, but John thought he was worth a hundred dollars more. When negotiations stalled, he took Maurice Clark up on his offer to form a partnership. Clark & Rockefeller was founded in 1859, brokers dealing principally in vegetables. The little firm prospered as canals and railroads brought traffic and the Civil War brought a wave of profiteering. Young Mr. Rockefeller was already a man of means in his mid-twenties, with few reasons to complain. One of them was the vile substance that had begun polluting the air and water around the company office overlooking the Flats.

Oil. The smell of oil was in the air that Rockefeller breathed and colored the waters of the Cuyahoga River flowing past his office. Little wonder that he and his partner should have considered the advantages of investing in "petroleum," so named by Sam Kier, the little man who first found use for the black muck that seeped out of the ground in the hills of Western Pennsylvania as a liniment and home remedy. Some Cleveland chemists analyzed the stuff and determined it would be even more useful as a lubricant and illuminant. After refining, oil and kerosene were produced. The worthless remains, a dangerously flammable liquid called "gasoline," was disposed of, usually in the closest river.

By 1865, there were 28 refineries in Cleveland, ports and train stations were clogged with shipments and people started using the word "millionaire."

After careful study of the situation, Johnny decided that drilling for oil was too speculative to meet his requirements for a sound investment. It was his judgment that the firm should skirt this get-rich-quick stuff and concentrate on processing and distribution.

Through that wonderfully mysterious element of chance that is almost always a part of great success stories, there had arrived in

Cleveland at this critical juncture a young Englishman named Samuel Andrews, a candlemaker by trade. He had developed a new process for refining kerosene from crude petroleum, but he needed financial backing to put his idea to work.

Rockefeller and Clark took the plunge, with help from John's friend, Henry Flagler and Flagler's relatives in the Harkness family. It was risky business, committing several hundred thousand dollars to an industry that didn't even exist a few years prior. In the end, all were happy with the outcome. Oh boy, were they happy.

Andrews' methods were years ahead of the competition. But only Rocky had the foresight and the financial savvy to use the advantage to catapult the company to the corporate stratosphere, an altitude where no businessman had gone before. He developed the systems to facilitate transportation and handling as well as the schemes to dispose of rivals through acquisition, imposition or demolition. Whatever it took. In 1870, a multitude of oil companies, refineries, transport and holding companies owned by John and his friends were united under the banner of the Standard Oil Company---gold dollar signs and silver barrels superimposed on a currency-green field. Rocky owned the most stock and exercised the most control. He was president for the next forty-one years. In all that time, there was not one gloomy stockholders meeting.

For several years, the company doubled its net income every few months, then Rockefeller increased the pace. Figures have been bandied about by a variety of sources, but a comprehensible value of the profits generated by Standard Oil in an age before income tax or government regulation is beyond realistic estimation. Using percentage of GNP as a yardstick, the Rockefeller family alone had accumulated a net worth equal to over 100 billion modern U. S. dollars.

Cleveland's John D. was recognized as the world's first official billionaire. "God gave me my money," he said, and maybe he was right. There wasn't anyone else around in 1900 who could get his hands on that much cash.

A look at the offspring of the Standard Oil behemoth---forced to divest many of its component parts by the landmark antitrust legislation of the early twentieth century---tells a story of commercial might beyond imagination---Sohio, Exxon, Mobil, Conoco, Standard of Indiana, SoCal and more. Along with cousins and in-laws like British Petroleum, Chase Manhattan and Chemical Bank, they have made the Fortune 500 their playpen, jostling among themselves over the years for room at the top. As for society, the annual Blue Books of the past century have always included dozens of family names owing their lofty status to a single employer---Standard Oil. Harkness, Clark, Flagler, Payne, Andrews, Eaton, Blossom, Ingalls and Grasselli are only a few.

The old man officially retired in 1896, but he kept a sharp eye on Junior and the grandkids. He lived a comfortable but modest and upright life. Lean and healthy, he assumed a wizened look as the years went by, partly because of chronic alopeceia, a harmless but embarrassing disease that left him completely hairless, head to toe. He wore a wig and fake eyebrows in public appearances.

Rockefeller abstained from alcohol and disdained most social activities. His only serious hobby was golf, a game that he played passionately and quite badly, usually at his own course in his backyard at Forest Hill.

Some say he was a greedy and ruthless financial tyrant who used an array of dirty tricks, underhanded tactics and downright illegal machinations to wipe out his competition and seize American industry by the throat. Maybe so. But it's hard to condemn a man who not only led American business into the 20th century, but American philanthropy as well, personally donating hundreds of millions of dollars to worthy causes and creating the foundations that have contributed billions more, all over the world.

Cleveland was the recipient of a fair share of the Rockefeller largesse for many years. Rockefeller Park, Shaker Lakes, Forest Hill, Case and Western Reserve---too many to count. It's likely that he would have done much more and maintained strong relations with his home town if not for the bitter memory of Laura's funeral. Ohio lawmakers had caught the fever from Washington and passed a stiff income tax of its own. Rockefeller was fighting it in the courts when he returned to Cleveland for the gloomy funeral of his wife of more than fifty years. Vindictive state officials couldn't resist. They served him with a tax summons as the mourners gathered in Lake View Cemetery. John D. was seething when he left Cleveland. The highest achiever in the history of capitalism and Cleveland's most distinguished citizen never returned.

66 Henry Sherwin

(1842-1916, Brook Farm, Vermont)

What was it about Cleveland in the post-Civil War era that drew so many energetic youngsters---Rockefeller, Mather, Chisholm, Flagler, Hanna---and here comes another one. Little Henry Stoddard Sherwin arrived in 1859, worked hard as a clerk and bookkeeper, saved his money, and, in 1866, invested in a paint company. He didn't know much about paints, but he had a simple theory. Cleveland was a growing port city. A port city meant plenty of sailors. The toll of wind and water made painters out of sailors and it often became habitual. Even on dry land, they couldn't help themselves. If it was standing still, they'd paint it. It wasn't a very scientific theory, but it was good enough for Henry to bet all two thousand of his hard-earned dollars on a future in the paint business. A few years later, his partners abandoned paint to get in on the oil boom and Henry was left to carry on alone.

He found a new partner, Edward Williams. The two decided to call their new outfit the Sherwin-Williams Company. Not very creative, but it sure didn't hurt business. Sherwin was a born salesman and Williams a steady hand at the helm. Cleveland was a town in a hurry, with new homes and buildings coming out of the ground like dandelions and Sherwin-Williams quickly turned profits that were plowed right back into more inventory and a new factory in the Flats.

The first years were good but they paled in comparison to what happened in 1880. Up until then, most paint was sold in its component parts---oil base, catalyst and color---to be mixed by the customer. A few pre-mixed paints had been introduced but their quality was dismal. Henry Sherwin swore he would develop a consistent and durable "one-part" paint. His promise became a reality in 1880. The paint was so good and Sherwin so confident, he offered his customers a money-back guarantee. SWP took the market by storm.

Expanding to other prime locations, Sherwin-Williams opened a plant in Chicago to service the rail industry. It became the largest paint factory in the world. Regional plants and subsidiaries opened their doors across the U. S. and Canada. New divisions catered to the automotive, industrial and retail markets. After World War I, foreign expansion and major acquisitions propelled the company to greater heights. In World War II, with crucial paint ingredients rationed or unavailable, the company made another breakthrough comparable only to Henry Sherwin's introduction of ready-mix SWP. Kem-Tone was a water-based coating, almost as endurable as oil-based. Easy to apply, easy to clean, safe and moderately priced, Kem-Tone was a dream for salesman, a friend to homemakers and a miracle for Sherwin-William stockholders. Once again, the company revolutionized the industry. By the second half of the 20th century, it was the largest paint producer on the planet.

Still number one in architectural coatings as the century drew to a close, Sherwin-Williams generates over three billion dollars in annual sales and continues its consistent growth pattern with more acquisitions, adding Pratt & Lambert to the fold in 1996.

"We cover the world," they say. And they're not joking. Henry Sherwin's $2,000 has gone a long way.

Henry's daughter, BELL SHERWIN, was an educator and reformer who ranks among the city's leading feminist and consumer activists. She was the first president of the Consumer League of Ohio, president of the National League of Women Voters and a co-founder of the Women's City Club.

162 George Steinbrenner III

(1930 - , Cleveland)

Could the Cleveland Indians have won a title in the late 70s or early 80s had Vernon Stouffer stuck to his deal to sell the team to George Steinbrenner? We'll never know. When he was rejected (for still unknown reasons), he and a group of local investors paid about the same price for the legendary Yankee franchise.

It wasn't George's first involvement in sports. He had purchased the Cleveland Pipers basketball team in 1960 and brought the city the American Basketball League championship in the 1961-62 season. George practiced his future style by often coming down from his seat in the stands to yell at his coach and players on the floor. The venture ended badly when the ABL folded, leaving Steinbrenner $125,000 in debt.

He redoubled his efforts at the family shipping business, Kinsman Marine, to recoup some of the money. Kinsman had become part of the American Shipbuilding conglomerate and George moved up rapidly through the corporate ranks, leading a takeover of the board of directors in 1967. At 37, Steinbrenner was CEO of the largest shipping company on the Great Lakes.

At a time when other shippers were retrenching and ore shipments were falling, George saw the potential for grain. He expanded the business to include operations in Toledo, Chicago, and Tampa. In the 1980s,American Shipbuilding again changed direction, concentrating on ocean shipping and government contract work. Headquarters were moved to Florida.

Business was good, but George was itching to get back into sports. He had been an athlete himself, racing hurdles in high school and college, competing---but never winning---against Harrison Dillard. He earned his masters degree in physical education at Ohio State. He spent some time coaching football, as an assistant at Northwestern and Purdue, but had to give it up for the boat business. By the early 60s, his only avenue into pro sports was as a fan...or an owner.

He bought an 11% share of the Chicago Bulls but sold it soon at no profit (should have held on to that, George). What he really wanted was a piece of the American Pastime. A baseball franchise. The opportunity to own the Yankees presented itself immediately after George was snubbed by the Indians. At $10 million, Steinbrenner paid $3.2 million less for the Yankees than CBS had paid for them nine years earlier. Twenty years later, the storied Yankees team was valued at over twenty times the purchase price.

George said he wasn't going to get involved in running the team, but he was just kidding. Within a few years, he became the most visible and controversial owner in sports. He lavished money on the team and enticed the press with posh parties and quotable quotes. Steinbrenner signed the first huge free agent, pitcher Catfish Hunter, for a then incredible 3.5 million dollars. He signed Reggie Jackson as designated star, and hired Billy Martin, creating a winning but volatile combination, like gin and vermouth.

He made no secret of his feelings about individual players, but he could never make up his mind about Billy Martin. He hired Billy, then fired him. Hired him again, then fired him. Finally, he hired him back. Then he fired him.

Once he tried to fire him, but he was informed by underlings that Billy wasn't working for him, so he immediately announced he was hiring Billy Martin as manager of the Yankees. And then he fired him.

Every now and then, George takes some time off from the game he loves to serve a suspension. The longest wasn't for a baseball violation, but a political offense---making illegal contributions to the 1972 Nixon campaign. Steinbrenner got a slap on the wrist from the courts (a smaller fine than Albert Belle received for yelling at a reporter) but was served a two-year pass from pinstripes by harsher judge Bowie Kuhn.

Somewhat mellowed through the years, George remains an impulsive and demanding boss and one of baseball's most colorful and outspoken owners. His Yankees seem to be regaining some of their old prowess after a stretch of mediocrity, and he does have one thing no Cleveland Indian alumnus of the past 48 years can match---a World's Series ring. Damn Yankees.

140 Vernon Stouffer & Family

(1901-1974, Cleveland)

Building on his father's modest lunch counter at the Arcade, Vernon Bigelow Stouffer constructed one of the country's most successful diversified food service companies. Vern Stouffer joined father Abraham and brother Gordon after graduation from the Wharton School of Business. In less than a decade, Stouffer's was a bustling chain of restaurants and the family business went public.

Stouffer was among the first to implement Clarence Birdseye's frozen food process, marketing high quality prepared meals as early as 1951. Frozen foods became a major component of the corporation. Hotels and real estate were added to the portfolio in the 60s and 70s.

In 1966, Vern Stouffer came to the rescue of the floundering Cleveland Indians. Ineptly operated on and off the field since the mid-50s, the team was on the brink of joining the exodus of other financially troubled franchises to better prospects out west when Stouffer entered the picture. He purchased controlling interest, installed veteran Gabe Paul as general manager and poured in dollars to resuscitate the ball club. Nothing worked. Five years later, after absorbing millions in losses, he sold the team to Nick Mileti's investment group. The resurgence of the Indians was still 20 years away, but Stouffer deserves credit as one of those long-suffering Clevelanders who held the fort until help arrived in the 90s.

175 Jeremiah Sullivan

(1844-1922, Canal Fulton, Stark County, Ohio)

Cleveland's history is replete with classic American success stories and Jeremiah Sullivan's is among the most notable. The son of Irish immigrants, Sullivan served with distinction as a teenager in the Civil War, a volunteer in the Third Ohio Artillery who saw action at Vicksburg and Atlanta, serving under Generals Grant and Sherman.

Denied a formal education because of his Irish background, Sullivan took work in a general store in Holmes County and ended up owning the place within two years. He opened a hardware store in Millersburg and established a reputation as a principled businessman. In 1887, President Grover Cleveland named him government bank examiner for Ohio, the first Irish-American to attain such a lofty position in the financial world.

Two years of studying the methods and operations of banks all over the state gave Sullivan an invaluable education in the inner workings of the financial world. In 1890, at 48, Jeremiah moved to Cleveland to begin his own banking career. Over the next three decades, he distinguished himself as one of the most respected financial experts in the nation and founder of one of Cleveland's foremost financial institutions.

In 1890, Sullivan founded the Central National Bank of Cleveland. While still President of Central, he also founded the Superior Savings and Trust in 1905. Both thrived as service-oriented operations. In 1921, the two banks were merged into Central National Bank Savings & Trust Company, among the largest privately-owned banks in the country outside of New York.

Sullivan's contributions went beyond his philosophy of making funds available to a whole new class of merchants and entrepreneurs. In 1913, he was instrumental in the passage of the Federal Reserve Act, using his considerable influence to lobby for passage of the law that would unify the many regional banking independents under the singular power of the federal reserve system. The Fourth District Federal Reserve Bank, a prize that propelled Cleveland into the top rank of national finance centers was awarded to Cleveland primarily as a thank you to Jeremiah.

Colonel Sullivan continued to lead the institution he founded until his death in 1922. After a lifetime of good health without a single day lost to illness or injury, Jeremiah Sullivan was felled by the postwar influenza epidemic and died at his home on Millionaire's Row. He was buried in Lakeview Cemetery.

25 Charles Edwin Thompson

(1870-1933, McIndoe Falls, Vermont)

Charles Thompson was a very interesting man, successful at many things, but it's hard to get past the single fact that this man was the principle founder of what is now TRW. Do you know how big TRW is? Started from scratch in 1901, it now has a gross national product larger than most countries. It has multi-billion dollar divisions that do magical things in aerospace. Does your company have any aerospace divisions? A giant in electronics. A titan in the automotive field. Satellites. Precision tools. Electronic research and development. Major federal contractor. Very big company.

How do these guys do this? Charles Thompson never went to college. He learned how to weld, a talent in great demand in the new age of the horseless carriage, and went to work after high school. Charles and some friends saw they could do as much welding work as they could handle, so they opened their own place, Cleveland Cap Screw Company ("We Weld Anything"). Winton Motor Carriage, then the largest automobile manufacturer in America, placed an order large enough to change the company's focus ("We Weld Wintons") and its fortunes.

Winton provided a tremendous boost, but it was Thompson himself who punched the ticket to the big time. He developed a welding method for more effective sealing of valves, an important key to reliable engine performance. The advantage over competitors was insuperable. Renamed Electric Welding Products, then the Steel Products Company after it broadened its product and customer base, it provided welded products to virtually every auto maker in the U. S.

In the next decade, the company expanded to include airplane valves and parts and built a vast distribution system for automotive replacement parts, dominating in both those fields as well. In 1926, the company was renamed Thompson Products, a tribute to the man.

It was Charles Thompson who started the Cleveland Air Races. The competition he envisioned as a promotional boost for high-speed engines turned into the airplane industry's annual showcase.

At the time of his death in 1933, Thompson's company was an unqualified success, with international sales in the tens of millions. Today's TRW, under CEO Joseph Gorman (another TRW commander revered in the international business community and the local civic community) is more than a hundred times larger.

126 James Van Dorn

(1848-1898, York, Ohio)

A steadfast man of pure Dutch ancestry, James Van Dorn traced his roots to the noble Van Doorn family of Holland, including Stephen Van Doorn, high sheriff of Antwerp in 1088. In America, the Van Dorns were among the earliest settlers, with family members living in New York as early as 1642, often noted as superior constructors. Peter Van Dorn moved his family to Ohio in 1828 and established a reputation as "the finest barn builder in Northern Ohio."

One of his ten children was James H. Van Dorn, born in York, Ohio. As a youth he was greatly influenced by his aptly named brother, Cleveland Van Dorn, a Civil War veteran, teacher and Baptist minister. It was Cleveland who urged James to use "God's gift"---his powerful forearms and shoulders---and ply his trade as a blacksmith.

It was sound advice. James apprenticed in Elyria, then worked in Akron at Aultman & Miller, buying a modest home there in the 1860s. It became the site of a shrine to clever marketing.

James spent almost six months handcrafting an ornate, wrought iron fence that he erected on his property. The fence was such an unusual masterpiece that it drew crowds of admirers (there wasn't much to do in Akron in those days). More than that, it demonstrated his remarkable talent with iron and attracted investors when he sought to establish his own company a few years later.

After years in the Van Dorn & Goodrich partnership, James came to Cleveland and established the Van Dorn Iron Works in 1898, prospering not only as a manufacturer of wrought iron fences and furniture, but monumental steel work as well. Van Dorn's sons expanded the business over the years to include auto parts, tanks and armor plating. Subsequent generations brought about more diversification into modern plastic and aluminum products. By the 1980s, the company included operations throughout the U. S. and overseas, thousands of employees and hundreds of millions of dollars in annual sales.

Jim Van Dorn's showcase fence had stretched around the world.

14 Jeptha Wade

(1811-1890, Romulus, New York)

Many of the major industries that made Cleveland a great city did not exist when the first settlers arrived in 1796. Railroads. Petroleum. Electricity. Automobiles. All came from nothing and became pillars of world economy. But the last is the greatest phenomenon. An entire industry, inconceivable two centuries ago, that expends little in actual labor and depletes no natural resources, yet it dominates the business, political and social circles of the globe. Communication.

The world's first communications mogul was Jeptha Wade, a talented and creative youngster with an eye for new products and the courage to believe he could accomplish tasks others dismissed as impossible.

Jeptha Wade arrived in Cleveland in 1856, just as he was in the process of putting together the area's first telegraph network. He had learned about the little gadget when he traveled to Baltimore in 1847 and saw Samuel B. Morse himself transmitting messages to Washington by wire, an enchanting demonstration that immediately converted Wade into a believer.

Wade had little to offer in the way of finances or business experience. Son of a surveyor, his only inheritance was a good education in mathematics and mechanics, but his artistic nature led him to an early career as a portrait artist. While active as a painter, he became aware of the camera, newly introduced to America in 1839, and begin experimenting with photography. Wade is credited with taking the first daguerreotype west of New York, in 1844.

His interest in art and photography were swept aside when he first laid eyes on the telegraph key. It was the key to the future. He formed a small company with meager capital and hired on as a subcontractor to erect the first telegraph line in the Midwest, from Detroit to Jackson, Michigan. Wade not only completed the work through difficult circumstances, he operated the Jackson office after the line opened, even though he had no training in telegraphy and Morse had not even sent him the code yet.

Wade won new contracts and new investors. He started stringing telegraph lines across the middle U. S. like popcorn string on a Christmas tree---Detroit to Chicago and Milwaukee, Toledo to Cleveland, Cleveland to Buffalo, Cleveland to Columbus to Cincinnati to St. Louis. Cleveland's name kept popping up on the interchange list, so Wade settled there. He fell in love with his adopted city. It remained his home for the rest of his life.

The rapidly expanding telegraph business was not without its problems. There was no FCC, so any clown with a roll of wire could set up shop and call himself a telegraph company. Plenty did. Early service was sporadic, with wide variances in quality, consistency and costs leaving the public confused and dissatisfied. It was Jeptha Wade who sorted the tangled wires and made sense of it all. He moved past his competitors by inventing the Wade Insulator, enclosing his lines in a protective shield that made them far more impervious to weather. Later, he added an iron enclosure, enabling him to traverse the Mississippi with the first underwater cable.

Recognizing the ruinous effect of wildcat competition on reputable companies, Wade conceived and executed his personal plan for consolidating the industry into a cohesive, inter-connected whole.

With the central regions of the nation solidified, Wade turned west. Using Pacific Telegraph Company as a vehicle, he rolled through California in less than two years, providing continuous lines of communication from San Francisco to Los Angeles and San Diego. It was all prelude to his most daunting task, the one that even had Wade's admirers shaking their heads in dismay---cross-continental wire service. Between the populous east and the western shoreline lay 2,000 miles of trouble. Rugged mountain terrain and vast forests, wetlands and waste lands, hostile Indians and wild animals---all waiting for Jeptha Wade. It wasn't easy, but he made it look that way. In 1861, the final links were set in place and St. Louis went on line with Pacific Telegraph Company, uniting America for the first time, coast to coast. The corporate entity that emerged to control this first network in American history was called Western Union. Its first president was Jeptha Homer Wade.

The taxing ordeal of fifteen years of fanatic dedication to the task finally caught up to Jeptha. Bedridden by exhaustion and serious illness, he resigned as Western Union's leader a year later.

He returned to Cleveland in poor health, expecting to live out the brief remainder of his life quietly and obscurely in the city he loved. But the Cleveland climate proved exceptionally good for Jeptha and he was further reinvigorated by his own civic generosity.

He owned a sprawling estate just east of Doan's Corners and spent months recuperating there. His spirits rose as his health returned. He became active in business again, as co-founder and first president of Citizens' Savings & Loan. He was involved with Henry Chisholm in the steel business and part owner of many railroads. He groomed his son to replace him, but Randall Wade's sudden death at 41 devastated Jeptha. After months of grief, he found solace in the companionship of his grandson, 18-year-old JEPTHA WADE II. The two Jepthas became inseparable. Like his grandfather, Jeptha II became a whirlwind success with interests and expertise in a dozen different businesses. He continued the family tradition of philanthropy as well, granting the city the rights to many more acres of the Wade Park lands and donating millions more to the museums and universities that thrived there.

The whole world is wired, now, from Barberton to Bangkok and Toledo to Timbuktu. Instant communication is taken for granted by anyone with a phone, a fax or a plug in the wall. But don't forget who started it all. Jeptha Wade, Clevelander. Dot-dot-dash-dot-dash.

43 Thomas White

(1836-1914, Phillipston, Massachusetts)

White Sewing Machine Company. White Steam Car Company. White Motors. White Consolidated Industry. White-Sundstrand. The abundance of "White" company names identified with Cleveland isn't because of any local infatuation with color. It's all because of Thomas H. White, another east coast native who came to Cleveland to turn his American dream into reality.

Tom held the patent on a rotary bobbin sewing machine. It took him a few years to convince local lenders that a product more useful to women than men could make money, but he gathered enough cash to set up shop in the Flats and by the mid-1870s, White Sewing Machine was a multi-million dollar company.

White's inventive spirit led him to diversify his company. Within another decade, he offered automatic lathes, machine tools, kerosene lamps and roller skates. Later, he added bicycles, phonographs, even a steam-powered automobile invented by his son, Rollin.

In 1906, the success of White Steam Car led to the formation of a separate business, White Motor Corporation. Half a century later, a new regime at White Motor, led by Vollmer Fries and Roy Holdt, took the company on a whirlwind ride to the higher altitudes of the corporate world. Through a series of mergers and acquisitions, White became White Consolidated Industries, a world leader in appliance and industrial manufacturing with sales measured in billions of dollars. Today, WCI's stable includes thoroughbreds like Frigidaire, Westinghouse, Philco, Kelvinator and Hamilton. Through Cleveland's prism, White has emerged as a rainbow of famous name products and equipment.

179 William White

(1850-1923, Rice Lake, Ontario, Canada)

Bill White grew up in Cleveland and started in the candy business with a small store in the 1870s. In 1884, an innocent mistake changed his life. He purchased a barrel of nuts from a local wholesaler only to discover it contained Mexican chicle, the hardened resin from a tropical evergreen, used sparingly as a flavor enhancer. Instead of returning the useless chicle, White kept it for his wife, who tried it in the kitchen with various recipes. She discovered that boiling the chicle made it soft and chewable. Adding mint made it palatable. Soon, White was selling it in his candy store. They called it "Yucatan" at first, after the region of origin, but people quickly began calling it "chewing gum." Sold in little sticks wrapped in paper, it became the most popular item in the store. By the late 1880s, it demanded his full time attention. In 1890, he founded the American Chicle Company. The company headquarters on the near west side produced millions of pounds of gum annually.

Production almost doubled after White joined forces with Dr. Edwin Beeman to produce Beeman's Pepsin Gum, a serendipitous merger of gum, sugar and pepsin, a therapeutic digestive aid discovered by Beeman as accidentally as White had discovered gum.

Using his new fortune as a springboard into politics, William White was elected mayor of West Cleveland, then won a seat in Congress in 1894. At the same time, his personal tastes went from moderate to absurd. He built a huge mansion on Lake Avenue and filled it with expensive art and furnishings. He bought land, a racetrack and an ocean liner-sized yacht called the *Say When*, a phrase that he used for his boat but never employed in his thirty-year shopping spree. White divorced his wife in 1906 and married his girl friend the next day. His most extravagant moment was surely the evening in New York when, on a lark, he gave a hundred thousand dollar diamond necklace to a showgirl. Must have been some performance.

Back in Cleveland, things got a little sticky for Bill. The bubble started to burst in 1915, after a flurry of wild spending and bad business decisions depleted his cash reserves. Partners who had grown weary of his behavior bought him out of American Chicle. He rebounded, forming another gum company of his own, but he had overlooked the "non-compete" clause in his buyout agreement with American and was wiped out again in the court battle that followed.

In 1922, he was on his way back up for the third time when he took a nasty fall on a Cleveland side street---some insist he caught the sole of his shoe on a wad of gum---and went head over heels. He never recovered, dying of an infection brought about by his injuries.

American Chicle is still one of the world's largest gum manufacturers, with sales in the billions. The Gum King is buried in Cleveland's post-mortem Hall of Fame, Lakeview Cemetery.

161 George Worthington

(1813-1871, Cooperstown, New York)

In 1835, 16-year-old George Worthington arrived in Cleveland in an ox-drawn wagon to sell a load of tools he had purchased in New York with a loan from his brother. George had heard Cleveland was bristling with construction activity and hoped to fetch a fair price.

He was sold out an hour after he arrived, doubling his money. This is my kinda town, said George.

He raced back to New York to reload and was back in town a few weeks later to establish the George Worthington Company. Within twenty-five years, it was the largest hardware company west of New York City.

A business and community leader for forty years, he built a massive company headquarters at West 9th and St. Clair. Destroyed by fire and rebuilt in 1874, the building remains standing today. George Worthington is buried in Lake View Cemetery. Isn't everybody?

183 Alonzo Wright

(1898-1976, Fayetteville, Tennessee)

Alonzo Wright worked as a garage attendant at a downtown hotel where his infectious energy and enthusiasm caught the eye of customer Wallace Holliday. It was a good connection for Alonzo. Holliday was president of Standard Oil. He offered Wright an office job with the city's biggest company, but, to his astonishment, the young man turned him down. He was set on owning his own business, no matter what it took. Holliday was so impressed that he returned with a better offer and Alonzo Wright became the first black man awarded a gas station franchise in the U. S.

Wright's place at 93rd and Cedar became the busiest pit stop in town. There was no such thing as customer service until Alonzo opened up shop. He introduced cleaning windshield, checking tires, oil and radiators. Customers flocked in. He opened a second station a few years later, then a third. By the 1930s, he owned 11 of them. Not only did Alonzo flourish, but he took the community with him, hiring as many attendants as he could from the neighborhood. By 1940, he was the largest employer of young black men in the nation.

When gas sales were restricted by World War II rationing, Alonzo moved quickly to protect his hard-earned fortune. He sold his stations and invested in real estate, applying the same business principles of unexcelled service and sound management. In the next decade, Wright became one of the largest property owners on the East Side, acquiring the Majestic and Carnegie Hotels along with apartments, retail shops and a nursing home. By the 1950s, his net worth was well into the millions.

In spite of his achievements, Wright still felt the sting of blatant racism. When he moved into a luxury home in Cleveland Heights, the all-white neighborhood welcomed him with a fire bomb. As late as the 1960s, his luxury yacht was turned away from the dock at Lakeside Yacht Club. He never let it dampen his spirits or diminish his enthusiasm. In 1961, he was officially declared Cleveland's "richest and most prominent Negro" by *Ebony Magazine*.

Badger
Cleaveland
Corrigan
Doan
Eastman
Grdina
Green
Halle
Hughes
Humphrey
Johnson
Kingsbury
Krol
Miller
Niagara
Pilla
Russell
Ruthenberg
Stinchcomb

Culture & Society

130 Joseph Badger

(1757-1846, Wilbraham. Massachusetts)

The first Christian clergyman in the Western Reserve, Joseph Badger earned his degree at Yale Divinity School, then served at a number of Massachusetts churches before accepting the daring assignment as missionary to the new lands.

He was shocked to find a small group of pioneers who expressed little interest in religion, but, in Badger's eyes, seemed more fond of whiskey and debauchery. Poor Reverend Badger must have run into some ancestors of the Dawg Pound residents.

Undeterred, he delivered the first sermon in the Western Reserve in 1800 and remained for over thirty years, establishing several churches and assisting others in their development. For Cleveland's first two generations, he was a voice crying in the wilderness and contributed much towards establishing Cleveland as the Midwest City of Churches.

197 Moses Cleaveland

(1754-1806, Canterbury, Connecticut)

A dour veteran of the Revolutionary War, Moses Cleaveland spent less than a full season in his namesake city, arriving in July of 1796 and scurrying back home to Connecticut before the harsh winds started blowing in off the lake, never to return.

Except for negotiating final terms of a treaty with the Indians on his way into the Western Reserve that insured his little band of pioneers would not have to return home scalpless, Cleaveland contributed little to the city that bears his name except for Public Square, pacing off a two acre plot on the bluff overlooking the lake that remains the official town center two hundred years later. The townsfolk kept his name---it was either that or the cumbersome "New Connecticut"---but were cavalier enough about old Moses to drop the "a" to economize on newsprint.

In all fairness, Moses did lead the people to the promised land. But the truth is, he was an uneasy Connecticut Yankee in the court of the wild Western Reserve, and couldn't wait to get back to civilization.

Moses Cleveland died back in Canterbury, his grave marked with a simple slab until the city of Cleveland paid to erect a memorial on the site a hundred years after his death. A large bronze plaque mounted on stone salutes the founding father:

> *In this cemetery rest the remains of Moses Cleaveland founder of the City of Cleveland. He was born in Canterbury January 29, 1754, and died there November 16, 1806. He was a lawyer, a soldier, a legislator and a leader of men. In grateful recognition of his services, this memorial is erected by The Cleveland Chamber of Commerce on November 16, 1906, the one hundredth anniversary of his death.*

178 Laura Mae Corrigan

(1888-1948, Eau Claire, Wisconsin)

In its entire history, who was Cleveland's most internationally prominent socialite? No contest. Laura Corrigan. Paid homage in later years as the closest thing to American royalty, sovereign of the social set from London to Paris, Laura Mae Whitlock McMartin Corrigan was not well received when she first ventured into the arched halls of Cleveland society. Married after a whirlwind romance to Jimmy Corrigan, playboy heir to a family steel fortune, Laura Mae tried her best to ingratiate herself to the high and mighty on Millionaire's Row, using Jimmy's money like a calling card, throwing lavish parties and bestowing large contributions on charities.

Nothing worked. Maybe it was her previous divorce or her decidedly underclass background. Maybe she came on too strong for the staid

Baptist and Presbyterian blue bloods. The lengthy romance she carried on with his father before taking vows with young Jim might have been a factor. Whatever. It didn't take long for Laura Mae to realize she was *persona non grata.* Conceding the battle but not the war, Laura Mae cut her losses and moved with Jimmy to New York City, hoping to make her mark in Manhattan.

Didn't happen. The Big Apple, closely allied with (and often related to) Cleveland's old line families, gave Laura Mae the same icy reception. Disappointed but unbowed, she uprooted again, re-locating again, this time to London, the pantheon of English-speaking society.

Jimmy was forced to return to Cleveland to defend his interests in the family business, Corrigan-McKinney Steel. Prolonged conflicts required him to stay, but Laura Mae stayed at their London home, spending the money almost as fast as Jim could make it.

The third time was the charm. The most important lesson Laura Mae had learned from her humbling rejections in Cleveland and New York was that money could not buy a place in society---unless you spread enough of it around. In America, she was lavish. In England, she was unbelievable.

Laura Mae was not just a party animal with an unlimited checkbook. She was a charming woman of boundless energy and flaunting style, doling out compliments and largess with pleasant equanimity. Before long, counted among her appreciative friends were the cream of British society, including members of the royal family. Jimmy's death in 1928 brought a mourning pause in the action, but only served to free up more of the Corrigan millions for Laura Mae to convert to social cachet. It is said that, in 1930 alone, the first full year of the Great Depression, Laura Mae Corrigan consumed over five million dollars just on entertainment.

In 1938, Mrs. Corrigan precipitated one of Cleveland's most memorable fiscal moments when she decided to switch banks and directed that her cash assets be transferred from Union Trust to National City. Hundreds of people lined the route for the impromptu parade as three Brinks trucks, flanked by dozens of armed guards, solemnly proceeded down Ninth Street with the cash.

Such a lifestyle would lead one to believe she was a shallow and frivolous woman, but World War II changed the legacy of Laura Mae. She was visiting her beloved Paris when war broke out. She barely escaped with her life when the Germans invaded. Instead of returning to safe haven in the U. S., Mrs. Corrigan sacrificed her extravagant life style to devote herself to humanitarian efforts, founding La Bien Venue to aid French refugees and operating the Wings Club in London for British and American officers. With access to her fortune in America blocked by war restrictions, she sold her personal belongings, including her jewels, to finance her munificent efforts. After the war, she became one of the few women ever awarded the French Croix de Guerre and the British King's Medal.

150 The Doan Family

Matriarch of one of Cleveland's stalwart pioneer families, SARAH DOAN moved to Cleveland from Connecticut with husband NATHANIEL in 1798. The trip, now less than an hour on a commercial airliner, took 92 days.

Nathaniel set up his blacksmith shop, Cleveland's first industry, just west of Public Square. Sarah didn't like the location. The wetlands near the water were infested with mosquitoes and snakes. In 1799, she persuaded Nathaniel to move up the hill and away from the lakefront to a prominent point on the main road east. Nathaniel opened a tavern instead of a blacksmith's shop, again at Sarah's suggestion. Profits on whiskey were much better than on horseshoes. The Doans were able to build a modest inn and a cluster of shops to cater to the needs of travelers. "Doan's Corners," several acres of property located at what is now East 105th and Euclid, burgeoned into an active hub of business and social activity, second only to downtown, with churches, apartments and a theater.

Nathaniel passed away in 1815, with Doan's Corners still in its formative years. Sarah survived him by almost forty years, an icon of the neighborhood and a living link between Cleveland's first steps from the wilderness and the bustling pre-war era of canals and railroads.

We know her niece only as "MISSY DOAN," one of the ten children of TIMOTHY DOAN and his wife, Mary Carey, who had arrived in Cleveland in 1801 after a brief stay in Buffalo, coming here to join brother Nathaniel. Both Doan men were trustees when the township of Cleveland was officially formed, but only Missy Doan could claim the romantic distinction of starring as the female lead on *Cleveland's First Date*.

Like America itself, Cleveland has shown a powerful affinity for the Fourth of July. It was on that date that Moses Cleaveland first entered the Western Reserve, arriving at Conneaut by boat. Many more great events, human or cosmic in origin, would come to transpire on that same date as the city's history unfolded, including speeches by famous orators, notorious murders and devastating acts of God. The second notable Fourth was 1801, when the first real social event was held in the rough-hewn home of Lorenzo Carter.

Miss Doan, "a lady but fourteen years old," was the belle of the ball. Her escort was Gilman Bryant, seventeen-year-old son of a most appreciated man---the local distiller. He recalled the enchanting evening in a letter later published by Colonel Whittlesey, Cleveland's first historian, then retold by Crisfield Johnson in 1879:

> *The cavalier attired himself gorgeously, in what he assures us was the prevailing mode; wearing a suit of gingham, a good, wool hat and a pair of substantial, brogan shoes. His long hair was bound behind in a queue about as long and thick as an ordinary corncob, tied round with a yard and a half of black ribbon, below which the hair extended in a small tuft. Those were the days of powdered wigs among the gentry, and the youth came as near the genteel*

standard as he could by anointing his hair with tallow, and then sifting on it as much flour as he could make stick. Thus attired, he mounted a horse and rode out to his lady's mansion of logs. She climbed upon a stump, and he rode up beside it; she kirtled her calico dress about her waist to keep it clean, spread her underpetticoat on the horse's back, mounted, and clasped her cavalier about the waist to steady herself, and away they went in splendid style to the double loghouse of Mr. Carter, on the brow of the hill at the west end of Superior street.

By all accounts, it was a wild night in Cleveland, with song and fiddle, merriment and Mr. Bryant's fine spirits. More than twenty people joined the festivities, from as far away as Euclid and Rockport, but Gilman and Miss Doan were the darlings of the evening, the freshest and youngest couple on the dance floor.

77 Linda Eastman

(1867-1963, Oberlin, Ohio)

The first woman to direct operations at a major metropolitan library, Linda Eastman's tenure saw the transition of the Cleveland Public Library from an innovator in modern systems to a major, multi-faceted institution, the worldwide standard for excellence.

Foremost disciple of William Brett, the nation's leading librarian and a fixture in the top post in Cleveland for two decades, Eastman served as vice-librarian under Brett, then succeeded him in 1918, after his sudden death in a street accident.

She assisted in the design and construction of the massive Main Library on Superior in 1925, added a Braille library section for the blind, access for the handicapped and specialized services for business and industry.

Linda Eastman was elected president of the Ohio and American Library Associations. After her retirement in 1938, she remained active as an advisor and consultant to her successors and others librarians throughout the country. In her 46-year career, she contributed much to the Cleveland Library's world prominence, with a peerless reputation it has maintained ever since. The library has continuously provided more free educational and entertainment services, always accessible to every resident of the area, than any other institution in the city's history.

Linda Eastman died at 95. Her library work was her life. She never married.

100 Anton Grdina

(1874-1957, Ljubljana, Yugoslavia)

The undisputed leader of the Slovenian-American community, not just in Cleveland, but throughout the United States, was Anton Grdina.

The World War I exodus of eastern European refugees flooded the streets of Cleveland with Slovenians, Serbs, Czechs, Croatians, Poles and Rumanians. Rich new ingredients were added to Cleveland's melting pot. The talents, crafts and customs of disparate cultures thickened the stew. Anton Grdina and his family had a 20 year head start, arriving in 1897. His established position as a businessman and banker made it possible for him to lead the welcoming committee.

President of North American Bank, the financial rock of the Slovene community clustered along St. Clair on the near eat side, he was patriarch of the largest Slovenian city outside Yugoslavia by 1940. But Grdina's emergence from among many fine Cleveland citizens to the ranks of the city's foremost humanitarians was a baptism by fire.

The East Ohio Gas Works #2, located on ten acres near East 55th and St. Clair, was the main storage site for the company's natural gas, liquefied and stored in four mammoth surface tanks. On October 20th, 1944, the cylindrical #4 tank exploded, transforming a million cubic feet of natural gas into a tidal wave of death aimed at

Norwood-St. Clair, Cleveland's Little Slovenia. The ensuing inferno burned for days, but, for all real purpose, twenty square blocks of the city were obliterated in the first moments. 130 people were killed---most incinerated beyond recognition---and over a hundred houses and factories leveled or severely damaged.

Anton Grdina fell to his knees and wept when he saw the devastated remains of the family neighborhood he loved, then summoned the strength to take command of its recovery. He led the survivors in mourning, then led the coalition of community and business entities that brought it back to life. He raised money in exhaustive fund drives, coaxed more from the city's major businesses and foundations, oversaw legal settlements and walked the charred streets, hearing personal complaints and brokering minor disputes. When it was over, Norwood-St. Clair came back, with new homes and new businesses. Grdina Avenue was built to link East 61st and East 62nd, and verdant Grdina Park was carved out of the scorched earth closest to the Gas Works.

Anton Grdina was the first American to receive the Third Order of the Crown, Yugoslavia highest civilian honor. In 1954, he was knighted into the Order of St. Gregory by Pope Pius XII.

86 The Halle Family

Halle's. The name still brings pleasant memories and wistful smiles to the faces of Clevelanders who remember the elegant department store that opened its doors in 1891 and served the community with style for more than 90 years.

Samuel and Salmon Halle purchased an existing furrier and haberdashery, expanded to include women's clothing and moved to a central location at East 12th & Euclid in 1910. A multi-faceted department store with a wide range of goods and services by the 1920s, Halle's was among the first to implement the branch store concept, opening suburban outlets that helped the business survive the depression.

Sam Halle was not just a leader in the retail industry. He certainly did his part to break down the local ethnic barriers. The German-Jewish businessman fell in love with Irish-Catholic Blanche Murphy the first time he laid eyes on the red-haired lass, and the two were married in spite of the howls of anguish emanating from both families and the fervent prayers of every rabbi and priest on the East Side.

It proved to be a marriage made in heaven, producing years of bliss and a second generation of Halles that combined the best attributes of both worlds---good business sense and a flair for fun and romance. Walter was the heir apparent, and several Halle daughters were active on the local social scene, but none outshone fair-haired Kay.

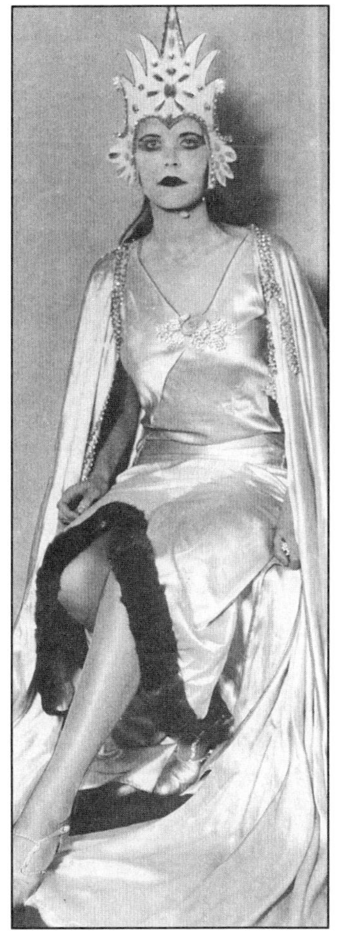

In spite of constant rumors that linked her to all the most eligible bachelors, Kay Halle never married, even though her escorts comprised an international Dream Team, including Randolph Churchill, George Gershwin, Winsor French and Isamu Noguchi. While the family store was never far from her mind, she responded to the call of patriotic duty, accepting an offer to serve in the Office of Strategic Services (predecessor of the CIA) during World War II and beyond. Her exploits as a spy have never been disclosed, although it's well known that she maintained an elegant home in Georgetown, hosting exquisite parties for the cream of Washington society and an endless parade of foreign dignitaries. She returned home often, and always found time to tour the flagship store downtown, dictating a list of criticisms and recommendations for brother Walter (who sometimes wished the her government superiors would send her on a lengthy assignment to Manchuria).

Envied and admired in Cleveland, Kay Halle was always the extra special guest at the poshest parties and sleekest events when in town, and absentee Mistress of the Cleveland Smart Set when she wasn't.

Meanwhile, back at the store, Walter was hard at work, making sure Kay and the rest of the clan had the wherewithal to which they had become accustomed. He presided over the second wave of expansion following World War II. With fifteen stores and the luxurious downtown centerpiece, thousands of employees and millions in income, Halle's earned its money and its reputation with a hallmark for customer satisfaction.

Walter Halle was succeeded by his dapper son, Chisholm, a better dresser than his father, but not quite his equal in business. The changing retail climate of the 60s, the deterioration of downtown and fierce competition from discount stores drained Halle's finances. In 1970, a "friendly" merger was arranged with the Marshall Field company in Chicago. Like Halle's, Marshall Field was a regional powerhouse owned and operated by a similarly proper family.

People are funny about money, even in the best of circles. In 1974, the amicability was removed from the equation by Field's accountants. Chisholm was forced out, Halle's was re-tooled as a lean retail machine to stop the flow of red ink. It didn't work. Reduced to a shadow of the showcase of the past, the store was still losing money when it was sold to an unsentimental group of investors who promised to maintain operations, then promptly closed the doors and liquidated the assets. Clevelanders attended the final closeout sale like mourners at a wake, there to somberly view the remains of a dear departed friend. Halle's was gone and a piece of Cleveland's heart with it.

172 Adella Prentiss Hughes

(1869-1950, Cleveland)

A child of Millionaire's Row, Adella Prentiss was a Vassar girl with an ear for music who toured as a pianist herself before returning to Cleveland to promote classical music in her hometown. She married Felix Hughes in 1904, and used his money to expand her crusade to improve Cleveland's musical tastes and stature.

A co-founder of the Musical Arts Association in 1915, Adella raised money from local businessmen to bring noted conductor Nikolai Sokoloff to town. Enthusiastic response to Sokoloff's orchestral concerts led to another round of fund-raising. In 1918, Adella Prentiss Hughes reached her goal. The Cleveland orchestras was formed, with Sokoloff as conductor and Hughes as manager.

Bravo!

73 The Dudley Humphrey Family

The George Humphrey family has been most active in Cleveland business and social circles at the highest levels. Various plaques and monuments downtown and in University Circle attest to their prestige and their philanthropy. But the Dudley Humphreys had a lot more fun. The George Humphreys were in the mining business. Dudley was in popcorn.

Dudley started out with one little popcorn stand at Doan's Corners and made a little money. Like all the rest of the smart Cleveland boys, he put his profits into expansion. Within eight years he was an early Orville Reddenbacher, king of a local popcorn empire.

In 1901, flush with cash and tired of hauling around big bags of nickels, Dudley invested all his money and most of his family's into a failing private park on the lakefront to the east of the city. The park catered to a fast crowd, featuring a bar, dances, gambling and a few carnival-type freak shows. Dudley had a different idea for Euclid Beach.

He remade Euclid Beach into a family amusement park, with thrilling rides, pleasant facilities and a fanatic dedication to good clean fun. For the next three generations, the Humphreys hosted Cleveland's best summer-long party, with Laughing Sal, saltwater taffy, the Flying Turns, roller coasters, funhouses, Dodgems and dancing 'til dark. And popcorn, of course.

Laughter, song and calliope music echoed through the summer nights. Dudley and his family expanded their wonderland and maintained it with loving care. Over the years, millions of contented visitors poured through the park.

The only problem was---and no one took serious note of it until the 1930s---that all the contented visitors were white. The Humphreys didn't believe in interracial amusement and Euclid Beach maintained a strict segregationist policy until a 1946 protest led to a riot, with several demonstrators and a policeman injured in the melee.

Euclid Beach continued to operate for another 23 years. The park's facilities were reluctantly integrated, but the harsh dose of reality had tarnished the name and the magic. Expansion stopped. Upkeep and maintenance declined. Newer and more glamorous theme and amusement parks lured the crowds away. In September of 1969, Euclid Beach Park closed for the season, never to reopen.

134 Lucy Bagby Johnson

(1841-1932, Wheeling, West Virginia)

Born to slavery, Lucy Bagby was raised on the Goshorn family's West Virginia plantation. In 1859, at 18, she traveled to Pittsburgh, attending to the needs of Miss Emma Goshorn, there to hobnob with her well-to-do Northern relatives. On Sunday, the slaves were transported to the local Negro church, mingling uncomfortably with the free black men and women of the North. It was there that Lucy met George Johnson, a towering man, taller than Lucy herself, who, at six feet, with striking bronze features and almond eyes, stood out like a monument to African beauty.

George was shocked to learn that Lucy was a slave, bound to return south in a few days. He urged her to take the "railroad" to freedom and promised to provide all the information she would need. But Lucy could not bear to leave her family: her mother and sisters had been treated well by the Goshorns. The two parted sadly, unlikely to ever meet again.

Returning home, Lucy caught the lustful eye of James Goshorn, but the stern and watchful looks of Lucy's mother kept him at bay. Goshorn took steps to resolve the problem. In 1860, he sold her mother and sisters to a Georgia buyer, ignoring their laments. The Bagby family was separated forever. Lucy's last word to her mother was a promise: I shall be free.

The following week, she walked away, hiding in the woods in daylight, trudging north at night. Fate led her to some sympathetic slaves near Wheeling who knew a man who knew another. Many helping hands reached out. She found herself a passenger on the Underground Railroad, arriving first in Marietta, then on to Cleveland. She found paying work as a cook and seamstress with the wealthy Benton family. Lucy Bagby was a free woman.

Cleveland was then at the forefront of the controversy over the infamous Fugitive Slave Laws, federal acts passed in 1850 to assuage powerful Southern interests. The laws mandated the return of runaway slaves to their owners, without trial or regard for any local anti-slavery laws. All that was required was identification and proof of ownership. Anyone who interfered with the return of slaves to "rightful" owners were subject to felony arrest and imprisonment.

In 1861, Lucy Bagby became the human lightning rod for the Fugitive Slave Law conflict. She was swept up in a series of events that some historians say helped precipitate the Civil War.

Mr. Goshorn came to town that year. Irked by Lucy's escape, he had placed ads in all the large Northern newspapers with an offer of a hefty reward to anyone who could help locate Lucy. A standout in any crowd, she wasn't hard to find. Goshorn's papers, presented to the local magistrate, were in proper order. Lucy was taken into custody.

But before Goshorn could leave the city with his property in tow, benevolent forces rushed to her assistance. The Bentons were not without considerable influence. They retained the eminent Judge Spaulding to represent her. Spaulding filed a flurry of legal motions, challenging her identification and the constitutionality of the law, and demanded a trial on the merits. As Lucy had committed no crime, he also filed a writ of *habeas corpus* demanding her release. Federal judge Daniel Tilden, Ohio's foremost jurist, was called into the controversy. The plight of a single slave girl had become a federal case. Abolitionists by the hundreds flocked to Cleveland to witness the outcome.

Under extreme pressure from both sides, Tilden started the trial. A phalanx of 150 deputies were needed to escort Lucy to the courtroom through a rowdy crowd that threatened to take the law into their own hands and free the girl by force.

Newspapers across the country headlined the story. Goshorn hired the finest lawyers to affirm his legal rights. Spalding was assisted by the leading abolitionist attorneys, fighting for justice. The two-day trial ended in a near riot when Judge Tilden, apologizing from the bench for the inherent immorality of the law, regretfully ruled that federal statutes prevailed: Lucy was remanded to Goshorn's custody and returned to slavery.

Back in West Virginia, Lucy was beaten and jailed, then packed off to Goshorn's cousin in Tennessee for hard labor. A few months later, the Civil War broke out. By a wondrous coincidence, Lucy was being returned by train to the Goshorn plantation when union troops crossed the border. Their commander, Captain Vance, spoke to Lucy. He advised her that President Lincoln had signed something called the *Emancipation Proclamation.* If she so desired, she was free to go. Lucy took him up on the offer and Vance put her on a train to Ohio. Lucy Bagby was free once more.

She made her way to Athens, Ohio and found work in a dry goods store. Another year passed before the most exciting moment of her life. A tall Union soldier entered the store to purchase provisions. Lucy heard a soul-shaking laugh and looked up to see the smiling face of George Johnson framed in Union blue.

They were married after the war. At Lucy's request, they returned to Cleveland, where Lucy was hailed as a heroine in the struggle for freedom and a living symbol of human endurance.

They raised a family. George opened his own store. Life was good. Lucy Bagby Johnson marched at the head of the city's Independence Day parade for decades. She died in Cleveland at 91.

87 Eunice Kingsbury & Family

(1767-1847, Alsted, New Hampshire)

You could count the families living in Cleveland on the fingers of one hand when JAMES KINGSBURY and his family arrived, determined to settle in the New Lands. The Guns, the Carters, the Hawleys and the Stiles were the only non-Indian residents a year after Moses Cleaveland and the men from Connecticut Land staked out the territory.

The Kingsburys dared to take a squatter's cabin across the river in Indian country at first, but moved into the tiny Cleveland neighborhood before winter, building a log cabin to the east of the future Public Square on the site destined, a century later, for the Federal Courthouse.

Mother of the first non-Indian child born in the Western Reserve, EUNICE KINGSBURY gave birth to a son in the cruel winter of 1797. It was a season of disease and deprivation. The baby did not live to see the spring.

The rest of the family not only survived, they thrived. James became a successful Cleveland merchant and builder. In 1800, he was appointed judge by governor of the territory, General St. Clair. James was later elected to the state legislature and in 1810 he was among the first trustees of the newly formed village of Cleveland. Eunice bore another son, ALMON, one of the first native born Clevelanders, who grew to become a leading local citizen and business partner of his father.

108 John Krol

(1910-1996, Cleveland)

John Krol became the highest ranking Roman Catholic clergyman in city's history. The only way to break his record is for a Clevelander to become Pope.

Son of Polish immigrant parents, he graduated from Cathedral Latin High School and went to work in a general store. Animated religious discussions over the cracker barrel roused him to his calling. He attended St. Mary's Seminary and was ordained in St. John's Cathedral in 1937. Fr. Krol served briefly at Immaculate Heart of Mary Church before his assignment to Rome.

Forced to leave Italy by the war, he continued to pursue his studies in church law. By the early 1950's, he has considered among the Church's foremost legal scholars. Often summoned to contribute his expertise in theological conferences and tribunals, Krol preferred working with parishioners and children, but his administrate skills were undeniable. In 1953, he was consecrated bishop and remained in Cleveland for years as auxiliary bishop and vicar general. In 1961, he was named Archbishop of the Diocese of Philadelphia.

Inevitably, Bishop Krol took his place among the leading American Catholics of the day, a reasoned voice in a strident chorus. While his historic opposition to abortion and social mores remained constant, he was boldly progressive in calling for reform of military policies, integration and higher moral standards in industry and the media. As president of the National Conference of Bishops, he presided over tumultuous times, striking the right balance between impatient reformists and troubled traditionalists.

In 1967, Krol was elevated to the College of Cardinals.

His good friend and classmate, inducted with him into that most exclusive of colleges, was Karol Wojtyla, the man destined for the top floor of the Vatican some years later as Pope John Paul II. The two had become close while serving on the Vatican II reform convention and it is widely believed that John Cardinal Krol, the most respected member of the small but influential American contingent, was an important factor in Wojtyla's selection as the first non-Italian to assume the papacy in more than four centuries.

84 Sam Miller

(1921- , Cleveland)

Never a candidate for public office and never clearly affiliated with a single party or faction, Samuel H. Miller has somehow managed to hold the title as the most influential private citizen in Cleveland politics for more than a generation.

Son of a poor junk dealer, Miller joined the Forest City Enterprises company in the 1940s and quickly rose through the ranks. By the 60s, he was chairman of the national real estate and development firm and the most trusted ally of the owners, the Ratner family. Imbued with a sense of civic and religious pride, he has been a lifetime activist for Jewish and Israeli causes. Charming, irritating or intimidating as required, he established an early reputation as a peerless fundraiser. In the last forty years, his ability to raise money for worthy organizations and charities has become legendary, not to mention a similar talent when it comes to politicians he favors.

The list of Miller allies in business and politics reads like a Who's Who of Cleveland, crossing all lines of race, creed or national origin. In 1996, he gave his friend Bishop Pilla a lesson in monetary policy when he was called upon to help aid the Bishop's ambitious plans to revitalize the inner-city neighborhoods. "I told him you close the door and don't let anyone out until they've written a check. The Catholics send people home with envelopes. You can't raise money that way."

A true rags to riches to rector story, Sam Miller may be the only Jewish rector of the Catholic Church on the planet. He was appointed honorary rector by Pilla as a token of his gratitude for Miller's ecumenical spirit and unhesitant support.

Still going strong as chairman of Forest City at 75, he has overseen the company's successful expansion into the mega-mall field, owning and managing one of the largest retail and residential property empires in America. Business may be his life's work, but civic and philanthropic efforts remain his life. Mayor White calls him a "second father." Political VIP's and wannabes line up at his cluttered office on Brookpark Road, hoping for his blessing and a check.

Through it all, his self-deprecating sense of humor has remained his saving grace. In a recent interview about his charitable works, Miller gruffly advised, "Just don't make me into a little Jesus."

51 Oghema Niagara

(@1865-1950, Lewistown, New York)

One of the first spokesmen for Native Americans, Oghema Niagara was nationally known as "Chief Thunderwater," an eloquent and solitary voice for the rights of the dwindling number of survivors of the great tribes of the Iroquois nations who had peopled the Western Reserve for centuries before being shunted aside for the new civilization.

Born on the Tuscarora Indian reservation, he was the son of a Seneca chief and grandson of Keokuk, respected warrior chief of the Black Hawk War. In the late nineteenth century, his regal bearing caught the eye of Buffalo Bill Cody. He was invited to join Buffalo Bill's Wild West Show and given the stage name, "Chief Thunderwater." Tiring of the theatrics, he kept the name but quit the show and began his work to improve the Indian's plight.

Chief Thunderwater settled on Cleveland's east side, selling his own herbal remedies and compounds to make a living. Over the next fifty years, he devoted himself to the cause, organizing the Supreme Council of Tribes, a reincarnation of the confederacy of the Great Nations, and serving as its supreme chief. His own home became the council's headquarters, where he administered medical and charitable services to hundred of Indians over many years.

Thunderwater lectured Indians on the evils of intemperance and the benefits of education while promoting Native American rights and values to the whites. Welcomed and respected in the local community, Chief Thunderwater appeared at many local functions and celebrations as the "official Indian of Cleveland."

120 Anthony Pilla

(1935- , Cleveland)

The son of Italian immigrants, Anthony fulfilled the dream of his mother Libera, (and every Catholic mother of the era) by entering the seminary and finding his vocation in the priesthood. Quietly efficient and universally respected, the young priest rose through the ranks, from parish priest to monsignor, auxiliary bishop, then prelate of the Cleveland diocese, one of the largest in the country, in 1980.

The 9th Bishop of Cleveland sincc 1847, Pilla appeared shy and reserved. His soft-spoken manner and gentle demeanor gave no indication of his forcefulness and determination as a religious leader, first on the local scene, then nationally, and even in Rome.

In 1995, Pilla was elected president of the American Conference of Bishops, the closest thing to a ruling body for the Church in the U. S. He promptly broke the traditional, non-partisan stance of American bishops by voicing his opposition to the "welfare reforms" of the Republican congress. His belief that the Church is obliged to take an active role in diminishing the ills of the secular society led to his commitment to the inner city.

88 Ralph Russell

(1787-1846, Goshen,Connecticut)

Ralph Russell was the founder of the local community of the United Society of Believers in the Second Appearing of Christ, an obscure Christian sect known for diligence, a socialist community spirit and the incorporation of dancing into their worship that astonished and frightened outsiders. These manifestations of religious enthusiasm which found their way into the services of this otherwise staid and restrained group have been catalogued under the names of: The Falling, The Jerks, The Dancing and The Barking. The most common was The Shaking, hence their common name, the Shakers.

Russell's group settled on lush lands to the east of the city, owned by Ralph's father. At its peak, the Shaker settlement included over 600 believers living and worshipping together on almost 1,400 acres. The Shakers were accomplished farmers, builders, weavers and craftsmen. An inventive and industrious lot, they dammed Doan Brook to form Shaker Lakes, erected over 50 buildings and sold their produce and wares to the surrounding communities to support their efforts. Among other clever gadgets, the Shakers invented the clothespin and the rotary bobbin.

But there was one serious flaw in the Shaker philosophy that inevitably led to their demise. The Shakers believed in celibacy. Absolute celibacy for all. That became a most difficult deterrent to survival through the generations. The Shakers didn't believe in generating. With only a handful of loyal members remaining, the North Union Shaker Community disbanded in 1889.

118 Charles Ruthenberg

(1882-1927, Cleveland)

Youngest child of German immigrants, Charles Ruthenberg studied at Lutheran High School and Dyke College before finding his apparent place in Cleveland's turn-of-the century middle class as a bookkeeper.

His Progressive politics were radicalized by the influence of friends who espoused utopianism and the writings of Karl Marx. In 1909, he joined the Socialist Party, rapidly becoming one of the most active and most radical proponents of socialism in America.

As journalist, essayist and political candidate, Ruthenberg rose to the highest ranks of the party in the U. S. and his tireless efforts contributed much to the rise of socialism as a powerful political force in the first decades of the 20th century.

Offered a lucrative bonus, raise and promotion by his employer to abandon his political activities, Ruthenberg decided to pursue them full time with even greater vigor instead. He organized rallies, led protests, waged his own political campaigns and managed others, all to advance the cause. He was imprisoned for speaking out against World War I and arrested dozens of times for incitement to riot, treason, sedition, obstruction and even charged with assault to commit murder in connection with the infamous May Day Riots in Cleveland in 1919.

The bloody May Day clash proved his downfall. Instead of the major breakthrough for the Left that Ruthenberg anticipated, the riots ushered in an era of swift and often brutal reactionary policies that blunted the movement and portrayed its leaders as violent and treasonous.

During World War I, Charles Ruthenberg joined forces with John Reed as the left wing broke from the Socialist Party and formed the Communist Party of America. Ruthenberg was its first Executive Secretary. Like Reed, he died suddenly at a young age, and like Reed, he is one of three Americans whose remains are kept within the walls of the Kremlin in Moscow, as close as you can get to a sacred resting place if you're a Commie.

103 William Stinchcomb

(1878-1959, Cleveland)

An engineer and surveyor who began working for the city at 17, William Albert Stinchcomb was elected county engineer in 1912. He oversaw construction of the Detroit-Superior Bridge and approved plans for the Lorain Bridge (now Hope Memorial). But those were minor accomplishments.

Bill Stinchcomb's primary contribution to his fellow citizens, past, present and future, may put him in a class by himself. He knew the geography of Cuyahoga County better than most, and loved it more than any. After lobbying for passage of state laws to permit him to undertake his grand design, Stinchcomb provided the greatest single gift one person has ever given to Clevelanders. The Emerald Necklace.

He drew the maps, laid the plans and oversaw creation of the Metropolitan Park System, the meandering stretches of valleys, forests, rivers and flatlands that encircle the county with the beauty and tranquillity of nature, open and accessible to all, free of charge.

Stinchcomb put it all together, piece by piece, with loving care. He bought the land, co-ordinated efforts by federal, state and local workers, approved construction of shelters, trails, ball parks and playgrounds, planted trees and paved the roads. It took him 45 years.

Sometime, when you're down in the valley playing ball or flying a kite, wading in the river or fishing along its banks, sledding down a steep hill or cross-country skiing, playing golf or having a picnic, or maybe just relaxing in the sun, listening to the birds and the gentle running water, remember Mr. Stinchcomb. It's his gift to you.

Allen
Benesch
Burton
Burton
Butler
Celebrezze
Creighton
Day
Garfield
Grossman
Huntington
Ingalls
Kidd
Kohler
Ness
Payer
Squire

Law & The Military

37 Florence Ellinwood Allen

(1884-1966, Salt Lake City, Utah)

Setting off on a career as a classical pianist, Florence Allen was injured in an accident while studying in Berlin in 1906. Permanent nerve damage ended her career in music and led to a far more distinguished one in law.

Allen returned to Cleveland as a music critic and teacher while studying politics and law at Western Reserve University. In spite of impeccable academic credentials, she was rejected by Western Reserve Law School because she was a woman. Undismayed, she received her law degree at NYU and was admitted to the Ohio bar in 1914.

Florence Ellinwood Allen was the first woman to serve as: common please court judge, county prosecutor, Ohio Supreme Court justice and chief justice of a federal district court. Her books on constitutional and international law garnered national esteem. She was the first woman seriously considered for appointment to the U. S. Supreme Court. She was, without question, the First Lady of Law in the city, the state and the nation.

Finally, in 1921, Florence Ellinwood Allen was the first female judge in Ohio to pronounce a death penalty verdict, becoming the first Ohio woman to formally order the execution of a man.

151 Alfred Benesch

(1879-1973, Cleveland)

Alfred Abraham Benesch was a bright local lad who graduated from Central High School and went on to Harvard. From ancient history books, it seems that roughly 50% of the high school graduating class of the Cleveland public school system, represented primarily by Central High, went on to matriculate at Harvard or Yale. Among the changes over the years has been a precipitous decline in that percentage.

Albert Benesch returned to Cleveland to practice law. An early leader in *pro bono* work, Benesch is the barrister modern hot dog vendors have to thank for making the streets safe for business. He fought for an end to the harassment of Jewish street peddlers 90 years ago, winning favorable city ordinances and police protection that applied to all those selling their wares on the street.

A believer in Tom Johnson's Progressive philosophy and a protégé of Newton D. Baker, Benesch was elected to city council in 1912, then appointed Safety Director by Mayor Baker in 1914. His highest civic priority was education. Benesch served on the school board for 27 years, including a lengthy term as president, and was influential in maintaining the high standards that characterized the city's school system during the first half of the century.

Benesch was a persuasive speaker and relentless advocate of reform. He is credited with leading the crusade to end the infamous "10% Quota" restricting Jewish enrollment at Harvard, an unwritten but ironclad rule that had endured for centuries. He eschewed confrontation in favor of low-profile lobbying. Patient but firm, his gentle persuasions ultimately convinced the crimson patricians that "quotas on freedom" were not compatible with the best interests of America's most hallowed learning institution. The coincidental decline in contributions from important Jewish and Cleveland benefactors, long a mainstay of Harvard endowments, emphasized his point. The Harvard quota was ended in the 1930s.

52 Harold Burton

(1888-1964, Jamaica Plains, Massachusetts)

A Harvard graduate, Harold Hitz Burton came to Cleveland to practice law. A few years later, he found himself in the front line trenches near Antwerp, one of over 8,000 Cleveland volunteers serving in World War I. Burton won a Purple Heart and the Belgian Cross.

After the war, he returned to Cleveland and began a career in politics. A state legislator and city law director in the 20's, he was interim mayor in 1931, then elected to three straight terms beginning in 1935. Cleveland was among the hardest hit major cities in the Depression and Burton's problems were compounded by an uneasy relationship with FDR Democrats in Washington. Still, he persevered, gaining the confidence of business, labor and the people with a diligent and even-handed style that engendered trust and confidence in City Hall.

The wild days of the Roaring Twenties and a lax attitude toward enforcing Prohibition laws on the part his predecessors had left Burton with some serious problems. The police department was rife with graft and corruption. Other city administrators were eager to look the other way, but Burton would have none of it. He appointed the legendary Eliot Ness as Safety Director and gave him a free hand. Dozens of indictments and hundreds of resignations later, the reputation of Cleveland's finest was restored.

In 1940, Harold Burton was elected Senator from Ohio. In 1945, President Truman appointed him to the United States Supreme Court. A career that spanned three decades of public service saw its finest hours on the federal bench. Burton formulated the majority opinion in the first landmark desegregation decision in 1951 and lent his hand to the *Brown vs. Board of Education* case, outlawing racial discrimination in public schools.

Cleveland has had more than its share of mayors of national repute---Tom Johnson, Newton D. Baker, Anthony Celebrezze, Carl Stokes, George Voinovich, Mike White---but perhaps none has served the city, the state and the country, each in turn, with such consistent honor and distinction.

68 Theodore Burton

(1851-1929, Jefferson, Ohio)

A graduate of Oberlin and University of Chicago Law School, Theodore Burton started his practice here in 1875 with $150 borrowed from family members. In the 1880's, he was elected to City Council, then to Congress in 1888, where he became a close confidant of Canton's William McKinley. He retired to private practice after two terms, but was drafted to run again in 1894, defeating Tom L. Johnson.

In the next 14 years, Burton established himself as the nation's leading authority on rivers, waterways and harbors. He was first chairman of the Inland Waterways Commission and chairman of the National Waterways Commission. Burton was instrumental in the construction of the Panama Canal and the conservation of Niagara

Falls. His other leading strength was finance. He crafted the important turn-of-the-century legislation that shaped the nation's financial structure, including the Federal Reserve Act.

In 1908, Burton won a classic campaign for the U. S. Senate over Joseph Foraker and Charles Taft. In 1916, Ohio Republicans drafted him for their presidential candidate but he fell just short of the nomination. Returning to private life, he accepted the post as president of Merchants National Bank of New York, one of the nation's largest, but only after the trustees accepted his special condition: he would not move to New York City, preferring to administrate from his Cleveland residence.

When the U. S. entered World War I, Burton was in the forefront again, as special ambassador of the President, conferring with leaders in Japan, China and the Philippines. In spite of his personal inclination to finally retire from public service after World War I, Burton acquiesced to voter sentiment and returned to Congress in 1920. Once more, he was the point man on major policy, drafting the international debt settlements settled on U. S. war loans to Europe.

In his later years, he wrote extensively on politics and macroeconomics. His book, *Financial Crisis and Depressions,* accurately foretold the chain of events which would lead to the Great Depression less than a decade later.

Author, lawyer, councilman, representative, senator, commissioner, presidential candidate, presidential adviser, international emissary and statesman: Theodore Burton.

153 John Butler

(1905-1996, Cleveland)

Acclaimed by many as the greatest criminal defense lawyer in the city's history, John Patrick Butler was as colorful outside the courtroom as he was adept within.

He matriculated along the classic Irish-Catholic-Cleveland course, attending St. Ignatius High School and the University of Notre Dame. A fine athlete as well as an outstanding student, Butler starred as an end on the most famous Notre Dame football team of all, the fabled Four Horsemen squad of the 1920s. Years later, his undying loyalty to his alma mater and a penchant for regaling others with anecdotes of his gridiron days earned him the nickname, "the Fifth Horseman."

Butler was complicated man of many talents. He graduated from college with the highest grade average ever posted at Notre Dame, a record unbroken for over forty years. A mesmerizing speaker with Shakespearean style and a peerless mastery of the language, Butler was a natural for the legal profession, but other careers beckoned. He was popular as a singer, with a lilting baritone voice and a wonderful stage presence. That avocation was cut short in 1938 when he was accosted by thugs on a downtown street, robbed and beaten. He recovered from the skull fracture, but his mellifluous singing voice was gone forever.

His theatrical talents served him well in the courtroom. Prosecutors rued the day they faced Butler across the aisle. His eloquence was so forceful and his persuasive powers so unique that, on more than one occasion, awestruck jurors approached him after delivering an acquittal for one of his clients and asked him for an autograph.

He practiced law for more than sixty years and successfully defended some of Cleveland's most notorious citizens, including Shondor Birns and Danny Greene. A man of impeccable personal standards, he never refused a case because of the odious reputation of a defendant. He lectured others on the right of every American to a vigorous defense, and he practiced what he preached.

Butler's brilliant legal mind was not lost on the political community. He served as official legal advisor to Mayors Burke and Lausche, and unofficial advisor to dozens of other politcal leaders.

A physical fitness iconoclast , he kept in shape well into his eighties with a regimen that seemed unthinkable to men half his age. He would take bracing swims in Lake Erie in March, sleep on his porch in January and bicycle for miles with twenty pound weights wrapped around his waist. Irish to the core, his only weakness was an occasional tendency to be over-served when enjoying an aperitif or two after a long day in court.

Cleveland has had a proud history of skilled masters of the courtroom since the day Alfred Kelley starred in the dramatic case of the city's first homicide. Sherlock Andrews, Moses Kelly, Andrew Squire, Frank Ginn, Harry Payer, Chester Gillespie and William Corrigan are among those that held jurors spellbound with their eloquence. In modern times, Gerald Gold, Michael Climaco, Fred Weisman, Bob Rotatori, Harold Pollock and James Burke have added luster to that reputation with more legal wizardry. Courthouse veterans swear that none outshines John Butler. His voice was so commanding, his language and logic so precise that other attorneys often filled the seats to learn from the master.

59 Anthony Celebrezze

(1914?- , Cleveland)

American-born son of Italian immigrants, Anthony Celebrezze earned his law degree at Ohio Northern and opened his own practice in Cleveland in 1939. One of the first Italian-Americans active in both local and state politics, Celebrezze was elected to the state senate in 1950 and re-elected two years later. A diligent but little-known legislator, he was persuaded to run for Cleveland's highest office by retiring mayor, Tom Burke, and Louis Seltzer, editor of the *Cleveland Press* and a powerhouse in local politics who sought a dark horse to oppose Democrat heir apparent, Albert Porter.

With Seltzer's ringing endorsements and his own relentless campaigning, Celebrezze shocked Porter in the primary and easily defeated Republican William McDermott in the November election. One of the city's most popular elected officials ever, Tony Celebrezze was re-elected four times and swept every ward in his final campaign.

As mayor, his accomplishments had a long term effect on the city, providing the foundation for its subsequent emergence as a major port city and the impetus for urban renewal through Erieview and other downtown complexes.

The methodical confluence of highways through the city's mid-section are another part of his legacy.

In 1962, Celebrezze was tapped for a cabinet post, serving as Secretary of Health, education and Welfare under Presidents Kennedy and Johnson, steering the landmark Medicare program through Congress. In 1965, he was appointed federal judge and served with distinction until retiring from the bench in 1980.

Cleveland has always played rough with its elected officials. Many careers have been launched with great expectations only to founder in the dangerous waters of public sentiment. Sooner or later, the tide shifts, and few have managed to emerge unscathed.

Anthony Celebrezze is a rare exception to the harsh rules of city politics. He remains revered today as among the most publicly honored and personally honorable men ever to serve the people of Cleveland.

185 William Creighton

(1837-1863, Pittsburgh, Pennsylvania)

A printer at the *Cleveland Herald*, William Creighton, dedicated patriot and a veteran of the Cleveland Light Guard Zouaves, raised his own company of infantry after the outbreak of the Civil War and reported to the hastily set up Camp Taylor in Cleveland. This hardy group was mustered into the Union army as Company A of the 7th Ohio Volunteer Infantry. The city's blue ribbon regiment of the Great War, the 7th Ohio fought with valor and distinction from Antietam and Chencellorsville to Gettysburg and Clear Mountain.

Over 600 men at full strength, the 7th suffered the loss of 12 officers and 261 enlisted men in wartime service. Colonel Creighton was one. Cited for gallantry at the Battle of Winchester, Creighton was badly wounded at Clear Mountain but returned to his command only a month later. In November of the following year, Creighton led the 1st Brigade in an assault on Taylor's Ridge in Georgia, charging the summit under withering fire. Near the summit, Creighton rushed to the aide Lt. Colonel Orrin Crane, his close friend and commander of the 7th Ohio. Without thought for his own safety, Creighton personally tended to Crane's wounds. He was shot and killed instantly, falling beside his close friend and comrade in arms. Crane succumbed to his wounds before help arrived.

They were the two highest ranking Cleveland officers to die on the battlefield in the Civil War. The bodies of Creighton and Crane were returned to the city in December. Thousands of mourners stood silent in an icy rain to witness the funeral procession after joint services at Old Stone Church. William Creighton and Orrin Crane were buried together, side by side, in Woodland Cemetery. Creighton is one of the heroes immortalized in bronze at the Soldiers and Sailors monument on Public Square.

65 Luther Day & Family

(18xx - 19xx, Canton, Ohio)

Great-grandson and grandson of Ohio Supreme Court justices, and son of a U. S. Supreme Court justice, Luther Day and his brother, William, were born heirs to Cleveland's foremost legal family. William became a federal judge, but Luther preferred private practice, promptly establishing himself among the most astute corporate counsel in the area. Among his heavyweight clients were names like Eaton, Van Sweringen and Hanna. Luther was so successful that brother Bill left the bench to join him in the firm of Day & Day, telling Teddy Roosevelt that he couldn't afford to live on the salary of federal judge.

After the death of Frank Ginn, managing partner of the esteemed firm of Tolles, Hogsett & Ginn in 1938, Thomas Jones took the helm as his hand-picked successor. His first decision, only days after Ginn's funeral, was to merge the firm with Day & Day. It turned out to be one of the best. The two managing partners wanted to call it "Jones, Day." Some of the associates lobbied for space on the marquee, and the final choice was "Jones, Day, Cockley & Reavis." Over the years, it evolved into the largest, most powerful law firm in the world: Jones, Day, Reavis & Pogue. Most people call it by the founders' first choice: Jones, Day.

40 James A. Garfield

(1831-1881, Orange Township, Ohio)

The illustrious career of a Northeast Ohio native son who rose from humble roots in nearby Orange to the presidency of the United States was cut short by an assassin's bullet less than four months after assuming the nation's highest office.

After attending local schools, Garfield went on to Williams College and a brief but conspicuous academic career. An outstanding teacher at Hiram, he was named college president while in his mid-20's, leaving to serve in the Ohio Senate in 1859.

Garfield's courage and character were evident in the Civil War. His success as a military strategist and his chivalry in battle were notable at Shiloh and Chickamauga. He retired as a Major General and was immediately elected to the House of Representatives, serving for 17 years before stepping across the hall after his election to the Senate in 1880.

1880 was a career year in the life of James A. Garfield. After his successful run for the Senate, he attended the Republican convention as campaign manager for Ohioan John Sherman, the leading candidate for the nomination. A three-way race among Sherman, former President Grant and Senator James G. Blaine ended in a bitter deadlock, broken when competing camps agreed on Garfield as the only compromise candidate whose candidacy would not irrevocably split the party.

Supported by powerful Cleveland financial forces, Garfield waged a surprisingly spirited campaign to upset Winfield Scott Hancock and win the presidency by a margin of less than 10,000 popular votes.

The new president was forced to focus on repairing party rifts during his first few months in office, and was tragically denied the chance to realize his potential as leader of the nation. On July 2, 1881, en route to a college reunion, he was approached at the Washington train station by a disgruntled politician, Julius Guiteau, and shot in the abdomen. Months of medical efforts failed to save him. He died on September 19th. President James Garfield was 49 years old.

When the news of the President's death reached Cleveland, on the night of September 19th, all the city's church bells began a tolling that lasted all through the night. Cannons along the lakefront intermittently boomed their tribute to the martyr president until dawn. The following day most of the city's downtown buildings were draped in black and white with the help of the city fire department.

The funeral train arrived in Cleveland on Saturday, September 24, and the hearse carried the President's body through silent, crowd-lined streets to the measured beat of the military escort. Around the high catafalque on the square where the slain Garfield would lie in state for two days was an honor guard of Cleveland Grays.

In like manner only sixteen short years before, a catafalque at the same place had held the martyred remains of President Abraham Lincoln. A canopied pavilion had been erected over the casket which was banked with white flowers. Between early morning and ten that night, more than one hundred thousand persons from all sections of Ohio and surrounding states moved past the casket.

At least as many mourners---probably more---passed by the body of President Garfield in America's last tribute to him in Public Square, and they included the great names of the nation. Two ex-Presidents, Ulysses S. Grant and Rutherford B. Hayes, came to pay their respects, as did Generals Sherman, Sheridan and Hancock; all the members of the cabinet and ranking foreign dignitaries.

James A. Garfield is buried at Lakeview Cemetery in Cleveland.

83 Mary B. Grossman

(1879-1977, Cleveland)

The first woman to serve as a municipal judge in the United States, Mary Grossman was a hometown girl, a Central High graduate, and a student at the Euclid Avenue Business College. She became familiar with legal work as a stenographer and soon came to believe she could outperform the men whose words she recorded. Mary attended law school at Baldwin-Wallace and passed the bar in 1912. In 1918, two years before she became eligible to vote through Constitutional amendment, she was among the first women admitted to the ABA. Mary Grossman was one of the area's leading suffragettes, head of the local League of Woman's Suffrage.

With the right to vote came the right to hold office. Grossman was elected municipal judge in 1923, and quickly distinguished herself as a righteous jurist. The voters knew a good thing when they had one. Mary Grossman held her post for 36 consecutive years.

Her reputation was just as strong, if not as favorable, among the city's criminals. She was known as "Hard-boiled Mary," and a trip to her courtroom was rued as a certain ticket to the Big House.

A charter member of the Women's City Club in 1916 and the league of Women Voters in 1920, Mary Grossman ranks alongside Belle Sherwin and Florence Allen as a pioneer in the struggle for women's rights in law and society.

128 Samuel Huntington

(1765-1817, Norwich,Connecticut)

He came to Cleveland in 1800. His name rings a distant bell with students of American history---his namesake uncle's signature appears on the *Declaration of Independence*. Young Sam decided to make the area his home and returned the following year with his family. He described the journey in a letter to Moses Cleaveland:

> *I have moved my Patriarchal Caravan through the wilderness to this Canaan. I was nine days on the Journey, with two Waggons, ten oxen, three horses, seven Cows and Eighteen persons in my Retinue. We slept seven nights in the open air after leaving the settlements in New York State.*

He was among the first landowners of Cleveland Township. His blue blood name won him appointment as lieutenant colonel, commander of territorial troops in the Western Reserve, and his legal background won him appointment as the area's first judge. When Ohio achieved statehood in 1803, Huntington presided over the first state legislature and served in the first session of the state's supreme court. In 1808, he was elected governor of Ohio. Later, he was among the first trustees when Cleveland was incorporated as a village.

145 David Ingalls

(1899-1985, Cleveland)

The only naval aviator to make "ace" in World War I, Ingalls shot down 7 enemy craft while assigned to a squadron of Sopwith Camels. He received the Distinguished Service Medal and British Distinguished Flying Cross for his valor.

He deserves another medal for good thinking and good luck. He returned home and made two wise decisions. The first was to join the law firm of Squire, Sanders & Dempsey. The second was to marry Louise Harkness, heiress of one of the great Standard Oil fortunes.

He accepted President Hoover's appointment as Assistant Secretary of the Navy in 1929, then returned to active military service in World War II as a ranking officer in the Pacific Air Corps. Ingalls received the Bronze Star and the Legion of Merit. By the end of World War II, David Ingalls sported a sizable fruit salad covering most of the left side of his uniform.

He was invited by fellow aviator Charles Lindbergh to join Pan Am after the war and retired as vice-president of what was then the largest airline in the world. David Ingalls was elected to the Aviation Hall of Fame prior to his death in 1985.

142 Isaac Kidd

(1884-1941, Cleveland)

Commanding officer of the *U. S. S. Arizona*, Admiral Isaac Campbell Kidd declined to leave his ship when it was first attacked while anchored at Pearl Harbor. Instead, he went to the bridge and took charge, issuing orders to man the guns and directing others to care for those wounded by the first wave of Japanese attack planes. Moments later, the Arizona was rocked by explosions as the second wave swept in, dealing at least three mortal blows to the vessel's hull and midsection. Badly wounded, Kidd refused to relinquish command and went down with his ship.

Admiral Isaac Kidd was Cleveland's first reported fatality in World War II. A symbol of American courage under fire and an inspiration to the millions of men at arms who would take up his fallen mantle and carry on to victory in the world's greatest conflict, Admiral Kidd was posthumously awarded the Congressional Medal of Honor.

71 Fred Kohler

(1864-1934, Cleveland)

One of Cleveland's most enigmatic and entertaining public officials, Mayor Fred Kohler was constantly making news, good and bad, from the time of his days as fearless police enforcer in the 1890's. Mayor Tom Johnson appointed him chief of police in 1903 and Kohler wasted no time in laying down the law. He imbued his men with a sense of discipline and an esprit de corps that gave the Cleveland police force an enduring reputation as one of the most efficient and least corrupted in the nation. President Theodore Roosevelt called him the country's finest chief of police.

Kohler's brusque style and contempt for political favoritism did not lend itself to strong alliances with influential members of either party. His enemies list grew longer as the years passed. As soon as Johnson was out of office, opposition forces gathered to rid the town of Kohler. The chief was hauled up on immoral conduct charges only weeks after the new administration took over. But Fred beat the rap and was restored to full rank.

His victory proved to be only one battle in a long war. In 1913, he was back in court, this time in an ugly divorce action, with an irate husband naming Chief Kohler as the chief amorous correspondent of his adulterous wife. His opponents had a field day with the scandal in the papers and Kohler was fired. Adding injury to insult, a month later he was set upon by hired thugs in an alley off Short Vincent Street and very nearly beaten to death with brass knuckles and blackjacks.

It took him weeks to recover, but Kohler was not a quitter. Instead of resigning himself to defeat and leaving town, he plunged headlong into politics, losing several elections before getting elected county commissioner in 1918. Crusading against graft and corruption, he restored his good name and earned a reputation as an honest reformer. In 1921, support for this political loner by either party was unthinkable, so he ran for mayor as an independent Republican. Not only did he win against stiff odds, but Kohler and his family put their money up with local bookmakers and won a hefty sum to boot.

Vindicated at last, big Fred was in his element. Payback time for all those who had kicked him when he was down. He had promised to clean up the mess at City Hall and he got right down to business, firing 850 patronage employees and slashing municipal expenses. Before long, he was battling with his own police force, the public utilities, the newspapers, city council and even boxing fans. Miffed by the decision in a bout he witnessed first hand, he banned the sport for the duration of his administration. Just as arbitrary and dictatorial in other matters, he took on all comers and rarely lost so much as a minor skirmish.

Toward the end of his term in office, Kohler took to erecting billboards to proclaim his deeds and his philosophy to his constituents. "I kept the Wolf from the Door----Fred Kohler, Mayor" said one. "I Alone Have Been Your Mayor" trumpeted another. Many cringed at his arrogance, but few could argue with his results.

Cleveland's charter was changed to a city manager government in 1924, and Kohler could not stand for re-election. He ran for Sheriff instead, winning handily. Running for re-election in 1928, he was dogged by new rumors of graft in office and defeated. Kohler never returned to public office.

Fred Kohler suffered a stroke in 1932 and passed away in 1934. Stories about the former mayor's sticky fingers were re-circulated when it was discovered he had more than half a million dollars stashed in a safety deposit box, but it was too late to do anything about it. They didn't have Fred Kohler to kick around any more.

13 Eliot Ness

(1903-1957 Chicago)

If Eliot Ness hadn't died before telling Oscar Fraley about his time in Cleveland there likely would havc been a sequel to the film, *The Untouchables*. It would have been called something like...*The Untouchables II.* Hey, if you got a title that works.

In many ways, his Cleveland story was even more dramatic than his prohibition battle with the Capone mob in Chicago. Ness came to the city as safety director, rooted out corruption, reduced crime and literally made the streets much safer, but he was eventually done in by personal problems and a demented killer who taunted him for years.

Reform mayor Harold Burton lured Eliot Ness to Cleveland in 1935. At the time, Cleveland was known as Fun City, USA. Speakeasies, gambling clubs and red light joints abounded. Word in the underworld was that Cleveland cops were willing to look the other way at all but the most heinous of crimes, if the price were right. Bad boys like Moe Dalitz, Alvin "Creepy" Karpis and Pretty Boy

Floyd all spent time here, owing to the genial hospitality of local gendarmes. Mayor Burton gave the young Ness (still only 32, four years after ringing up Capone) just what he demanded---complete control to do whatever was required to restore law and order.

Eliot went to work right away when with a raid on the notorious gambling spot, the Harvard Club. When tainted suburban police and politicos refused to participate, Ness deputized two dozen downtown boys, armed them with shotguns and led the raid himself. Gangsters at the club had sworn they would shoot it out with anyone who tried to take them on, but they meekly surrendered when the new lawman strolled up to the front door alone and loudly announced that they had one minute before he and his posse came in, guns blazing.

Over the next few years he cleaned house at the police department, ferreting out corrupt cops, including precinct captains and lieutenants, several of whom were charged and convicted on bribery charges. Over a hundred more officers resigned, replaced by educated, upstanding men in blue, survivors of a rigorous entry exam designed by Ness.

Eliot took on union racketeers too, culminating in the extortion conviction of ringleaders Donald Campbell and John McGee. The key witnesses against them were the owners of a popular family restaurant---Gordon and Vernon Stouffer.

While the Capone conviction was a singular accomplishment in Chicago, Ness scored several here. He saw the need to keep juveniles off the streets and out of trouble, so he developed the idea for "Boys Town." In a few years, juvenile crime in the city decreased by 80%.

His innovations became standards for police departments nationwide. He insisted on new, brightly painted police cars to make the law a high profile presence. He equipped cars with two-way radios and established a central police phone number. Response time was reduced dramatically. Crime plummeted 38% in a single year.

Ness instituted on-the-spot drunk-driving tests ("Close your eyes and touch your nose with your finger---that's not your nose, sir, that's your knee."), with immediate arrest the penalty for flunking. He set up a separate traffic court, initiated mandatory automobile inspections and provided ambulances manned with medical personnel. These changes precipitated a decline in traffic fatalities by half. Cleveland, which had been the seconds worst city in the nation for auto deaths, was named "Safest City in the USA." Insurance rates dropped a corresponding 50%. Eliot Ness was so popular he could have run for mayor.

Trouble was, he did. But he waited until 1947, five years after his last day as safety director. He could have won earlier, but a series of personal misadventures tarnished his tin star. He divorced his second wife and wasn't shy about being seen around town with various women on his arm. He was scandalized by one incident involving a married woman and by embarrassing headlines about a woman, liquor and a hit-skip accident. Worst of all, he never did solve the mysterious torso murders.

Some psychopath had been killing vagabond residents of the decrepit Kingsbury Run area, decapitating and dismembering his victims. A body (or worse, portions of a body) turned up every few months, beginning in September of 1935. There were at least 12 known victims, and strong suspicion that many more may have died at the hands of this gruesome killer. In his defense, it should be noted that Ness never really controlled the case. His strength and his authority were administrative. He had never been a detective in the Sherlock Holmes mode and had little experience in sleuthing. Regardless, the unsolved case became his albatross.

A political novice who wasn't able to measure up to his charismatic press clippings with his unimpressive oratory, Ness was easily defeated in 1947. The campaign took a heavy toll on his finances. Concurrent business setbacks almost ruined him financially.

In 1956, in poor health and in need of money, he agreed to collaborate on the story of his glory days. The Chicago chapters were completed and journalist Fraley wanted to follow up with more about Eliot's time in Cleveland. He never got the chance. Eliot Ness died of a sudden heart attack in 1957.

Ness didn't live to see *The Untouchables* become a best-seller, a hit television series and a blockbuster movie. The righteous law enforcer who loved media attention and never missed a chance to enhance his reputation would have loved it. In death, he had become what he always wanted---the most famous lawman of the 20th century.

165 Harry Franklin Payer

(1875-1952, Cleveland)

While the Cleveland Old Guard dominated the fields of law and politics for more than 150 years, an occasional outsider broke through the barrier through sheer force of will and extraordinary talent.

Harry F. Payer was born in Cleveland, son of a Bohemian immigrant and a working class Cleveland mother. Another Central High School graduate, his academic performance and an early reputation as a skilled orator and debater earned him entry to Adelbert College, where he graduated Magna Cum Laude. More honors followed at Cleveland Law School. In 1899, he met two men who would greatly influence his career, Tom L. Johnson and Newton D. Baker. Johnson was so impressed with the impeccably dressed young man that he enlisted Payer, at 24, as his campaign manager. Johnson was elected in 1900.

No cushy cabinet job for Harry. He served in the trenches as assistant city solicitor under Baker, point man in the legendary legal struggle for control of the city's streetcar lines. Out-standing in the courtroom, Payer won many notable cases, in both civil and criminal trials.

Harry Payer was one of Cleveland's most colorful and personable characters as well. With a vast personal library and magnificent east side home, Payer was a philosopher, philanthropist, lecturer, diplomat and connoisseur. Always dressed in formal wear, a gracious host and spellbinding speaker, gentleman Harry was considered the leading Czech-American citizen of his time, president of the Czech Club of America. When visiting the United States, the president of Czechoslovakia was a guest at Payer's house. Payer delivered a 1920 Fourth of July oration to over 60,000 people in Prague, in both English and Bohemian.

He served as assistant secretary of state for Franklin D. Roosevelt, co-founded the Cuyahoga County Bar Association and led a lengthy campaign for judicial reform.

23 Andrew Squire

(1850-1934, Mantua, Ohio)

You can squander your money on Harvard or Yale or you can emulate the senior founder of Squire, Sanders & Dempsey. One of the most respected legal practitioners and scholars in the city's history never spent a day a law school.

Son of Dr. Andrew Jackson Squire and Martha Wilmot, Andrew Squire attended the Western Reserve Eclectic Institute, fancy name for a liberal arts prep school at Hiram College. When he graduated there in 1872, young Andrew set off for Cleveland just as the city began its dizzying ride to the heights of the industrial boom.

Squire carried an enviable pair of introductory letters, one from the president of Hiram and future president of the U. S., James Garfield, and another from the eminent educator Burke Hinsdale. He found a position as law clerk, was admitted to the bar a year later without ever attending law school, and soon established a reputation as an accomplished practitioner of business law.

In 1890, he joined forces with Judge William Sanders and James Dempsey to establish the firm of Squire, Sanders and Dempsey. Over a century later, it remains one of the city's most eminent firms.

The ensuing years were among the most legally contentious in the Cleveland's history, with powerful Republican forces arrayed against the progressive populism of Tom L. Johnson's New Democrats. Squire's loyalties lay on the GOP side. He and his firm were on the front lines of most of the crucial battles. Squire himself was noted not only as a superb litigator, but a peacemaker, broker and conciliator, capable of uniting widely disparate personalities and finding common ground.

Baker
Baldwin
Blossom
Carter
Case
Clark
Green
Ingham
Johnson
Kelley
Kirtland
Mather
Mitchell
Peak
Rappe
Scranton
Seneca
Severance
Silver
Van Sweringen

Lifetime Achievement

15 Newton D. Baker

(1871-1937, Martinsburg, Virginia)

One of the most astute legal minds in the city's history, Newton Diehl Baker, Jr. met former Cleveland Congressman Martin Foran while working for the Postmaster General in Washington. In 1899, he came to Cleveland to work in Foran's firm. It was there that Newton D. Baker was introduced to Tom L. Johnson. The alliance forged between these two men became the lightning rod of Cleveland politics for a generation.

Baker was Johnson's strong right arm in the battle to reinvent municipal government for the 20th century. As City Solicitor, Baker orchestrated the offensive against entrenched interests opposed to a city railway system (forerunner of RTA and prototype for municipal transit across the nation), home rule and city-owned public utilities.

These were times of high drama in Cleveland politics as the city became the battleground for the confrontation between government, personified by Johnson and Baker, and the mighty new industrial monopolies, symbolized by hometown Standard Oil.

Johnson was finally defeated in 1909 by a Republican coalition, but the highly respected Baker was retained as solicitor. With Johnson's death in 1911, Baker assumed leadership of the local Democratic party. He ran for mayor himself and returned the reformers to office in 1912. It was during his administration that Muny Light, public transit and home rule became realities. In 1916, he retired to private practice, founding the law firm of Baker, Hostetler & Sidlo. Only months later, he was summoned by President Woodrow Wilson.

Baker was named Secretary of War and served through World War I as chief architect of a military effort unprecedented in scope and complexity. He continued to serve until de-mobilization was complete and all contracts, loans and negotiations were finalized. America's victorious emergence from the World War as a global superpower was due, in no small part, to the organizational and administrative skills of Newton Baker. He was as loyal to Woodrow Wilson as he had been to Tom Johnson, touring the country after the war as the president's leading spokesman for the valiant but futile effort to support the League of Nations.

In 1921, Baker returned to Cleveland and resumed leadership of the law firm. While officially retired from public service, he continued to fight for Cleveland in private practice. He was the city's attorney in the successful battle to force local utilities to act in the public interest.

In 1928, Newton D. Baker received long overdue recognition for his contributions to the nation. He was one of the first civilians ever awarded the United States Distinguished Service Medal.

79 The Baldwin Families

Cleveland has a collection of people named Baldwin that makes that family of Hollywood hunks look like a bunch of dim-witted lugs in comparison. They comprise a coincidental blend of achievers linked by surname and common Connecticut heritage, yet mostly unrelated by blood. Pioneer sheriff Samuel S. Baldwin; prominent banker Norman Baldwin and Judge Charles C. Baldwin, founder of the Western Reserve Historical Society---all arrived from different points of origin in the Mother State to make their mark in Cleveland. Judge Baldwin's wife, Sophia, and his son, Samuel, continued his important work in ornithology, establishing the famous research center on the family estate in Gates Mills.

Baldwin-Wallace College, the area's oldest institute of higher learning; Baldwin Reservoir, the largest man-made water storage facility under roof in the world; Baldwin Institute, the first non-discriminatory preparatory school in Cuyahoga County; Banks-Baldwin, the country's largest legal publishing firm; Baldwin Bird Sanctuary; Baldwin Park; Baldwin Avenue. If this is Cleveland, it must be Baldwin.

The most fascinating Baldwin story belongs to John, the grandson of a blacksmith and son of a Revolutionary War hero who came to Cleveland in 1827 to homestead a small farm in the Middleburg area. While digging a cellar for his home, Baldwin stumbled on the vein of rock that would make him a rich man. "Berea sandstone" proved to be the world's most efficient grinding stone. John quietly bought up most of the land that would become the Berea quarries over the next few years.

Self-educated and self-motivated, John began by hacking out chunks of rock himself, with chisel and hammer, in 1828. As his profits grew, he added stonecutters. In 1833, he invented a method for turning stone on a lathe, supplanting the work of dozens of hand laborers. The Baldwin Quarry Company was made. In the ensuing century, the tonnage of stone shipped from the Berea reservoir counted in the millions.

A humble and deeply religious man, John Baldwin put his money to work for the community. Ardent proponent of education as the cure for most of society's ills, he founded the Baldwin Institute in association with the Methodist Episcopal Church, donating all the necessary land and most of the start up costs. It was certified as Baldwin University in 1855, and later merged with nearby German Wallace College.

Baldwin was also the catalyst for the memorable Lyceum Village experiment. Along with a cluster of other Methodist idealists, he established this Christian socialist community in Middleburg, dedicated to the principles of community sharing and equality.

The utopian enclave struggled valiantly, but failed after a decade. Many departed. Baldwin and others remained for the transition into the more traditional settlement called Berea. John Baldwin served as first mayor of the village, officially incorporated in 1850.

A civic and social activist throughout his life, John Baldwin was one of the nation's earliest advocates of absolute parity under the law---"all people, all races, all colors, all creeds---all equal."

168 Dudley Blossom

(1879-1938, Cleveland)

You better be rich if you're born with the name Dudley Blossom, or you're going to have a tough time your first few years in school. Fortunately, this Dudley Blossom arrived a bona fide blue blood and carried his high born moniker with dignity and aplomb.

Successful standard bearer of the family name in business, Dudley was involved with the Blossom Lock Company, the Payne conglomerate and Central National Bank. He married Elizabeth Bingham, heiress to the Payne family Standard Oil fortune in 1910. The rich get richer. There wasn't any reason to dedicate himself to further financial pursuits---he had enough to build an Olympic-sized swimming pool like Uncle Scrooge's in his basement, fill it with hundred dollar bills, and spend his time working on his backstroke.

It's a good thing for Cleveland that he didn't. After returning home from voluntary service with the Red Cross on the battlefields of World War I, Dudley blossomed into one of the few "super-philanthropists" Cleveland has been blessed with over the years---outstanding citizens who found their life's work in contributing their considerable time, influence and money to the city that they loved.

As Cleveland Welfare Director for a dozen years, he oversaw the expansion of charitable services at City Hospital, which stands today as Cleveland Metro Health Center, one of the finest and oldest continually operating, publicly funded hospital complexes in the nation. It still provides medical services to more needy people than any other hospital in Ohio.

It was Dudley who assured the Cleveland Orchestra of a permanent home by raising the necessary millions to match the challenge grant of the Severance Family, making Severance Hall a reality. He raised millions more for University Hospitals, the Musical Arts Association and the Negro Welfare Fund. The Blossom Hill School, Blossom Hill Home and Blossom Music Center honor his contributions to education and the arts.

Dudley was the man behind the Great Lakes Exposition, the spectacular celebration of life in the Midwest that gave Clevelanders a welcome respite from the dreariest days of the Depression. A combination amusement park and international exhibition center, the Exposition was the greatest tourist attraction in the city's history, luring over eight million visitors after opening on the lakefront in June of 1936.

Any accurate profile of his accomplishments is incomplete without a sense of this man's personality. When you're asking very wealthy people to give you millions to spend on high-minded public projects, it helps to be charming. Dudley Blossom could charm money out of a dried turnip, which he once did. It is said that, as a child, he was the only kid who worked an extra dime out of old man Rockefeller. In his adult years, he worked extra millions out of the Rockefellers and other wealthy families, all for the benefit of the people of Cleveland.

2 Lorenzo Carter

(1767-1814, Rutland, Vermont)

The real original Clevelander and the prototype of the American pioneer, Lorenzo Carter was almost 30 when he first set foot in the Western Reserve with his wife Rebecca in 1797, less than a year after Moses Cleaveland and his band of Connecticut troopers first staked claim to the territory.

While the surveyors, land owners and speculators soon returned home and other families moved on to more hospitable territory away from the waterfront, the Carters came to stay, building the first log cabin on the site that would come to symbolize the location of a great city, on the bank of the Cuyahoga River where it meets Lake Erie.

In the mold of Davy Crockett and Daniel Boone (who paid Carter his highest compliment----"a man of trust"), Carter blazed the first trails, fought for survival against the wilderness and the weather, and earned a reputation as a man of unflinching courage, great physical strength, common sense and rock solid integrity, powerful virtues in a land where civilization was no more than an idle thought.

The Indians revered Carter as a white medicine man. It was widely believed he could not be harmed. He could speak the Indians' language and treated them with respect, welcoming them to fish and hunt along the river. It was Carter who hosted the seasonal feasts that established a friendly rapport among Indians and whites as they celebrated together, sharing food, good will and whiskey under Carter's roof.

The first home, the first building, the first school (opened in his home by Ann Spafford in 1802), the first frame house, the first commercial lake vessel (the *Zephyr*), the first ferry, first crop farm, the first rule of law (Carter was constable), the first trial, the first liquor license (granted by the Court of Quarter Sessions), the first tavern, the first marriage (in his house), the first society ball (1801)---all of these and many more inaugural events of Cleveland history involved Lorenzo Carter as the undisputed leader of the tiny community.

Countless distinguished citizens in every walk of life would leave their mark on Cleveland in the ensuing two centuries, but first among them, standing tall with Rebecca and his family, long rifle in one hand, wood ax in the other, was Lorenzo Carter, Cleveland's leading man.

16 Leonard Case & Family

(1786-1864, Westmoreland County, Pennsylvania)

Credit goes to Leonard Case as the Father of the Forest City. As one of the early presidents of the village, Case decreed that shade trees be planted alongside new streets as early as the 1820s, a practice that endured for more than a century, forever cloaking the community in lush verdant hues.

A title clerk for the Connecticut Land Company, later a bank clerk and lawyer, Leonard Case became more familiar with Cleveland property values than any other man of his time. Over the years, Case developed a keen sense of business and an eye for a bargain, acquiring thousands of acres of prime county land when the Panic of 1837 forced many to liquidate their holdings. The windfall made Leonard Case one of Cleveland's first truly wealthy citizens and it transformed him into the city's first resident philanthropist. He endowed a number of Cleveland's charitable and public service institutions, with special attention to education and the arts.

His sons, LEONARD CASE, JR. (*1820-1880, Cleveland*) and WILLIAM CASE (*1818-1862, Cleveland*), went on to surpass their father as citizens of extraordinary public service and generosity. Both were plagued by poor health, suffering since childhood from chronic diseases that limited their activities and cut their lives short, yet both inherited a sense of civic pride and responsibility that has benefited Clevelanders for more than a century since their passing.

Leonard used his inheritance to generously endow many of Cleveland's most noble establishments, from school libraries to museums, and provided a million dollars to establish the Case School of Applied Sciences. At his death, he bequeathed 200 acres of prime downtown real estate to Case, a windfall that propelled the school to the realms of high finance and higher learning.

William Case was so sickly as a child that he took to the outdoor life to build up his constitution. In his years of hiking through Ohio and the northwest country, he became a nature lover. Among the people he met in his travels was the great Audobon, whom he served as an assistant. When he returned to Cleveland to settle down, he and some fellow naturalists who shared his interests in the mysteries and beauty of the environment would come together frequently for discussions. In 1835, the Case family provided a permanent home for their gatherings on Public Square. They aptly named it the "Ark." The Arkites became Cleveland's most renown club, with the leading minds of the day coming together to exchange their best ideas.

William Case was elected mayor in 1850, Cleveland's first native-born leader. While ably presiding over the beginning of the town's evolution to major city status, William also followed in his father's footsteps, instituting a second planting program that made certain that the urban tree population would keep pace with the explosive increase in people.

Neither of the brothers survived their father by more than fifteen years, and neither ever married. The book was closed on the generations of the Case family, but not before many of the city's most benevolent and most enduring institutions were as deeply rooted as the trees that still line the streets of Case's Forest City.

117 Harold T. Clark

(1882-1965, Derby, Connecticut)

Tennis, anyone?

An attorney with a Yale-Harvard pedigree, Harold Clark came to Cleveland to practice law with Squires, Sanders & Dempsey. After years with the firm, he opened his own practice to specialize in wills, estates and probate. In time, he became the designated Keeper of Trusts for many of the city's wealthiest families. It was in this capacity that he encouraged Cleveland's elite to provide a steady cash flow for civic benefit. Because of Harold, a respectable stream of charitable giving became a Niagara of generosity.

Clark played an important role in providing the foundations of many of the area's outstanding cultural institutions. The Cleveland Metroparks, Cleveland Zoo, Holden Arboretum, Museum of Natural History, Museum of Art, Karamu House, Society for the Blind and the public spaces that breakup the downtown skyline with touches of class---all bear the imprint of Harold T. Clark.

Civic arts and culture were his forte, but tennis was his first love. A fine player in his youth, Clark was among the sponsors of the new East End Tennis Club in 1920, a posh facility on Carnegie for the smart set. He steered the funding for numerous public courts as well, earning a tennis-friendly reputation for the city. Harold's groundwork paid off years later when Cleveland was chosen to host the Davis Cup finals in 1961, and many times thereafter, along with dozens of other amateur and professional championships.

82 John Patterson Green

(1845-1940, Newberne, North Carolina)

The first black man elected to office in Cleveland and the only black citizen elected to a northern state senate in the nineteenth century, John Patterson Green emerged as the first patriarch of Cleveland's black community, a leader and activist in the area for more than fifty years.

Migrating to Cleveland in 1857, John Green worked at menial jobs. For a time, as a teen-ager, he lived alone on the downtown streets. He often worked for books instead of money. In 1866 he published his first book, *Essays on Miscellaneous Subjects by a Self-Educated Colored Youth*. The modest publication was hailed as an important work and Green gained favorable local attention and support.

With overwhelming support in the growing black community and some critical assistance from white progressives, John Green ran an exhausting campaign for Justice of Peace in 1872 and was elected by a narrow margin. His shocking victory was national news.

He served ably and dared to reach higher, running for the State House in 1877. Well-spoken, popular and respected, Green waged another spirited campaign and appeared to be victorious before some election board shenanigans brought home a last minute victory for his opponent. Many believed the election was blatantly stolen by racist Democrats, but no official action was taken.

Four years later, Green was not to be denied, winning election as a State Representative by a large margin.

In 1891, John Patterson Green wrote and submitted the Labor Day bill, recognizing a state holiday as a salute to all working people. The bill was passed into law, and, in 1894, became the model for legislation in Congress establishing Labor Day as a national holiday. Clevelanders and all Americans owe a debt of thanks to Mr. Green, and not only for his exemplary character and civic-minded spirit. Thousands of politicians have been promising citizens a smorgasbord of pleasantries since the republic began, but, thanks to John Patterson Green, everybody has one more day off every year. If he was around today, he'd have an excellent chance of becoming the first African American President of the United States.

170 Mary Bigelow Ingham

(1832-1923, Mansfield, Ohio)

There's no escaping the fact that *The Cleveland 200* is overpopulated with males. The opportunity for women to achieve prominence in any field did not exist at all in the first century of the city's history and hardly improved through most of the second. Business, finance, law, politics, science and sports---all were exclusive men's clubs. Even the arts were hardly accessible to females until well into the 20th century. Considering such discouraging circumstances, the few women who managed to make important public contributions, especially those whose achievements came in the face of 19th century chauvinism, are all the more remarkable.

Gentle Mary Ingham was one. Born and raised in a devout Methodist family, she was educated in the arts and theology. She was a local teacher, then a college professor and administrator. In 1866, she married wealthy publisher William Ingham, but continued her career in academia for another twenty years. Active behind the scenes in religious and civic activities all her life, she overcame a natural shyness and humility as well as contemporary social restrictions to become a respected public figure.

Ingham was a co-founder of the Women's Foreign Ministry in 1870, and promulgated that organization's religious goals for decades. Locally, she established and administrated inns and hospices for indigents at several locations. In 1882, Ingham's efforts to promote art education led to the establishment of what would become the Cleveland Institute of Art. A prodigious writer and speaker, Mary Ingham wrote a column on women in the *Cleveland Leader* for years under the pseudonym of Anne Hathaway. She wrote and published women's history books, short stories and a play.

Her most fervent crusade was against what she perceived as mankind's worst enemy: John Barleycorn. She was very active with the Women's Christian Temperance Union and one of the leaders of the landmark WCTU national convention in Cleveland in 1874. She lived to see the reality of the group's ultimate goal---Prohibition became the law of the land three years before her death at 91.

If Mary Bigelow Ingham were alive today, she would be disappointed to learn that Mr. Barleycorn is back, with a vengeance and some friends. But then again, if she were alive today, she'd be 164, and probably wouldn't care.

5 Tom Lofton Johnson

(1854-1911, Blue Springs, Kentucky)

An old line, Confederate loyalist family, the Johnsons lost everything in the Civil War and young Tom was forced to strike out on his own in his mid-teens to make a living. Success was not long in coming to the imaginative Mr. Johnson.

While working for pennies on the Louisville Street railway system, he invented a see-thru glass farebox that put an end to the constant haggling over who paid what. The simple but practical invention remains in use today on the buses and streetcars of the world.

With a tidy profit from his inventive wits in hand, Johnson was determined to move up in the railway business and found himself a most suitable partner, one of the fabulously wealthy DuPonts. Mr. Deep Pockets put up the money and Tom did the work. They acquired, re-built and sold the Indianapolis Street Railway, reaping a huge profit. Similar successes followed in St. Louis, Detroit and Brooklyn.

Tom L. Johnson arrived Cleveland in 1879, already a millionaire, determined to work his streetcar magic here. He began efforts to gain control of the Cleveland lines only to find himself confronted with a large and difficult obstacle: Marc Hanna. It was a consummate battle between an irresistible force and an immovable object. It took years of wrangling, financial dueling, political infighting and back room brawling, but when the dust settled, Tom L. Johnson emerged the victor and new champion of Cleveland.

Flush with success, Johnson made yet another fortune with Lorain Steel Company and was poised to join the ranks of America's affluent elite when the course of his life was dramatically changed in a matter of days. He read a book on political philosophy by American Progressive, Henry George. The impact was profound. Johnson virtually abandoned his business interests and dedicated the remainder of his life to the Progressive principles of efficient, populist leadership. He ran for Congress and was elected as a Progressive Democrat in 1890, re-elected in '92. Reform-minded, bold and charismatic, he ran for Mayor of Cleveland in 1900, waged a spirited campaign and won out against the powerful array of Republican forces led by nemesis Marc Hanna.

His controversial years at City Hall marked the zenith of Progressive politics in America. Loved by the people and hated by the power brokers and bosses, Johnson battled for true democracy in the city's government, municipal ownership of utilities and idealistic expansion of public services. Under Tom Lofton Johnson, the city was described as the "most honest and efficient government in the U. S."

The Johnson Era finally ended with his defeat in 1909 by Herman Baehr, backed by the largest war chest ever amassed by Republicans in a local campaign.

It's all too common for a politician to enter office with nothing but a pocketful of promises and depart, years later, inexplicably well-to-do. Tom L. Johnson turned that tradition on its ear. A man of means when he became mayor, Johnson gave everything he had to the people of Cleveland, leaving office exhausted, emotionally and financially drained.

He died two years later at 57, leaving a legacy as Cleveland's most selfless and most memorable political leader.

3 Alfred Kelley & Family

(1789-1859, Middlefield, Connecticut)

The real First Family of Cleveland was the remarkable Kelley clan from Connecticut. Foremost among the Kelleys was Alfred. If this were Europe, they'd call him Alfred the Great.

Without him, it is almost certain that the city would be no larger than Lorain, no more a metropolis than Mentor. It was Alfred Kelley who arrived at a wilderness outpost with hearty Lorenzo Carter riding herd on a few loose knit frontier families and molded it into the city of Cleveland.

He was intrigued by the glowing reports of his older brother, Datus, the first of the Kelleys to visit the area, and made the journey west in 1810 with two other men destined to leave their mark on area history: Dr. Jared Kirtland and Judge Joshua Stowe. His knowledge of law earned him admittance to the Ohio bar and he became Cleveland's first and only lawyer and the first prosecutor in Cuyahoga County. In 1812, he successfully prosecuted Indian John O'Mic for the murder of two trappers, resulting in two more firsts, Cleveland's introduction to capital crime and the death penalty.

The primogenitor of Cleveland mayors, Alfred Kelley was the city's first formal leader, elected President of the Village of Cleveland in 1815. A year later, he resigned that post to represent the northern counties in the Fifteenth General Assembly of Ohio. It was there that he made his mark as Father of the Ohio Canal, leading the legislative battle over the northern terminus of the waterway that would link the Western Reserve to the Ohio River and the Mississippi beyond. As a result of Kelley's efforts, Cleveland emerged victorious, and Alfred saw the massive project through to reality, personally supervising the work that began in 1825.

Among his achievements as a state legislator was the first bill passed anywhere in the world to abolish imprisonment for debt (without Al, we'd need a jail the size of Alcatraz in every neighborhood). Kelley also drew up the state banking statute that eventually became the model for national banking laws.

He returned from his tour of duty in Columbus to become president of the Cleveland's largest bank and resume his role as a leading local citizen. In the 1840's, Kelley assured the city's continuing rise by leading a second major crusade, this one to link Cleveland by rail to the great cities east and west. He served as president of three of the city's earliest railroad companies, overseeing the rapid expansion that made Cleveland the largest rail terminal between Philadelphia and Chicago.

Alfred Kelley devoted a lifetime of service to the city and the state and contributed more to its early growth and prosperity than any other individual. He arrived to find Cleveland an unincorporated village of less than a hundred people. At his death in 1859, it was already one of the largest cities in the Midwest.

DANIEL KELLEY (1755-1831, Norwich, Connecticut) was Alfred's father and patriarch of the family. Distinguished son of a proud family harking back to the earliest Connecticut settlers, Daniel Kelley had already attained considerable personal success as the leading figure of a pioneer settlement in upstate New York years before Cleveland came into existence. In 1814, after 4 sons had already been lured to the promise of the Western Reserve, Daniel and his wife reluctantly joined them.

When Alfred resigned as president of the Cleveland Village to speak for Cleveland in the State Assembly, his father was elected to take his place, serving four consecutive terms. Daniel Kelley is buried in the Erie Street Cemetery.

DATUS, JOSEPH and **IRAD KELLEY** carried the family's flag into the cultural and business arenas, building the first brick buildings in town and operating the post office. Irad's interests in a commercial shipping venture led him to the western islands of Lake Erie. He and Datus eventually purchased the largest of these and renamed it Kelley's Island, mining its superior limestone quarries.

THOMAS KELLEY was the last of the Kelley brothers to arrive in the new lands, hastening here in 1815 after hearing that brother Al had been elected village president. As soon as Alfred's canal was completed, Thomas launched a lucrative shipping career, making enough money by 1848 to assume the presidency of the Merchants' Bank. He subsequently followed in Albert's steps to the state legislature, served with distinction, and was named to the lofty post of U. S. Marshal for Ohio by his friend Daniel Webster, then Secretary of State. Thomas Kelley's career may have been the first instance of nepotism in Cleveland politics, a tradition that has survived intact to this day.

19 Jared Potter Kirtland

(1793-1877, Wallingford, Connecticut)

As a doctor, naturalist, sociologist, academician and philanthropist, Dr. Jared Kirtland left many lasting contributions to the city that he loved. His brilliance in the natural sciences was evident from an early age. After graduating from medical school at Yale, he practiced in his home town for several years. then followed his father, a Connecticut Land Company agent, to Ohio.

One of America's leading naturalists, he was expert as well in natural history, geology, etymology, botany and horticulture.

His contributions to the Cleveland area still permeate the local landscape. Dr. Kirtland introduced dozens of varieties of non-indigenous trees, flowers and shrubs to the area. He is responsible for 26 varieties of cherries and 6 different pears still grown in Ohio today. It was Kirtland who discovered that the Ohio shoreline was ideal for grape growing, with its underpinnings of moisture laden shale.

With James Nicholson and Mars Wagar, he developed the lakefront wilderness west of the river into a community. Whippoorwill, Kirtland's 200 acre estate in the middle of what is now Lakewood, was a lush testing ground for his experiments.

Dr. Kirtland had a commanding presence. Tall, with riveting blue eyes and a shock of unruly white hair, he was revered by his peers, neighbors and students as one of the area's most brilliant citizens.

27 The Mather Family

Who is the most famous "Sam" in Cleveland history? You might say Sam Sheppard, if you're into mystery or Sam McDowell if you're a baseball nut. It better be Sam Miller of you're running for office. Maybe Sam Gerber if you're medically minded, even Sammy Kaye for Big Band fans, Samuel Andrews for stockholders and Samuel Huntington for political historians. Never mind. It's a trick question. The answer is Samuel Mather. All of them.

A distinguished American family long before the first white man set foot in the Western Reserve, the Mathers counted among their ancestors the appropriately named Increase Mather, founder of Harvard, and, of course, Samuel Mather, Jr., who walked shoulder to shoulder with Moses on the road to the Forest City. Of all the names listed on the first deeds of the Connecticut Land Company, only "Mather" has remained indelible.

Landowners and community leaders from the earliest days, the Mathers prospered as traders and service providers. In the early 1800s, Samuel W. Mather also provided mortician services, an important necessity when the life expectancy was not that many years past puberty. Samuel H. Mather was there when the first dollar changed hands at the Society for Savings (today's Key Bank) in 1849. Samuel L. was part of Cleveland Cliffs iron before the first shovelful of ore was taken from the Lake Superior mines. And then there was Samuel, born in 1849 to Georgiana and (who else?) Samuel Mather. With Jay Morse and James Pickands, young Sammy started Pickands, Mather. His success in international mining and metals exceeded the sum total of all other Sam Mathers combined, and they were all very wealthy gentlemen. With the departure of the Rockefellers, he was said to be the wealthiest man in Ohio. It was certainly enough to be equitably magnanimous with virtually every worthy cause and institution in Cleveland: there isn't a notable hospital, museum, university or charity in the area without a Mather endowment to its credit.

Samuel's greatest success may have been his marriage to Flora Stone, a young lady with a distinguished if star-crossed heritage of her own long before joining the Mather clan. Her father was Amasa Stone, famous for his bridge-building as well a his impressive wealth, infamous for the tragic Ashtabula Disaster, the bridge collapse that killed 92 people. Make that 93. Disconsolate and depressed, Amasa Stone took his own life a few years later.

After a privileged childhood and a proper education at the best schools, Flora was enjoying life as a lovely princess of Cleveland's aristocracy when three events changed the course of her life. First, her sister Clara married dapper John Hay, former personal military aide to President Lincoln, U. S. diplomat, New York *bon vivant* and future Secretary of State. This family tie introduced Flora to an even grander scale of life and thought. Then, in 1876, disaster struck. The Ashtabula Disaster was blamed on Stone's ill-considered design. Years of litigation and recriminations followed. Flora Stone emerged, tempered in character and spirit, to marry Samuel Mather in 1881.

Flora Stone Mather was an important influence in the development of the Ohio Consumers League and Legal Aid Society. University Circle is a sprawling monument to her generosity. The CWRU campus, University Hospital, the museums, historical societies and serene public gardens are a living expression of her love of children, the arts, humanities and education.

The Mather mansion, one of the grandest on Millionaire's Row, still stands at 2605 Euclid Avenue, one of two survivors of the gilded age. Erected in 1906 at a cost equivalent to more than fifteen million modern dollars, it was built of New Hampshire brick (the exact same hand-made, water-struck bricks used at Harvard) and Indiana limestone, with hand-carved, black oak walls, mahogany floors and rosewood parquet. There was a third floor ballroom that could accommodate 300 and fourth floor living quarters for a dozen servants.

166 Lottie Pearl Mitchell

(@1890-1974, Wilberforce, Canada)

A lifetime of dedication to the cause of equal rights, boundless energy, good humor, endless enthusiasm and an indomitable spirit made "Lady Pearl" synonymous with the NAACP in Cleveland and a respected presence in the national movement.

A neighborhood activist from her early days, Lady Pearl led a Negro "splash party" at city-owned Garfield Pool in the 1930's. They drained it to avoid integration. With a group of others, she paid a surprise visit to Euclid Beach Park, long a stronghold of segregation, intent on joining the dancers at the bandstand. Park officials stopped the music and called police.

Lady Pearl never stopped. A graduate of Wilberforce University, she led the respected Alpha Kappa Alpha sorority as an alumna, lending a helping hand to hundreds of younger "sisters" through the years. She attended Oberlin's School of Music and became an accomplished singer and musician. A talented actress, Lady Pearl appeared in the first integrated production at the Cleveland Playhouse and was active for years with the Playhouse Settlement (later Karamu House).

Her life's work was a personal crusade for human rights, and she remained involved in the struggle well into her eighties.

30 George Peak

(1722-1827, Maryland)

The first known African American resident of the Western Reserve, George Peak and his family were the very first West Siders, daring to settle across the river in what was still the official territory of the Indians (we hadn't gotten around to breaking that treaty yet).

Wily old George was far more than a curious statistic in Cleveland's past. By all accounts, he was a wealthy man, with a mysterious horde of silver coins that was said by some to be found treasure and by others the tarnished yield of the theft of a British army payroll in the French & Indian War. George just said that it was his money, and that was good enough. It was rare enough in those days for a man to pay in real currency that questions about the source of the money were considered rude and foolish.

George Peak was highly regarded by his white neighbors as a good friend and helpful citizen. George introduced the stone grinding wheel to the area, an innovation more valuable than cable TV to all the ladies who had been spending most of their days grinding wheat by hand with mortar and pestle. They thought the world of him.

He raised a large family and was always there to lend a hand to anyone in need. No one seemed to care what color it was. George became a landowner at 90, buying over 100 acres in Rockport. He lived to a ripe 105 and was mourned at his death throughout the city as one of Cleveland's most respected pioneers.

47 Amadeus Rappe

(1801-1877, Audrehem, France)

There were only five Catholic families in Cleveland when the first Church, St. Mary's on the Flats, was organized by Reverend John Dillon. The building on Columbus Street was not yet complete when Fr. Dillon died in 1837. St. Mary's survived and its parishioners multiplied in numbers as Irish immigrant families flocked to fill Cleveland's growing demand for laborers.

The Catholic community was overwhelmingly Irish and German, but it was a Frenchman, Louis Amadeus Rappe, longtime missionary to the Maumee Valley area, who came to St. Mary's in 1847 and began the work of transforming the tiny parish into the third largest Catholic diocese in the U. S.

Rappe was consecrated Bishop the same year. He immediately launched a campaign to erect St. John's Cathedral and undertook a wide range of ambitious plans. Bishop Rappe oversaw the establishment of numerous parishes, including St. Stanislaus, St. Patrick's, St. Wenceslas and St. Malachi's. Charitable institutions were also high on the Bishop's priority list: St. Vincent Charity Hospital, St. Vincent's Orphanage, St. Mary's and St. Joseph's Hospital were among the tireless prelate's projects. He founded St, Mary's Seminary to ease the demand for new priests and organized the Sisters of Charity of St. Augustine. Starting with a group of four nuns, this order blossomed to service generations of the city's sick, poor and needy while also providing the core staff of parish schools and churches and Catholic hospitals.

In spite of his achievements, Bishop Rappe became embroiled in controversy over his 23 years as head of the diocese. In the 1850s, he promoted the Total Abstinence Movement to combat the growing problem of alcoholism, denouncing Demon Rum in a series of blistering sermons:

> *Among the evils which prevail...is one which is more frightful than any calamity that could befall you; which threatens not only to put an end to all decent observances of the Sunday, but to eradicate piety and*

to destroy every sentiment that elevates and ennobles the Christian soul, to bring inevitable ruin upon reason, honor and fortune---the drinking shop, the sink wherein all that is good is buried.

This attitude was considered overly harsh in the Irish parishes. In the late 1860's, they lobbied for higher Church officials to relieve Bishop Rappe, claiming he abused his authority by favoring German and French priests. Rappe denied the charges and many of the faithful rallied to his support, but he steadfastly refused to defend himself and resigned in 1870 to avoid a rift in the diocese. The foundation and the framework for the area's largest and most active religious institution, the Diocese of Cleveland, remains virtually intact as built by Amadeus Rappe.

Bishop Louis Amadeus Rappe died in 1877 and was buried at St. John's Cathedral. His statue stands in the cathedral's courtyard, gazing past East 9th Street to the West

80 The Scrantons

Joel Scranton (1793-1858, Belchertown, Massachusetts)
Irene Hickox Scranton (1800-1858, Durham, New York)

Cleveland's most poignant love story, the Scrantons, is over 150 years old. A merchant who came to Cleveland with the canal, Joel Scranton made his living selling leather for tools, horses and clothes. Joel was Mr. Leather. He opened a store on Superior, soon expanding to a whole dry goods line. He invested his profits in riverfront real estate, then developed the property with roads and rail service. He literally paved the way for one of the most productive industrial centers in the world. Scranton's Flats, they called it, the center of the city's pre-Civil War boom.

Beyond the Flats, he owned tracts of land all over, including one on Public Square that he graciously sold to First Presbyterian in the early 1830s as land for the Old Stone Church. The tough trader became a philanthropist and civic volunteer over the years. Everyone gave the credit to Irene.

Irene Hickox came to Cleveland as a school teacher. Proper and well-educated, Miss Hickox was welcomed as an educator and a shining example for youth, both badly needed in the rough hewn Cleveland of 1825. She was principle at one of the city's first schools for girls.

It was meant to be. Cleveland's most eligible bachelor and most admired young lady. They were married in 1828. She stopped teaching shortly after, but never stopped caring for the young people of Cleveland. Over the next thirty years, Irene was involved in founding, operating or endowing most of the area's important charities, civic and religious. Hospitals, orphanages, museums, poverty programs and shelters---Irene Scranton even kept a small hospice in her own home, ready to comfort whomever might pass by in need.

After Joel had made more than he could ever spend, she roped him in to the volunteer life. He came to love her more for it. He supported her plans and ideas, financed her crusades, stood by her and worked with her.

Early in 1858, Irene returned feverish from a mission of mercy and took to bed. Doctors were called. Joel fretted and paced while they tried to treat her for the dreaded "ague." She rallied, then faded again. The doctors shook their heads. She lingered long enough for a bittersweet farewell, then died in Joel's arms on March 15th.

Joel Scranton was inconsolable. He tended to her funeral, simple as she wanted, then retired to his home, spending hours alone in a straight-backed rocker. He died suddenly, cause unknown, on April 9th, twenty-five days after the passing of his beloved wife Irene.

32 Seneca

(@ 1760-1816, Unknown)

The noble chief of the Seneca tribe, his name was variably Anglicized as "Stigwanish" or "Stigoneesh," but he was known to the white man simply as Seneca, named for the once great tribe he led in both war and peace.

Seneca's warrior days ended with the decisive Indian defeat by General Mad Anthony Wayne at the Battle of Fallen Timbers in 1794. In the subsequent treaty conferences, the tribes relinquished much of their homeland, but were guaranteed "eternal" Indian domain west of the Cuyahoga, in exchange for peace to the east.

Unlike the white men, the Indians were true to their word. In the history of the Western Reserve, there was never again any organized resistance to white settlement or expansion. Seneca was among the most influential peacekeepers.

When Cleaveland's survey party arrived in 1796, Seneca advised them on the lay of the land he knew so well, providing invaluable advice for future residents. Without Seneca, it is possible that the inchoate Cleveland settlement would have died out completely. In that brutal first winter, it was Seneca who provided game and provisions that sustained the pioneers.

Seneca remained in the area for another twenty years, assisting his new neighbors in countless ways as teacher, scout, confidante and ombudsman. Almost all white settlements west of the Alleghenys encountered violent hostility at one time or another from Indian tribes provoked by the ominous and seemingly endless encroachment on their territory. All but Cleveland. Seneca kept the peace.

America's most valuable double agent in the War of 1812, Seneca reported on British efforts to enlist Indians as supplemental troops and lobbied against alliances with the redcoats.

A fastidious man who was unmoved by the white man's lure of trinkets, money or whiskey, Seneca was described by General Edward Paine as a man with "...the honesty of Aristides, the dignity of a Roman senator and the benevolence of a William Penn."

In the end, the reward for his good deeds was death.

A white settler whose wife and son had been murdered by a renegade Indian took his revenge on the innocent Seneca, killing him in a rage in 1816.

21 The Severance Family

There is only one of Cleveland's most illustrious families that can claim the distinctly modern trait of gender equality in familial prominence and accomplishment since the first generations set foot in the Western Reserve. Severance.

Even marriage at 20 to Cleveland banker Theodoric Severance and the task of raising five children did not deter CAROLINE SEYMOUR SEVERANCE (*1820-1914, Canandaigua, New York*) from her life's calling as one of the earliest and most eloquent spokespersons for women's rights in America.

She read and studied history and philosophy while fulfilling her duties as homemaker. In the 1850s, she was influenced by the great Sojourner Truth. For the following half century she dedicated her efforts to the struggle for equality. Caroline Severance was among the founders of the Ohio Women's Suffrage Association and a lifelong crusader for women's rights in law and society.

Her landmark treatise, *Humanity*, a plaintive and forthright call to action, became the rallying cry for women's groups around the nation. An inveterate organizer, she was instrumental in establishing a number of women's clubs in Cleveland, Boston and Los Angeles. Caroline Severance toured the nation as a lecturer on women's legal rights. She was also active in anti-slavery and international peace movements.

Her sister-in-law, MARY LONG SEVERANCE (*1816-1902, Cleveland*) married Solomon Lewis Severance, a successful merchant who died suddenly five years later, leaving Mary and two sons, Solon and Louis. Both joined the ranks of Cleveland's most prominent business, civic and philanthropic leaders. Mary herself was a leading figure in religious and charitable causes, helping to establish two Presbyterian churches, the Protestant Orphan Asylum and Lakeside Hospital. During the civil war, she championed women's volunteer work in Union hospitals. It was mother Mary who instilled in her sons a sense of genuine public service and civic pride that ultimately benefited all of Cleveland.

"In all of the relations of life she went about trailing the beatitudes in her train, and her gentle and gracious life signified much to Cleveland." [*A History of Cuyahoga County and the City of Cleveland*, William R. Coates]

An impressive epitaph for a great Cleveland lady.

Meanwhile, back at the ranch, the Severance menfolk were taking care of business. Teddy, Louie, Sol and Lewis all brought home more than their share of the bacon in their respective careers as bankers and merchants, but it was Mary's grandson who really hit the jackpot. Before he came along, the Severances were living pretty high on the hog. By the time he was finished, they owned the pig sty.

JOHN LONG SEVERANCE (*1863-1936, Cleveland*) took the family into oil--- Standard Oil. A major stockholder in the petroleum titan, John L. Severance struck out on his own years later, founding a local company that became American Linseed Oil. Success spawned more new ventures. At one time or other, John was a major player in the local salt industry, construction, banking, manufacturing and real estate. Many of the companies he founded remain active today.

John Severance and his Rolls Royce

In later years, his appetite for business diminished and he turned his interest to social and philanthropic interests. He spent time hob-nobbing at exclusive haunts like the Union Club, but he spent a lot more finding ways to give away his money. At the height of the stock boom of the 20s, he donated over a million dollars to build a home for the Cleveland Orchestra. Unfazed by the Depression, he donated a million more in 1930 and Severance Hall became a reality.

John Severance was President of the Cleveland Museum of Art, donating millions himself and urging his Millionaire's Row neighbors to get in on the joy of giving. He is among the handful of benefactors who set the powerful example in civic spirit that led to Cleveland's reputation as the nation's most charitable city.

55 Abba Hillel Silver

(1893 -1963 Lithuania)

Abba is the Hebrew word for father. Both in size and stature, Abba Silver was the big daddy of the American Zionist movement.

A man of incredible intellect and strong convictions, Silver rose to a leadership position in American Judiasm in large part due to his spellbinding oratory. His presence filled a room and his words enraptured the audience. Virutally every review of an Abba Hillel speech contains the word "spellbound." Indeed, his weekly sermons were invariably given to standing room only crowds.

The passions of Rabbi Silver's oratory were not limited to strictly Jewish causes. He was a fervent supporter of the working class, community service to the poor and family values. But it was on the subject of Zionism that he struck the strongest chord.

Silver was a Zionist from his boyhood days. He believed in the cultural need for a Jewish State and immersed himself in the Hebrew language. He didn't ask his congregants and followers to go live in Palestine, but he expected that they contribute. Silver insisted that the establishment of a Jewish State was necessary for American Jewish survival. As head of the Zionist Organization of America, Rabbi Silver spoke to the United Nations in 1947, presenting a compelling case for the partition of Palestine. A year later he was instrumental in convincing President Truman to recognize the newly declared State of Israel.

Rabbi Silver gets the news that Israel has become a modern nation.

Considered a potential candidate as first president of the state of israel in 1948, he declined to give up his rabbinical work, deferred to his friend, David Ben Gurion, and returned to his work in Cleveland.

His dedication to Israel did not distract him from his local congregation or his scholarly pursuits. The Temple became the largest reform congregation in the country and the domed synagogue in Wade Park that was built under Rabbi Silver's watch remains one of the most beautiful in the country.

Abba Hillel published six major works in his lifetime including the well-known *Where Judaism Differed.* There are streets in nearly every city in Israel that bear Abba Hillel Silver's name. So was the Lone Ranger's horse and a Norwegian pop quartet.

11 The Van Sweringen Brothers

ORIS PAXTON (1879-1936, Wooster, Ohio)
MANTIS JAMES (1881-1935, Rogue's Hollow, Ohio)

In 1905, an odd pair of brothers took an option on a parcel of land in what had once been the Shaker settlement east of the city. Neither wealthy nor well-connected, these modest young real estate developers had a vision for the area as an idyllic suburban community. In the next quarter century, stoked by the fires of success, that vision grew brighter and larger, finally engulfing not just the east side, but the heart of the city of Cleveland. What these two curious men saw was the future. Thanks more to them than any other private citizens before or since, that future came to pass.

They couldn't make it on the West Side, so the boys went east.

The first real estate venture of Oris Paxton and Mantis James Sweringen was on Cook Avenue in Lakewood, where they purchased property and built homes. Neither one had any experience in real estate. Van babes in the Lakewood woods, they lost their shirts, defaulting on loans and suffering through an embarrassing foreclosure. For a few years, they were forced to do business under the names of their sisters, Edith and Carrie. They regrouped, and changed their name, reviving the "Van" prefix which the family had dropped long ago.

The Van Sweringens paid off their debts with profits from a modestly successful development in Cleveland Heights. Whether it was the fancy new moniker, the hard lessons they had learned or their success in the Heights, they managed to convince a high-powered group of investors to back O. P. and M. J.'s excellent adventure, the conversion of the Shaker Lakes area into the most expensive and exclusive suburban enclave in America.

For awhile, it looked as if the Shaker scheme was headed down the same road to ruin as the Lakewood debacle. Interest was high among the city's sophisticated crowd, but one serious obstacle made the buyers beware: there was no public transportation to downtown. The automobile was still just a cantankerous adolescent, fun on the weekends but too expensive and unreliable for daily commuting.

Cheap rail lines criss-crossed the city, thanks to Tom Johnson and his Populist programs. No one was going to pay the Van's steep asking price for a house in an isolated neighborhood.

The Vans tried to convince the Cleveland Railway to extend a line, but the idea was rebuffed as unprofitable. Their only option was to buy the right of way, six miles down Kingsbury Run, then through the inner city to Public Square, and build their own rail system.

It wasn't easy. The boys were determined to build their "Shaker Rapid," but before they were finished, a series of complicated business transactions were required, including acquisition of rights to a series of railroads---the Nickel Plate, the Chesapeake & Ohio, Toledo Railway, St. Louis & Western, Lake Erie & Western, the Erie Lackawana Chicago & Eastern, and the Missouri Pacific. They ended up controlling the largest railroad empire in America, over 30,000 miles worth of tracks, choo-choos and cabooses. In the process, Oris and Mantis had created that All-American entity that has since made millionaires of thousands and billionaires of a few: the Holding Company.

In less than a decade, the crafty brothers leveraged a half million dollars of their own money into a four-billion-dollar monolith and found themselves players in the main arenas of national finance.

O. P. and M. J. had Cleveland on a roll again, and they weren't about to give up the dice.

With rail rights secured, they completed the rail link and Shaker turned gold. From 1919 to 1929, Shaker Village added over 300 expensive new homes each year. The population of the suburb increased from 1,700 to 15,500 and the valuation of the property which had been purchased by the Van Sweringens for slightly more than $1,000,000 soared to $80,000,000.

They used a measly few million to build their dream home in Hunting Valley, Daisy Hill. The cost of elevating this country estate to the level of baronial grandeur eventually achieved has been estimated as high as three million dollars, but the cost was of no great importance. It took architect Philip Small seven years to complete the massive reconstruction of the barn into an imposing mansion. Their home was as elegant and lavish as any house owned by the elect of Cleveland society, but it never played any role in social capers of the era because the Vans were removed from society. They belonged to the right clubs, the Union Club, Shaker Heights Country Club, Pepper Pike Golf Club, but they didn't participate. O. P. couldn't even play golf, but he was Sam Snead compared to M. J. They didn't go to parties. They shied away from charity events, donating through a structured office program. They avoided journalists and reporters, paying a public relations expert to keep their names out of the papers. The Vans never married, had no independent hobbies and rarely traveled, except on business, always together.

O. P. and M. J. were closer than Siegfried and Roy. They spent half their time in the office, and the other half at Daisy Hill, each other's most trusted advisor, lifetime business partner and best friend.

Their railroads roared with the Twenties, filling the Van's coffers with more ammo. They invested in healthy companies like White Motor and Goodyear, and made even more. Because of the pyramid stacks of holding companies necessary to make all the transactions, the debts were as impressive as the assets, but the brothers Van, flush with other people's money, turned to the map of the city with a gleam in their eye.

After a classic tussle with the Johnson forces over who would control the city's architectural destiny, the Vans emerged victorious again, winning the rights to build the ambitious Terminal Tower complex. Completed in 1929, it changed the face of Cleveland, shifting the nexus of the city back to Public Square, away from both the East 9th Street financial center and the cluster of public buildings flanking the downtown Mall. The largest structure between New York and Chicago, Terminal Tower, with its stacked grids of rails serving the area and the nation beyond, luxurious department stores, elegant restaurants and four star hotel, became the city's signature.

The Vans didn't even show up for the dedication ceremonies. On June 28th, 1929, they were back at Daisy, having a quite dinner for two, another trophy project on the mantle, planning their next conquest. They looked to be invincible, a two-headed Midas, destined for even greater glory. What they didn't know then, and neither did any one else, was that the end of the line for the Van Sweringen brothers was exactly four months away. An eighteen-year run ended on October 29, 1929, when their hot dice on Wall Street turned up snake eyes.

The Stock Market Crash sent rail stocks into a free fall as the commercial and passenger traffic dried to a trickle. The Van Sweringens were way out in front and high above the crowd, atop a financial pyramid that was a much a marvel, in its own way, as the great pyramids of the Egyptians. The pity was that the mortar holding the bricks together had not had time to solidify. The Vans desperately needed time.

They turned to J. P. Morgan for financial help. Years later, economic historians would speculate that there was a clique of New Yorkers, led by Morgan and Charles Schwab, who welcomed the financial decline of the Van Sweringens and other Cleveland interests. The Morgan company provided just enough of an infusion to secure the ability to force the Van Sweringens' property into bankruptcy. Years of legal wrangling couldn't prevent the inevitable. The vast holdings of the Vans were sold at auction in September of 1935.

The boys were down, but they weren't out. In a last minute finesse, they managed to put together a deal with Mid America Corporation, another holding company formally owned by Van allies. It was a method for O. P. and M. J. to resume operations and control. The stage was set, but fate stepped in.

The Morgan auction took place in September 1935. Only O. P. was present. His brother was in Cleveland, desperately ill. His high blood pressure had worsened and an attack of influenza had complicated his condition. He rallied, but his health deteriorated again in mid-October and he returned to Lakeside Hospital, where he died early on the morning of December 13th. O. P. was at his bedside.

O. P. went through the motions, but mechanically. He was a man in despair. "I've always been able to see a way," he said, "but to this obstacle there is no answer." He walked in morning for less than a year. He died in his sleep on a train trip to New York in November of 1936.

Neither the Van Sweringens nor their sisters left any heirs. Their planned comeback, cut short by death, meant that their estates had little net worth beyond the property and furnishings at Daisy Hill. The liquidation sale in 1938 elicited a 220-page catalogue from Parke-Bernet Galleries, with over a thousand art works and other valuables.

The personal traces of the Van Sweringens soon vanished, but their heritage endures, in Shaker Heights, on the railroads that still run, and most of all, in downtown Cleveland. Remodeled and revitalized in the 1980's, Terminal Tower anchors the modern Tower City, with commuters and customers flowing in on Rapid lines from east and west, filling the shops and restaurants, trooping across the walkway to Gateway, pouring out into the downtown streets. It is still the city's signature. The Vans' spirit remains.

Armstrong
Barnaby
Cowles
Donahue
Douglas
Freed
Fuldheim
Gray
Hall
Holden
Randle
Scott
Scripps
Seltzer
Vail
Ward

The Media

70 W. W. Armstrong

(1833-1905, New Lisbon, Ohio)

The *Cleveland Plain Dealer* was in big trouble. After J. W. Gray founded the paper and built it into one of the city's largest, the publisher died suddenly, leaving it in the hands of less competent managers. It was a time of fierce competition in the news business, with many dailies fighting for circulation in the big cities. Less than a year after Gray's death, battered by the competition and plagued by bad management, the *Plain Dealer* suspended operations.

It lay dormant until W. W. Armstrong, successful publisher of the *Advertiser* in Tiffin, Ohio, decided to take a chance and buy the Cleveland paper's assets and equipment in 1865. He resurrected the *Plain Dealer* and restored it to prominence as one of the state's leaders. A skilled writer and editor and an ardent Democrat "...of the old school of Jackson and Benton, unswerving in favor of States rights, home rule and hard money, and these time-honored principles he was prepared to maintain against all opponents."

The *Plain Dealer* has operated continuously since William Armstrong published his first issue, 131 years ago.

190 Barnaby & Friends

Hey little neighbor!

That was the sprightly greeting that every kid in Cleveland looked forward to hearing every day from their favorite television host. Lynn Sheldon played Barnaby as a sweet, overgrown imp, with straw boater and string tie borrowed from his own vaudeville past and pointy elfin ears that Mr. Spock would borrow for *Star Trek* years later. Sheldon was a pioneer of local television, hosting more than two dozen shows on four different stations before landing the lead in in the *Barnaby Show*, a Cleveland mainstay for more than a quarter century.

Barnaby may have been the most charming, but he was only one of many local performers ingrained in the collective memories of apprentice coach potatoes. Ghoulardi, Mister Jingeling (the Keeper of the Keys is still around, doing Christmas guest stints at Tower City), Woodrow the Woodsman, Jungle Larry, Gene Carroll and his wonderfully terrible variety show, Don Webster and the *Big 5 Show*, Big Chuck, Hoolihan, Little John and even Superhost, the weekend afternoon movie host who was, as hard as it is to imagine, a poor man's version of Ghoulardi.

And who could forget the immortal Captain Penny with his signature sign-off: "you can fool some of the people all of the time, and all of the people some of the time, but you can't fool Mom…" In real life, Ron Penfound's story had the saddest and most bizarre denouement. Lonely and dejected over the loss of his wife and his flagging career, he committed suicide, leaping to his death from the High Level Bridge, just as his wife had done a few years before.

But tragedy was rare on TV in those days. Barnaby and his friends were fun, the guests were goofy, the cartoons were entertaining and their words of comfort and wisdom were well taken. They were as much a part of Cleveland history as the newspapers, the sports teams and the weather. Our first electronic friends.

"And remember, little neighbor, I think you're the nicest person in the whole, wide world. Just you."

39 Edwin Cowles

(Austinburg, Ohio, 1825-1890)

Co-founder of the Republican Party in Ohio and the first of many influential Republicans who made Cleveland the epicenter of GOP power for more than 70 years, Edwin Cowles was, first and foremost, a newspaper man.
A printer by trade, he helped create the *Cleveland Leader* in 1854 and became its sole owner and editor-in-chief a few years later. For the rest of his life, he ruled Cleveland's largest daily paper with an iron fist, as champion of Republican causes, outspoken voice against slavery and bitter opponent of the three factions Cowles considered vile plagues on society: Democrats, Catholics and the Irish.

Cowles was not timid when it came to touting his personal beliefs, and wielded his newspaper like a war club, bashing his enemies, real and perceived, with daily glee. His favorite targets included the Roman Catholic bishop and two rival publishers, J. W. Gray at the *Plain Dealer* and E. W. Scripps at the *Press*. Unlike today, high standards of decorum in journalism were not a priority in the late 19th century. Some of the printed exchanges among the newspaper moguls were scatological classics. The *Plain Dealer* variously described Cowles as "...the original ass that Balaam mounted" and "...one of the most base and infamous of creatures, who, wearing the garb of human, has nearly all the elements of a demon...a fellow whose fruitful brain can produce a whole catacomb of lies...[he] resembles so much the prince of the regions of Pluto that if he be not his Satanic Majesty in person, he is worst still, being one of his dastardly and treacherous imps...."

97 Phil Donahue

(1935- , Cleveland)

The originator of daytime TV talk, the father figure to Oprah, Sally, Geraldo, Jerry, Jenny, Grumpy, Sneezy and Doc, was born and raised a normal kid on Cleveland's west side, an altar boy and decent student at Our Lady of the Angels parish, then at St. Edward's High School in Lakewood.

In 1967, after a short stint as host of radio talk show in Dayton, he was given the nod to fill an idle daytime hour on local WHIO with his own "talking head" show, a poor man's version of *The Mike Douglas Show*, with more serious talk and little performing. Donahue was a good listener, not just with his guests, but his studio audience as well. Before long, everyone was chiming in.

Live audience participation was the novelty that propelled Donahue to national syndication in 1969. By the mid-70's, the *Phil Donahue Show* was a force in the industry and before the end of the decade it was the #1 syndicated daytime show in the nation. A fair-minded ombudsman to some, a liberal wolf in Republican clothes to others, Donahue became the superstar of talk TV, opening lines of communication between a nation of viewers and the biggest names in politics and show business. Along the way he married an American sweetheart, *That Girl!* herself, Marlo Thomas.

After more than 15 years as the undisputed champ of chatter, Donahue was overtaken by competitors eager for a piece of his daytime audience. To boost ratings, Phil expanded his format, mixing his high-brow guests and subjects with tabloid topics. Prime ministers one day, Chippendale dancers the next. His heart was never in the sleazy evolution of the genre. The show finally succumbed to ratings erosion in 1996.

He won over 20 daytime Emmy Awards and launched an over-populated generation of imitators, from the raunchy to the sublime, as producers, advertisers and syndicators flocked to the low production costs, high returns and apparently endless public fascination with hosts and guests willing to make fools of themselves in exchange for a little notoriety.

Caller, are you there?

74 Mike Douglas

(1926- , Chicago)

Determined to be a performer, Mike Douglas spent years scrambling for gigs and money. He traveled the country singing with Kai Kaiser's Kollege of Musical Knowledge, a big band in the waning days of big bands. He did some radio, worked in dinner theaters and even went solo, with a song and joke act, usually second on the bill to the feature show.

Mike Douglas learned how to play to the audience the hard way. His routine was fixed at a tight fourteen minutes until one night in Columbus, when the gangster owned of a nightclub poked him in the chest before the show and told him the star wasn't showing up. "Kid, you're doing an hour," said Guido. "Yes I am," said Mike.

In 1961, he was working at a late night club in Los Angeles when a friend at Westinghouse called and asked him if he wanted to audition for a new format show they wanted to try at KYW, their station in Cleveland. Club in L.A. 1961. The "talk-variety" show needed a host who could perform and converse with guests. They had already auditioned all the local personalities and weren't happy yet. Mike flew to Cleveland, won the job and started on the air with *The Mike Douglas Show.* Everyone involved was just hoping it would last until summer.

It was a blockbuster from the very first day. Within a year, it was being syndicated---a new word in television---to other Westinghouse stations. Soon it was on the air in every major market in the U. S. and many overseas.

By the late 1960s, *The Mike Douglas Show* was the biggest success in television history, the prototype for more than fifty talk and variety shows to follow.

Mike didn't rest on his laurels. It may have been "Easy Listening for Television," but it was entertaining, mainly because Mike himself was such an affable host with a sense for audience comfort and a great eye for talent. TV insiders marvel at what he did for some of Hollywood's biggest careers. He discovered Bill Cosby and featured him for a week (the weekly co-host was another Douglas innovation). He launched Barbra Streisand's career, touting the gawky teen as a future superstar. Sonny & Cher were offered their own show after appearing with Douglas. Over 21 years, everyone you could call famous sat down next to Mike Douglas, from Marlon Brando to Mother Teresa. Seven presidents were guests on his show. The highest rated week featured a couple of curious conversationalists, John Lennon & Yoko Ono.

Mike Douglas loved Cleveland, but they made him move the show to Philadelphia in 1965 because of some FCC snafu about where Group W could own stations.

He was having so much fun and making so much money, he never paid much attention to the business side of show business. The wave of imitators and competitors that had come along in the 1970s cut into his market share. In 1982, Group W suddenly canceled his show, replacing Mike with John Davidson, the star of the future according to Group W bigwigs. John wasn't around long and all the smart guys who made the decision were fired.

Mike Douglas retired, shocked but uncomplaining, uninterested in any other format but the one he loved and personified. More than any other personality, he is cited by his peers as the nicest guy in show business.

And where is he now? You'll be glad to know Mike Douglas is doing well. Healthy and content, he plays golf, sees his friends, spends time with his daughters and his grandchildren. And, oh yeah, he moved one more time. In 1994, back to Cleveland.

111 Allan Freed

(1922-1965, Johnstown, Pennsylvania)

He didn't invent rock 'n' roll, but he was there when it was born, and Allan Freed gave the noisy new baby its name. Like the music itself, Freed was an unrepentant Wild Child of the mid-century, eager to please, and willing to try anything to succeed, get noticed or have fun, in no particular order.

In the early 1950s, it was DJ Freed on WJW who introduced rhythm and blues music to white audiences. Freed was turned on to the music by Record Rendezvous owner, Leo Mintz. Freed loved being on the cutting edge and Mintz wanted to sell records. Even then, it was about the money as much as the music. Freed adopted the nickname, "Moondog," when he began playing "race music" on his show. Until then, segregation permeated the air waves as surely as it did society, with black music assigned to the back of the bus, played only on black stations. Freed would drum out the beat on his studio desk, clap his hands and yell things like, "Rock it out!" and "Roll on, baby!" He electrified the kids and horrified their parents. No one knows the exact moment, but one night he shouted "Rock and Roll!" Eureka.

Freed organized and hosted the famed Moondog Coronation Ball at the Cleveland Arena on March 21, 1952---the first rock concert in history. A tiny blurb in the Cleveland Press was the only mention of the event. Sponsors hoped to draw at least a thousand kids to hear the new music. Over 20,000 showed up, ready to party. An under-manned squad of nervous cops tried to get them to quiet down. It wasn't their best strategy. Neither was shutting down the show halfway through. That precipitated another inaugural event---the first riot at a rock concert. They got that part right, right from the beginning.

The Moondog Ball catapulted Freed to the twin peaks of popular music and radio. He became the arbiter of hip, introducing dozens of black artists and sponsoring tours with stars like Fats Domino and Chuck Berry. He even produced some primitive rock 'n' roll movies, often appearing in them himself. In 1954, he was signed by WINS in New York for a nationally syndicated show. It became so popular that, at one point, he had over 4,000 fan clubs.

Alan's star kept rising until 1958. Freed was in his usual frenzy, hosting a Chuck Berry-Jerry Lee Lewis concert. When the kids started getting out of hand, police tried to intervene. Freed grabbed the microphone and shouted, "The Boston cops don't want you to have a good time!" Not his best effort at crowd control. In the ensuing melee, a man was stabbed and dozens injured. Freed was charged with inciting a riot. It was the first slip in a long slide for Moondog.

In 1959, Freed was pilloried for his role in the payola scandal that rocked the business. Months of investigations and hearings revealed the shady practices and under-the-table payments common among music industry executives and leading disc jockeys. Freed was number one, with a bullet, and this was the wrong hit list. Disgraced and depressed, Freed was fired from WABC. The fallout was so severe that both Freed and his rock 'n' roll music went into a period of quiet decline. The music recovered when the Beatles came along a few years later. Freed never did.

He suffered financially, of course, but his health suffered more. Alan was as wild and reckless as his on-air personality. A heavy drinker, he was introduced to drugs by the musicians he dealt with and added them to his long list of vices. He died at 42 of uremic poisoning.

Thanks in no small part to his efforts at popularizing the music and creating the name, the Rock and Roll Hall of Fame and Museum was awarded to Cleveland, opening its doors in 1995. Alan Freed was elected to the Hall of Fame roster in 1986, the first class. No doubt he was looking down from that big studio in the sky, howling, stomping and screaming into a golden microphone.

"This is the Moondog rockin' at ya!"

44 Dorothy Fuldheim

(1893-1989, Milwaukee, Wisconsin)

Before the days of well-coifed beauty contest winners posing as television anchors, Dorothy Fuldheim wasn't just a news reporter or commentator. Dorothy was the news. Already a veteran journalist, she was hired by WEWS-Channel 5 less than two years after the station went on the air and soon established herself as a local television institution. Her no-nonsense reporting and incisive comments were a staple in Cleveland for 35 years. A sizable portion of the daily news on Channel 5 was set aside exclusively for Dorothy. What did she do? Anything she wanted.

Internationally respected as a serious journalist, she traveled the world, interviewing political leaders, royalty, the famous and infamous, always offering her candid opinion of events in progress to attentive viewers back home. No personality of note would dare pass through Cleveland without stopping in for a chat with Dorothy. By the 1960s, she was the *grand dame* of the airwaves.

Although gracious and mannerly, she was hardly demure. Outspoken when needed, she was one of the first in the media to openly challenge Senator Joe McCarthy during the Red Scare of the 50s, criticizing his tactics and character while others cowered in fear of retribution from Tail Gunner Joe and his ruthless henchman, Roy Cohn. In 1969, still feisty in her 70s, she took umbrage at the uncouth language and attitude of Yippie leader, Jerry Rubin during a live interview. Dorothy ripped off his microphone and booted the speechless Rubin out of the studio.

The old redhead never slowed down. She continued to travel, authored several books, toured the lecture circuit and, as a single mother, raised her only child. It should come as no surprise that the Miss Fuldheim, independent-minded years before feminism entered the language, named her daughter Dorothy Fuldheim, Jr. Her incomparable career finally came to an end in 1984 with a paralyzing stroke. At the time of her last broadcast, Dorothy Fuldheim was 90 years old.

67 J. W. Gray

(1813-1862, Brideport, Vermont)

In 1841, Joseph William Gray bought the *Cleveland Advertiser* with his brother, Admiral Nelson Gray, and renamed it the *Cleveland Plain Dealer*. More than 150 years later, Gray's paper endures as the oldest and largest newspaper in Ohio, and one of the oldest in the country. Admiral Gray (a name bestowed on him by ambitious parents, not a bona fide title) left the business a few years later, but Joseph William Gray found his life's work as owner, publisher and editor-in-chief of the *Plain Dealer*. The paper became a daily in 1845, and Gray, an unabashed Democratic, made it an outspoken champion of Democrat causes, local, regional and national.

A vigorous supporter of Stephen Douglas, Gray tried but failed to push his idol into the White House.

Although Cleveland was a staunch Republican stronghold, Democrat Gray was popular for his editorial style and wit and in great demand on the social scene. He may have made a far greater contribution to the city's journalistic and political history if fate had not stepped in. J. W. Gray died at 48 after a sudden illness.

164 Arsenio Hall

(1959- , Cleveland)

There was a time, many years ago when people used to applaud and dogs used to bark. That was before *The Arsenio Hall Show.* Appropriating the "Dawg Pound" cheer of his hometown Cleveland Browns, Hall put a canine spin on audience appreciation that woofed its way into the national consciousness. More significantly, he gleefully invaded the lily-white turf of late night television and gave it some long-needed color.

Arsenio was never the class clown in school. He was the shy kid who found his outlet on stage. He seemed to know very early that he wanted to be a TV comedian. He didn't just watch Johnny Carson, he studied him and emulated the late night king so much that when it came time for Arsenio to get his first suit, he insisted that it bear a Johnny Carson label. Like Carson, Hall started out with a modest magic act, making his first TV appearance as a prestidigitator before he could even pronounce the word. Arsenio made his television debut when was 12, stepping before the cameras at local Channel 8.

After graduating from Kent State, Hall worked in Chicago as a salesman, moonlighting on the comedy club circuit, looking for a break. It came when singer Nancy Wilson saw his shtick and signed him as an opening act. Subsequent warm-up duties for Aretha Franklin and Patti Labelle earned him a short stint as co-host on television's *Solid Gold.*

Arsenio hit the big time when FOX named him interim replacement for Joan Rivers after she was canned as host of the new network's abortive attempt to compete on the late-night talk circuit. Network brass figured there was nothing to lose. The ratings rebound was surprising. Arsenio soon returned with his own syndicated show. *The Arsenio Hall Show* was an unqualified hit, even besting the hallowed *Tonight Show* in occasional ratings. Arsenio's refreshing style won young followers. His ultra-hip guest list won more. He opened the doors to rap, hip-hop and other New Wave performers who had been snubbed by white bread hosts.

His nightly presence propelled his star to greater heights. By the late 1980s, he joined the exclusive ranks of celebrities known by a single name---Liberace, Madonna, Prince, Arsenio (there aren't that many guys named Arsenio anyhow). He was praised by some for expanding the late night horizons, criticized by others for his show's "narrow focus," not too subtle code for "too black." Arsenio's responded that no one ever complained about the *Tonight Show* being too white.

Hall also faced criticism from the NAACP and Spike Lee that he wasn't black enough. Arsenio ignored critics on both sides, cranked up his posse and did his thing. For a time he was considered a leading candidate for the *Tonight Show* chair after Carson's retirement.

Arsenio's historic run finally ended in 1994, a casualty of the Great Late Night War. When David Letterman shifted to CBS, local affiliates flocked back to the fold. Fierce competition for big name guests between Leno and Letterman caught Arsenio in the crossfire. When the ratings tumbled, he checked out to pursue his interests in feature films and program production.

His influence is apparent in the diverse guest lists and entertainment-oriented formats on after hours television and the plethora of black performers that have followed his path to starring roles on prime time series.

113 Liberty Holden

(1833-1913, Raymond, Maine)

Picture *Bonanza*, with old Ben Cartwright sitting around the Ponderosa reading the *Plain Dealer* and you have a decent image for Liberty Holden, founding father of another great Cleveland family name.

A precocious child and a college-educated teacher, Liberty Emery Holden married the sister of Charles Bulkley, a leading citizen of Cleveland in the 1850s. He left teaching to study law, then abandoned law for investing in real estate. His civic and social activities brought him into contact with a number of Cleveland's most successful men---Rhodes, Mather, Humphrey, Otis and Hanna. In 1872, he wisely decided to join them.

After learning the ropes in a modestly profitable investment effort in Minnesota, Holden turned west and boldly plunged into mining territory that was difficult and risky, but the rewards were immense. The silver mines in Utah were barely more than a wild rumor when Holden invested heavily in rights, then more for equipment and labor. They tapped into a mother lode. Without leaving Cleveland, Liberty Holden became one of the richest men in the West, and a leading spokesman for western interests in the powerful political circles of Cleveland and Washington.

In 1885, Holden purchased the *Plain Dealer*, already one of the city's largest daily papers, from Major Armstrong. Many believed it was just a lark for Liberty, acquiring the paper as a literary hobby, but he quickly demonstrated his dedication. He instituted morning delivery (a practice now more than a century old), re-invigorated editorial content and expanded circulation.

Active in the community from his first days here, Liberty Holden played a role in the creation of many of Cleveland's grand institutions, including Wade Park, Rockefeller Park, University Circle and Cleveland Museum of Art. He served as president of the Cleveland School Board and Western Reserve Historical Society.

His descendants include not only many notable Holdens, but the Vails, still a notable nameplate at the *Plain Dealer* a hundred years after Liberty first put his name under the masthead.

56 Bill Randle

(@ 1925- , Detroit, Michigan)

One of the most influential voices in modern music, Bill Randle was already an expert in music history, theory and the classics when he started his radio career as a logical extension of his personal interests.

Randle's sense of the cutting edge and confident, low-key style propelled WERE to the top ranks. First, it was the introduction of cool jazz and bebop. Then Randle and his famous peers, Alan Freed and Norm N. Nite, led the rock and roll expedition to glory as surely as Moses Cleveland led the trek to Cleveland.

It was Bill Randle who coached Elvis through his formative year of 1954 and Bill Randle who introduced him to the national audience in 1955, playing an Elvis Presley record outside of the South for the first time on his top-rated radio shows in Cleveland and New York.

A modern renaissance man, Randle's musical credentials are unique, yet his achievements in other fields would each constitute a full and impressive career. Author, film producer, historian, critic, academician, corporation man, geopolitical expert, CIA alumnus and practicing attorney---Bill Randle still maintains an arduous schedule today, a septuagenarian music legend. His musical showcase is top-rated on the radio again. He remains the most informed and insightful voice on the music scene, with firsthand familiarity with everyone from Art Tatum and Frank Sinatra to Whitney Houston and Coolio.

He may well be, by any fair standard, the foremost living expert on popular music. He's been a student of the game for over sixty years, and a major player for more than fifty.

106 Jane Scott

(1920- , Mentor, Ohio)

The oldest rock and roll critic on earth can often be found in her office at the *Plain Dealer* as late as 4 a.m. When a graveyard shift editor once asked her about it, she gave him her standard reply in that sweet, whispery voice, "Oh, I just like the quiet."

Quiet is not what Jane does for a living. Determined to be a reporter, Jane took a meager-paying job with a tiny paper in Chagrin Falls in the late 1940s, then finally landed a job on the P. D. staff in the 50s. Relegated to the dregs of daily fillers, Jane dutifully covered garden club meetings and library lectures until one day in 1964, when a savvy editor insisted someone cover the airport arrival of a shaggy-haired quartet from England that was making noise on the teen scene. None of the veteran reporters wanted anything to do with it. Jane Scott, meet the Beatles. The Fab Four took a liking to her and invited her backstage. Her story made the front page. Since then, Jane Scott has been welcomed into the inner sanctum of rock by the stars of two generations. She has covered over 2,000 concerts and interviewed thousands of performers.

A walking history of pop music, Jane Scott's personal anecdotes make other self-proclaimed rock experts drool with envy. She was Jim Morrison's buddy and a shoulder for Janis Joplin to cry on. She took Jimi Hendrix to buy his first Corvette, taught KISS about makeup and urged Alice Cooper to "get crazy." The reclusive Bob Dylan kissed her on the cheek. Bruce Springsteen jumped in the audience and give her a hug. Jane Scott, they say, is still "the best backstage pass in the world."

She doesn't look like a rock legend. Jane's style of dress can only be described as "60s bag lady." She wears garish scarves, leather skirts and white go-go boots, accessorized by her ever-present tote bag, loaded to the brim with God knows what. The leather skirt, she once confided, is perfect for rock concerts. "When the kids throw up, it's easy to clean."

Still working at a pace that reporters half her age find exhausting, Jane does have one secret for keeping her hearing after all these years---ear plugs. No wonder most of her reviews are so favorable.

31 E.. W. Scripps

(1854-1926, Rushville, Illinois)

The founder of UPI, the Scripps-Howard empire and its flagship paper, the *Cleveland Press*, Edward Willis Scripps got his start in the news business as a teenager when he helped his older brother launch the *Detroit News* in 1873. E. W. Scripps learned enough to set out on his own to Cleveland a few years later. At 24, with his brother's money and his own hard work, he was founder, publisher, editor, advertising salesman and copy writer for the innovative daily paper that sold for the unheard of bargain of one red cent, the *Penny Press*.

Soon to become the fabled *Cleveland Press*, it was that little newspaper that gave birth to the nation's first media empire, a sprawling conglomerate of big city dailies and news reporting services in sports, science, national and international, national news and photographs, along with syndicated features and cartoons that filled the pages of hundreds of publications in America and around the world.

Driven to relentless expansion, Scripps traveled the country, creating or acquiring major metropolitan dailies in Columbus, Toledo, Cincinnati, Pittsburgh, St. Louis and San Francisco. The growth of Scripps' major services, UPI, NEA Photographs and United Features Syndicate was exponential with the advent of wire service. For the first time, a single media source spanned the globe with stories and pictures of immediate interest and value.

Scripps himself was inexhaustible and totally dedicated to his work until 1890, when he suddenly withdrew from all active participation in the business or any of its publications. With an enormous fortune and growing income as primary owner, he retired to the life of a globe-trotting playboy. He died in 1926 at 72, in a mysterious accident aboard his yacht off the coast of Africa.

Scripps never married and had no children. The *Cleveland Press* is gone, liquidated by speculative owner Joseph Cole in 1982. UPI is still in existence, but a shell of the former media titan. Scripps-Howard is still in news and broadcasting, but no longer the dominant force in either field. The last remaining local icon of the empire is WEWS. Launched by the Scripps Company in 1947 as one of the earliest commercial TV stations in the nation and the first in Ohio, its call letters still salute founder E. W. Scripps, the first giant of the modern media.

18 Louis Seltzer

(1897-1980, Ohio City)

It is only fitting that Seltzer should follow Scripps because that's how it was---the young man's career path followed the fortunes of Scripps' ascent to power and was earmarked by the same success. Scripps was the champ when it came to financing and publishing strategy, but Seltzer knew how to run a newspaper.

He started in the business when he was 12, an office boy at the *Cleveland Leader*. Before he was 14, believe it or not, he had his own little Sunday column. At 18, he was a city editor. A good wordsmith and insightful political journalist, he learned the ropes quickly enough to become editor-in-chief of the *Cleveland Press* in 1928. He stayed at the helm for almost four full decades, putting over 10,000 editions of the *Press* on the streets of Cleveland.

He attracted fine writers and colorful characters like a magnet, and retained them with a contagious enthusiasm that engendered fierce loyalty to both Seltzer and the causes he championed.

His unabashed involvement in local affairs made him the most powerful political influence in Ohio since the days of Mark Hanna. Careers were made and broken on the front pages of the afternoon daily. The *Press* was never the same after his retirement in 1966. Circulation declined along with the sense of excitement generated in Seltzer's days. In 1980, the paper was sold to local businessman Joseph Cole. New marketing efforts failed and the *Cleveland Press* faded into history after its last edition on June 17, 1982.

116 The Vail Family

Harry Vail was born in Cleveland, son of a local judge and Civil War hero. Another alumnus of Central High School in its glory years, Vail went on to earn a law degree and returned home to begin his legal work. Instead, he found a job in journalism, working for the Cleveland Herald. It was the beginning of a hundred years of Vail family involvement with local newspapers.

Harry served admirably as a county commissioner, overseeing construction of several major projects, including the Detroit-Superior Bridge. He became a successful real estate owner and respected member of various local clubs and public service groups, but his first love was the newspaper business. He was the editor of the *Sunday Voice*, Cleveland's first Sunday paper and a spokesman for First Amendment rights. Harry's son, Herman, also started out in law, then veered off into the news business. He married Delia Holden, granddaughter of the *Plain Dealer*'s owner, and later became president of Forest City Publishing Company, taking over control of the paper himself.

Young Tom Vail

Herman's son, Thomas, didn't bother with law school. He went right into the newspaper business. He was the last person to assume the joint duties of publisher and editor-in-chief of the *Plain Dealer*, serving for more than 25 years and overseeing the paper's emergence as Cleveland's largest, oldest and only daily publication. Tom Vail retired in 1988, after negotiating the sale of Cleveland's most prestigious newspaper to the Newhouse media conglomerate.

53 Artemus Ward

(1834-1867, Waterford, Maine)

Charles Farrar Browne came to Cleveland in 1857, hired as an editor at 23, the "gawkiest, greenest-looking young fellow I had ever set eyes on," according to future *Plain Dealer* owner W. W. Armstrong. On a slow news day in 1858, he slipped in a tongue-in-cheek letter to the editor under the pseudonymic artifice of Artemus Ward, outspoken proprietor of a wandering freak show. The item delighted readers of the *Plain Dealer*. They chuckled so audibly and so encouragingly that in the months and years that followed, the snail-like progress of Ward's traveling show towards Cleveland (it never did arrive) continued to be reported in his hilarious "letters," along with Ward's cogent comments on the curious people and places he encountered in his meandering.

Among other things, ornery Artemus helped originate the Cleveland-Pittsburgh feud long before the Browns-Steelers clashes when he casual remarked that the city down the pike was a "1 horse town."

The columns became enormously popular, re-printed in newspapers throughout the area, and occasionally appearing in New York and London, where even the British begrudgingly admitted that, for a colonist, Ward was amusing indeed.

Browne approached notoriously parsimonious publisher J. W. Gray with a request to either allow him to sell his columns to *Vanity Fair* and other national magazines or pay him the unheard of salary of one hundred dollars a month. Gray shook his hand and wished him luck. Artemus Ward left for New York to take a lucrative offer from *Vanity Fair*.

From that platform, he gained national prominence, both as a writer and lecturer. The most impressive story of Ward's influence is told by Cleveland author George Condon in *Cleveland: The Best Kept Secret*. On September 22, 1862, President Abraham Lincoln began an historic cabinet meeting with a brief diversion:

> *"Gentlemen," he said, "did you ever read anything from Artemus Ward?" None of the group replied as Lincoln studied their faces.*
>
> *"Let me read you a chapter that is very funny!" he said as he opened the book to a chapter called, "High-handed Outrage At Utica," and began to read. The cabinet members listened politely, but some of them considered the reading inappropriate to the time, the place and the occasion. Secretary of War Edwin Stanton was open in his look of disapproval....When Lincoln finished reading, there was momentary silence as the president looked around at his cabinet....*

> *"Gentlemen," he said, "why don't you laugh? With the fearful strain that is upon me night and day, if I did not laugh I should die, and you need this medicine as much as I do."*
>
> *The President's tall shiny hat was resting on its top on the table beside him, and even as he spoke, he was removing from the hat an official document which he proceeded to read aloud to his astonished cabinet. It was the immortal Emancipation Proclamation, which would make that date in history one for all men to remember.*

The popularity of Artemus Ward's written commentaries and speeches continued to rise, both here and abroad. His first publication, *Artemus Ward, His Book*, met with "tumultuous success." He was just reaching full stride in a career that gave promise of joining the company of literary giants when the humorist took ill while touring England. He died at Southampton the following March, not yet thirty-three years old.

Birns
Chadwick
Czolgosz
Demjanjuk
Gabos
Green
Kaber
King
Mad Butcher
Menobsy
Modell
O'Mic
Presser
Sheppard
Sturman

The Notorious

122 Shondor Birns

(1905-1975, Hungary)

He admitted to a number of criminal offenses, undoubtedly committed hundreds more, but there was something likable about that old rascal, Shondor Birns. He came to Cleveland as a penniless, 5-year-old Hungarian. His first known offense was arriving: he was an illegal immigrant. Fending for himself in the back alleys of the teeming immigrant enclaves, Shondor Birns built an impressive underworld career. He had a way with numbers, a natural ability to organize, a colorful Damon Runyon vocabulary and no respect for stodgy statutes prohibiting games of chance. For decades, he was the central figure in the city's illegal gambling operations and dean of the after hours night life.

Twice convicted on tax and gambling violations, he served brief sentences, then resumed his official position as CEO of Vice. In his heyday through the Fifties and Sixties, Shondor avoided most of the violent infighting that plagued other syndicates by overcoming his competitors with generosity. He co-opted those that would challenge him, bestowing franchises and splitting the take like a munificent feudal lord.

Through the 50s and 60s, the travails of the city's biggest bookmaker played across the front pages like a gangster B movie. His vice and tax trials were grist for Birns' mill, full of theatrics and peopled with deliciously unsavory characters. His public persona was established at his uproarious 1954 income tax evasion trial. Facing certain conviction on abundant proof, he summed up his novel defense in one sentence: "I may have broken the law, but I didn't do anything wrong." The judge agreed, found him guilty, but handed down a light sentence. Shondor was back on streets in months, resuming full control of all operations.

The crime world finally passed him by in the 1970's. Higher stakes and lesser regard for life was the order of the day. Months of stakeouts and nefarious planning culminated in his ruthless execution in 1975 by opposing racketeers, including former protégé Danny Greene. Always cautious, Shondor varied his daily travels and had no established routine---except one. Still fond of the opposite sex at 70, Shondor kept a weekly appointment with a call girl in a West Side apartment near Kiefer's Tavern. It was there, one weekday afternoon, that his killers rigged his car with explosives. The checkered career of Cleveland's most notorious bookmaker ended with a thunderous blast.

Maybe it was the way Shondor would have wanted it. One last headline and a blaze of glory.

136 Cassie Chadwick

(1857-1908, Eastwood, Canada)

Some people are born to greatness and others born to mischief. Cassie Chadwick was born to great mischief, evident from the time she tried to mask her theft of a large sum of money as young girl by concocting an elaborate cover story about inheriting the money from a long lost English uncle. Betsey Bigley was caught that time, arrested for theft and forgery, but her uncanny acting ability led to a declaration of insanity and she was sent to an asylum for a year, then released.

A few years later she came to Cleveland to visit a sister and found her promised land. It was a matter of weeks before she was up to her old tricks. When her sister left to visit friends, she sold all her furniture, then moved out. She repeated the trick around the city, renting furnished houses then liquidating the furniture and pocketing the cash. With the heat rising in Cleveland, she took to the road, cutting a wide swath with her innovative frauds, posing as a wealthy widow, heiress, businesswoman, clairvoyant or madam of prostitution as appropriate. Finally arrested for swindling in Toledo, she was tried and sentenced to nine years in prison, but served less than three after ingratiating herself to the warden and securing a pardon from Governor William McKinley.

She returned to Cleveland in 1896 with a new identity (Madame Catherine Hoover) but no change in her incorrigible character. Maintaining an elegant low profile, she married Dr. Leroy Chadwick, a prominent Cleveland physician who resided at the east end of Millionaire's Row on Euclid Avenue. Using the unsuspecting doctor's tidy fortune as her foundation, the woman now known at every fine store in the city as Cassie Chadwick began work on her criminal masterpiece. Less than a decade later, it would explode across the front pages of the nation as Cleveland's most sensational scandal.

In 1902, Cassie asked a noted Cleveland attorney to meet her in New York on an urgent business matter. Her father, a man she identified as Frederick Mason, wealthy man and confidante of Andrew Carnegie, had passed away. She needed assistance in resolving some matters related to his estate. The lawyer accompanied Mrs. Chadwick on a cross-town carriage trip, which she directed to the magnificent Manhattan home of Andrew Carnegie himself. She asked the stunned lawyer to wait for her on the street while she took care of business. He watched in amazement as she was admitted after a brief exchange of pleasantries with a butler. Twenty minutes later she re-emerged, with a carefree smile and a bulging envelope. She said everything had gone well, no further legal services would be required, and seemed disposed against further discussion.

The lawyer could not restrain his curiosity. He badgered her with questions. What was she doing in Carnegie's house? What was in the envelope? What was going on? He had been retained as her personal attorney. He had to know. "Oh well," said Cassie, on the brink of tears, "I suppose I must tell someone, and I'm sure you're the one to trust with this most extremely confidential of matters."

He certainly was.

Cassie revealed the scandalous secret: she was the illegitimate daughter of the great rail baron. He had always acted responsibly and most generously with respect to her interests, regretful only that their true relationship must remain forever arcane. She also divulged the contents of the envelope: Caledonia Railway Bonds from Scotland and two demand notes personally signed, "Andrew Carnegie." The aggregate value was over ten million dollars.

The bonds and notes were forged and the trip to Carnegie's an elaborate sting. It was his house, all right, that was impossible to fake. But Cassie made her way inside under the pretense of inquiring about a housemaid who had applied for employment and submitted the Carnegie household as a reference. The butler, not wishing to offend the impeccably dressed and mannered lady, bade her come in and served her tea while patiently explaining no one had ever heard the name. He also gently intimated that the Carnegies never received impromptu guests and recommended securing an appointment before any future visit.

No matter. It went like clockwork. The attorney, who had been carefully selected by Cassie precisely because he could not be trusted to keep a secret, rushed back to Cleveland and began spreading the word. "Listen, this is completely off the record, but I just left Mrs. Chadwick in New York, and..."

By the time Cassie returned, most of the bankers in town were praying that she would stop by, all willing to give her a lot more than a toaster in consideration for the privilege of handling her accounts. The lottery winner was Wade Park Bank. Like everyone else, Iri Reynolds already knew what was in the envelope. He promptly issued Cassie a five million dollar line of credit (half the estimated value---just to be safe). Cassie played this instrument like a concert violinist, garnering a mountain of cash from eager financiers. Over a half million each in Cleveland and Pittsburgh. $150,000 in Boston. $200,000 in New York. The President of Citizens National Bank in Oberlin, Charles Beckwith, forked over eight hundred grand.

Never let it be said that Cassie was greedy with the money. In a city flush with fabulously wealthy philanthropists, her charity was boundless. She never rejected a request for alms, supported many needy families herself and was known to donate enough Christmas gifts to the Cleveland Orphan's Asylum to provide for every child in the institution. She hosted spectacular parties, traveled in lavish fashion and treated others to extravagant gifts. One day she bought a grand piano. On impulse, she sent 27 more to various friends.

The house of cards could not stand for long, and it was the Boston banker, Newton, who toppled it. Unable to get satisfaction on the amount owed to him, Newton brought suit in Federal Court in Cleveland for $190,800. Panic is a close relative of high finance, and it was a classic Pavlovian reaction when two other bankers jumped into court, seeking to collect on notes.

Now the panic was really on, and it struck immediately at the Citizens National Bank. Mr. Beckwith explained that there was a note from Cassie backing up all loans, and that they were endorsed by a man "who can pay it as easily as you or I could get a nickel." A man of his word, he refused to divulge the man's name. That was left to attorneys who became involved, and unhesitatingly announced that the mystery Daddy Warbucks was none other than Andrew Carnegie. As soon as the name was out in the open, bankers, lawyers and reports scrambled to get a statement from the steel king. "I know nothing of the woman," said the old Scot.

Cassie was arrested a week later, in the Hotel Breslin in New York. Banker Beckwith, laid low with a heart attack at the time his bank failed, had a relapse which his doctors called "paralytic dementia" and finally shot himself to death in February, 1905.

Cassie went on trial in March, 1905, in Federal Court. Among the throng of spectators was Andrew Carnegie. Asked if he were going to prosecute Mrs. Chadwick himself, his reply was: "Why should I? Mrs. Chadwick has shown that my credit is A-1." The judge and jury were not as appreciative. She was convicted and sentenced to ten years. Although she often mentioned another mysterious "trust fund" that she promised would be revealed at the right time to facilitate her release and ultimate exoneration, she died in prison in 1907.

Sting artists, con men and swindlers have scored more times than Clevelanders would prefer to remember in the past 90 years, some of them masters of the game. But there has never been another with the audacity, ostentation and incorrigible charm of Sassy Cassie Chadwick.

76 Leon Cszolgosz

(1873-1901, Detroit, Michigan)

Leon Czolgosz, nearly forgotten after a century of inconceivable violence, laid claim to the title of Cleveland's most notorious citizen at the turn of the century. His evil deed still sets him in a class by himself. Leon Czolgosz is the only Clevelander to have assassinated a President of the United States.

Little Leon was a smart kid, but a born troublemaker whose family arrived in Cleveland in 1891 where his Polish-born father found work as a saloon keeper. Fluent and literate in both Polish and English, Leon quickly found work in a mill in Newburgh. Embittered by the failure of a strike at the mill, Czolgosz fell in with the anarchist crowd, read extensively of the radical revolutionary movements gaining momentum in Europe and proclaimed himself an intellectual. In 1898, he quit working entirely and tried to become an activist in the movement. Leon fancied himself a charismatic leader who would rise on a swell of grassroots support as masses of working people flocked to the message of his fiery rhetoric and utopian philosophy, but it never happened. He was shunned by members of the Liberty Club, a loose knit group of Cleveland anarchists, because his opinions seemed so extremist, which is saying a lot for anarchists, and Leon grew sullen and withdrawn.

He fantasized about performing some spectacular feat that would earn the recognition he so rightfully deserved.

In May of 1901, legendary anarchist crusader Emma Goldman stopped in Cleveland on a national speaking tour and delivered a mesmerizing address on the need for action. A few months later, he began stalking President William McKinley, the rotund Republican from Canton whose trip to the White House was primarily financed by the captains of industry and politics in Cleveland.

After learning of the president's scheduled appearance at the Pan American Exposition in Buffalo, Csolgosz rented a room there and lay in wait for a week. On September 6th, he approached McKinley in a receiving line at the exposition. Face to face with the President, instead of shaking hands, Csolgosz pulled out a gun concealed by a handkerchief and shot twice at point blank range. Hit in the chest and abdomen, McKinley lingered for a week before succumbing to his wounds.

Leon Csolgosz was tried and convicted after a two day trial, sentenced that day and electrocuted on the 29th of October, 53 days after the attack and 45 days after McKinley died. In 1901, justice was still swift, certain and severe. Leon Csolgosz was buried in an unmarked grave in Auburn, New York.

139 John Demjanjuk

(@ 1925- , The Ukraine)

If John Demjanjuk is Ivan the Terrible, the despicable sadist at the Treblinka concentration camp in World War II, he is without question the most notorious of this section's unseemly bunch. If he is the simple auto workers who, as a nondescript guard at Trawinki deserved only the moniker, "Ivan the Pretty Bad," then he is a sad victim himself, an innocent man who finally won a measure a justice only because the Israeli Supreme Court put the rule of law above the desire for vengeance.

Rumors of a vicious war criminal living peacefully in Cleveland led to a federal investigation, then indictments. An eager bunch at the Justice Department trumpeted the news that one of the last remaining Most Wanted names on the list of missing Nazi criminals had been caught. A turbulent hearing in Cleveland federal court, presided over by high profile Judge Frank Battisti, ended in decision to deport Demjanjuk for falsifying his entry visa. It was thought by many to be the same as death sentence. Demjanjuk, appearing harmless and disoriented, bleated his innocence as he was packed off to Israel for a war crimes trial, and virtually certain conviction in the court of a nation where collective memories of the Holocaust still seared the minds of those who would never forget.

Rejected on appeal, Demjanjuk reported to Israel where he was kept under 24-hour guard in a maximum security cell while a legal process that lasted more than a decade came to its dreaded climax. Emotional testimony from death camp survivors scarred by unthinkable evil gave a vivid reminder of man's darkest days. When it was over, the honorable justices pointed to the flawed documentary evidence and decreed that guilt was not certain. The law was inviolate. John Demjanjuk was set free.

He returned to the U. S., hailed by his fellow Ukranians, reviled by many in the Jewish community who took the eyewitness testimony and Demjanjuk's porous alibi as adequate proof of his culpability.

He is back at his home in Cleveland. Guilty or innocent? Will you be the judge?

192 Cornell Gabos

(@ 1938- , Hungary)

Hey, buddy. Wanna buy a Picasso? Cheap?

You're not going to fall for that, are you? Nobody would? Guess again.

Take an avante garde East Side gallery, serve champagne and hors d'ouevres on silver platters, add a room full of suckers----er, art enthusiasts, and you have the makings of the biggest art scam in American history.

For Cornell Gabos, it was like fishing at a trout farm. With his charming Hungarian accent and pithy anecdotes about relationships with Dali, Miro, Chagall and the boys, unsuspecting patrons of the couldn't help but be captivated. Obviously an expert and apparently the best connected art dealer in the western world, Gabos was as credible as Mother Theresa and smooth as an oil slick. The artists themselves surely loved him. Otherwise, how could he possibly offer such exquisite prints at those prices, and still set aside so much for charity? What a guy! Let's hear it for Cornell. Hip, hip---wait a second.

After years of selling signed, limited edition prints by foremost modern artists, Cornell Gabos was recognized for his world class accomplishment---a multimillion dollar fraud. A crook with panoramic vision, Gabos conned hundreds out of millions in a classic swindle that worked so well for so long, he just couldn't stop.

Until the government's Operation Bogart (Bogus Art) came closing in, Gabos worked for years out of an inauspicious frame shop in University Heights, flying around the country to sell limited edition prints at glitzy auctions. One time he sold a Chagall print that had gone for nearly $7,000 a decade earlier, for only $850.

How did he do it? Volume. He had lots of limited edition prints. He sold at least 40 of one Miro work even though only 30 real copies existed.

Gabos talked a good game. Once he related how he had been given a wonderful price on a bunch of Miro's from the artist himself on a recent visit. No one bothered to check the facts: Miro had been dead for several years.

Gabos claimed doctorate credentials from UCLA, experience Europe's leading auction houses and particular expertise in appraisal. He was a doctor all right, Dr. Flim Flam.

His auctions were given additional legitimacy by Gabos' practice of bringing in repected artists as a special guests. Paid promptly and treated royally, the artists weren't in on the scam. Peter Max was among his favorite unwitting shills.

To enhance his charade, Gabos would print up phony certificates of authenticity. Once a work was purchased, he would diligently follow up with annual appraisals, unquestionable assurance that the value was increasing.

His fraud was discovered when Operation Bogart uncovered a storeroom at the Leon Amiel publishing company in New York with 75,000 fake works. Gabos was their number one customer. Cornell knew his time was running out. He burned all his records, but dared to stage one last auction in Washington, D. C. before flying off to Zurich to meet with his banker.

Authorities closed in a few days later, but managed to recoup only $55,000 for those who were duped out of an estimated $9 million. International arrest warrants were issued for Gabos, but the trail had gone cold. He was supposedly sighted a few times, on the French Riviera or at a Swiss chalet, but, like Bigfoot, the reports were vague and unreliable. Finally, in April of 1996, he returned to Los Angeles. Cornell was working on a new project with a respected sculptor when he was arrested on an anonymous tip. Held without bail, he is headed for trial and the prospects for an extended vacation with accommodations provided by the U. S. Department of Corrections. hasn't said much about the money.

Money? What money? Listen, I don't have any cash, but how about a few Dalis? Just signed last week by my friend Salvador…

167 Eva Kaber

(1880-1931, Cleveland)

Stabbed two dozen times, Lakewood businessman Dan Kaber lived long enough to tell police, doctors and anyone else who would listen, "My wife had this done!" Although the actual assault was carried out by two East Side killers for hire and included a clumsy attempt to make the hit look like a botched burglary, Kaber was certain his better half was behind it all.

Eva Kaber was one mighty unhappy housewife. She hated her husband. Loathed and abhorred him. She didn't just want a divorce, she wanted this guy dead. Deceased. Six feet under.

Dan Kaber seemed like a nice fellow. He not only supported Eva in a decent manner, but Eva's mother, Mary Brickel, and her daughter from a prior union, Marion McCardle, all living well and hating it in Kaber's handsome Lakewood home. Eva had convinced Mom and Marion that Dan was a despicable man, unworthy of life, and the three of them spent the better part of most days hating Dan together.

Eva decided to do something about it. She sought out a local psychic medium and conjurer with an unscrupulous reputation who provided some potions for Eva to slip into his food and drink. These were not love potions. Over the next several months, Dan's health deteriorated badly. He grew weak and constantly nauseous, suffered from severe headaches and abdominal cramps. He suffered, but he didn't die.

Frustrated by the lack of progress, Eva stepped up the pace. She arranged for the two men to finish the job, paying a $500 advance on a $5,000 murder contract. (The two lugs never collected another dime from Eva. If you're going to be a hit man, make sure you get at least 50% in advance at all times. Otherwise, it's just not worth it.)

On July 18, 1919, Vic Passelli and Sal Cala entered the house through an unlocked door, tip-toed up the stairs and found Mr. Kaber waiting for them. He heard them coming. (This was their first job.) A frighteningly loud and violent struggle ensued. Unarmed and outnumbered, Dan collapsed, mortally wounded, but not before he had bitten off part of Passelli's finger and broken Cala's nose.

Based on the sincere declaration of a dying man, the police made Eva their number one suspect. It took over a year to break the case, and they may never have charged Eva if her own mother had not finally broken down and confessed her part in the homicidal scheme. Eva was brought to trial in 1921, along with her mother and her daughter, who also figured prominently in the plan to do in Dan. It was the first and only time that three generations of women in the same family have been indicted for murder.

The trial was far more suspenseful than it should have been, thanks mainly to the young legal lion Kaber hired for defense. William Corrigan worked the insanity angle like an old veteran and almost got Evil Eva off entirely. He surely saved her from the electric chair. No one could save her from prison. In July of 1921, Eva Kaber became the first Cleveland woman convicted of first degree murder. She was sentenced to life in prison on the jury's recommendation of mercy. The state later waived prosecution of Grandmother Mary and Maid Marion was tried separately. She was incomprehensibly acquitted by a jury whose grandchildren probably served on the Simpson panel.

Eva never confessed, never expressed any remorse and defiantly insisted she would be free in a few months. She died of cancer after ten years in prison.

The last footnote to the story relates to attorney Corrigan. Thirty-three years later, he would be an old veteran when he took the lead in the trial that would surpass the Kaber Chronicle on Cleveland's all-time case list: the Sheppard Murder Case.

135 Don King

(1935- , Cleveland)

One of the most recognizable moguls in the nether world of sports, Don King used his street smart cunning and an uncanny sense of timing and promotion to jockey his way past a flock of cutthroat competitors and reach the top ranks of boxing's matchmakers, ruling the heavyweight ring for decades like the whimsical dictator of a third world nation.

And the hair. Oh, that hair. Electric, attention-getting and in your face. Don swears God gave him that hair in 1971 just as sure as He gave Rockefeller his money. It just happened one night. A miracle.

The real miracle is that Don King rose above his crime-scarred past and shady reputation to become a dominant figure in an international sport. A numbers racketeer who dodged one homicide charge by claiming self defense, King was convicted on manslaughter charges in 1965 after stomping a man to death on a Cedar Avenue sidewalk. He served his time and returned to the streets unbowed.

In spite of his past and a reputation for carving out the lion's share of everything for himself, King dazzled the world's best fighters with visions of mega-paydays. Many times he delivered, even if he was first in line at the pay window after the bout.

In spite of tax troubles and epithets from competitors and reformers, Don King still rules big time boxing. Just recently, he was recognized as a shining example of the efficacy of the American penal system. A fully rehabilitated and productive citizen, Don King won the Distinguished Service Award from the Cleveland NAACP.

81 The Mad Butcher

(Unknown)

This isn't some angry guy who works for Vienna Beef, we're talking about Cleveland's very own serial killer. Sure there have been your John Wayne Gacys and your Jeffery Dahmers of late, but they just built on an American tradition of psychopaths. The Mad Butcher was an American original in his serial killing, yet he kept the quaint European tradition of Jack the Ripper and never got caught.

Also known as the Torso Murderer, the perpetrator probably started his mayhem in 1934. In September of that year a dismembered body was found washed up at Euclid Beach. A year later the first two headless bodies were found. Over the next three years the victim count would grow to twelve. Seven men and five women. They were all decapitated and dismembered in such a precise, surgical manner that speculation rose that the killer had a medical background.

Most of his victims were transients, living the hobo life in the dilapidated shacks of Kingsbury Run. Only 3 of the 12 were ever identified. As the body count mounted, the headlines grew larger and the mood of the public more grim.

The Mad Butcher included one living victim on his list: Eliot Ness. Frustrated in his efforts to get his man, Ness was further discouraged by the taunting post cards boldly sent to his office, needling him for his inability to stop the murders. The wunderkind safety director's reputation eroded with each new grisly find. When victims 11 and 12 were discovered on August 16, 1938 Ness was desperate to find the killer. He had the shantytowns along Kingsbury Run burned to the ground, the vagrants rounded up for questioning, then run out of town. A building-to-building search for the killer's macabre laboratory was conducted. Nothing.

Finally, the killings just stopped.

A letter was sent to the police chief in December of 1938 by a man claiming to be the Butcher, stating that he had moved to California (apparently realizing what a great place California would become for psychopaths). Nothing conclusive.

A few months later, a man named Frank Dolezal was arrested and confessed to the crimes but his story didn't quite fit. Dolezal's suicide ended attempts to investigate him further. The most credible theory is that the killer was well connected, possibly even known to some as a member of respected West Side family, active in legal and political arenas. Some believe the family became aware of his gruesome activities and quietly shipped him off to a high security mental institution.

The other predominant belief is that he didn't stop, he just branched out. A headless body was found in October of 1939 near New Castle, Pennsylvania. Three more bodies turned up in nearby McKees Rocks in May of 1940. Similar murders have been documented in West Virginia, Tennessee and Indiana, dating well into the 1950s.

There's even a remote chance that the Mad Butcher is still alive today. Presuming he was very young when he started, he would be in his early 80's now. And if he kept himself in good shape, he just might be able to....

Hey Gramps! Where do you think you're going with that scalpel?

93 Menobsy

(@1750-1802, Unknown)

A Chippewa medicine man who moved easily among both the local tribes and the new white settlement on the east bank of the Cuyahoga, Nobsy was respected by both as a healer, story teller and medicine man. In 1801, the man called Nobsy became the unfortunate feature player in the city's first malpractice case, and its first recorded homicide.

Summoned to the bedside of the wife of Big Son, brother to Stigwanish, Nobsy performed his rituals upon the suffering woman and gave assurances that all would be well. She died the next day.

The rest of this story is told by historian Crisfield Johnson:

Big Son made some threats, but he was generally considered a coward, even by his brother, Stigwanish, who had treated him with coldness in consequence, and it was not supposed there would be any serious results.

Late one afternoon Menompsy was in Carter's tavern when the subject of Big Son's threats was introduced. "Me no fraid," said the medicine man; "me charmed---no ball, no knife can kill me. See!" he exclaimed, throwing open his blanket and displaying several ugly scars on various parts of his body, "see where Indian cut me; another Indian shoot me, and me no dead man yet---me no dead man yet."

Shortly after, he went down the hill to one of the trading houses at the foot of the hill. There he met Big Son, whose grief for his defunct spouse had been greatly stimulated by deep potations of Bryant's fiery whisky. A fierce altercation ensued, in which the Seneca renewed his threat and Menompsy again repeated, "Me no 'fraid---me no 'fraid."

They went out of the store together, and ascended the path which wound up the bluff, where Union lane had been laid out and now runs. It was then becoming quite dark. When partly up the hill Big Son held out his hand, as if to shake hands in token of conciliation. The same instant he pulled his knife and plunged it into the side of the unguarded medicine man. The latter fell to the ground, while the Seneca speedily made his way to the encampment of his brethren, below Carter's.

An outcry was raised, and several white men came running to the scene, Carter among them. The wounded man looked up in his face, saying: "Me dead man now---yes, Nobsy broke now," and soon afterwards expired.

The death of this Indian man of consequence heightened tensions throughout the area. A white contingent, led by the ever-vigilant Carter and Amos Spafford, held council with the Chippewas, urging them to forego vengeance lest the incident escalate to war between the Chippewas and the Senecas, with the Ottawas and Iroquois likely to join in and white settlers caught in the crossfire. Carter offered a gallon of Mr. Bryant's finest, to be distilled promptly the next day, as a sincere indication of their strong desire for a peace. The Chippewas agreed not to retaliate, partly as a concession to the whites, and partly out of awareness of the superiority of the fierce Iroquois. Bryant apparently spent too much time working on quality control that evening, overindulged in his own samples, and forgot to make the liquor as promised. Carter was needed to step in again, calm the Indians, scold Bryant and double the quantity of the offering. Two gallons of whiskey were duly conjured up by the following day and additional hostilities were avoided.

This time Bryant did not fail to perform, and the Chippewas obtained their consolation in time to remove the body to Rocky river the second day after the murder, accompanied by their friends, the Ottawas. When the mournful but fantastic procession passed out of sight into the western woods, the whites breathed much more freely than they had during the previous forty-eight hours.

Big Son was never prosecuted or punished. Far from being detested, the deed raised his reputation among his own tribe. Causing the death of a supposedly invulnerable medicine man, no matter the method, was seen as worthy of respect. Major Carter deemed the incident beyond jurisdiction of the Cleveland government, such as it was, and no action was taken. It was the first time in history someone got away with murder in Cleveland.

200 Art Modell

(1926- , Brooklyn, New York)

Once a privileged and respected member of the Cleveland community, Art Modell betrayed the city and the sport that had made him wealthy in so sleazy a fashion as to earn a berth in Cleveland infamy. Would you change your reputation from glorious to notorious for a measly three hundred million dollars? The smartest answer to that is: well, first let's see the money.

Art Modell made a big splash when he first hit town, arriving as the new owner of the cherished Cleveland Browns, a franchise only a few years removed from its days as the NFL dynasty and probably headed back to the top soon under football's most respected coach, Paul Brown. An advertising hustler in New York, Modell paid less than $4 million for control of the team and less than $50,000 of that was his own money.

A good schmoozer with reporters, Art was gracious and deferential. Paul Brown would run the team. Art was hardly more than a passive investor. Soon he was sure he had the game all figured out and started getting involved in football operations. Paul Brown was patient at first, then increasingly irritated with Modell's meddling. He hardly concealed the fact that, when it came to football, Modell was a dope.

Art fired Paul Brown in 1963, his first cardinal sin against Cleveland. The fans howled, but calmed down when Blanton Collier coached the team to the NFL title the following year. Paul Brown wasn't the kind of man to make a point of reminding everyone that it was really the team he had reconstructed, so Art took most of the credit.

Things didn't go as well over the next 31 years. In spite of repeated emotional promises from Modell, a series of hopeful coaching changes and more than few years of Stadium-shaking excitement, the Browns never won another title. The team never participated in a Super Bowl. Through it all, the Cleveland fans remained unswervingly loyal. They packed the stands, cheered the team, roared with the victories and moaned with heart-rending defeats. The NFL's stock soared with TV rights and merchandising. Modell went along for the ride. By the mid-90s, in spite of the team's distinctly mediocre record over three decades, Art was a millionaire many times over. His $50,000 investment had grown over a thousand times in value.

In 1995, Art Modell decided to do something to express his true feelings about the fans in Cleveland and his most personal beliefs about life itself. After a series of clandestine meetings and layers of skullduggery to confuse the press and the public, Art announced he was taking the Browns and moving to Baltimore, citing his desperate need for financial security.

The announcement was not well taken in Cleveland. Led by a visibly perturbed Mayor Mike White, the city struck back, launching a flurry of legal challenges, not to mention the awful things they were saying about Art and his son, Bozo, in the papers and on the streets. An agreement was reached whereby Cleveland will retain the name and colors of the Browns, and will be allowed to pay at least $300 million to get a replacement team someday. In spite of that underwhelming victory, some residual resentment about Art Modell is still present in the Cleveland community.

Art Modell is ranked last in the lowest category. He is ranked last in the entire *Cleveland 200*. That will not change until a century from now, when the sequel is published. He will then rank last on the *Cleveland 300*.

Hit the road, Art. And take the kid with ya.

96 John O'Mic

(Unknown - 1812)

There has not been a legal execution in the city of Cleveland in over 90 years, but the death penalty is part of ancient history here. In April of 1812, two white trappers were found slain along the banks of the Sandusky River. Two young Indians had been seen in the area and were arrested by Western Reserve authorities. One took his own life while in custody. The other, a Chippewa brave called John O'Mic, was taken to Cleveland for trial.

Judge Ethan Allen Brown presided. Sheriff Samuel Baldwin was the officer of the court. Future mayor Alfred Kelley prosecuted the case and Peter Hitchcock was appointed for the defense.

After a one day trial on April 29, O'Mic was found guilty and sentenced to hang. Most of the population of the Western Reserve turned out on June 26, 1812 to witness the execution on Public Square. There were some embarrassing moments when O'Mic refused to let go of one of the 4x4's bracing the gallows until he had a drink of whiskey. As usual, Lorenzo Carter was the man in charge of getting things done. He produced a jug of spirits and provided several rounds for O'Mic's. The Indian regained his composure, walked forward and submitted. The trap door snapped and John O'Mic plunged to his death at the end of a rope. His body was handed over to local doctors for medical research.

O'Mic's death was not without repercussions. The War of 1812 broke out a short time later. Many tribes in the Lake Erie basin supported the British in the conflict because of their resentment that the whites had so shamefully executed an Indian brother.

180 Jackie Presser

(1926-1988, Cleveland)

For a guy who weighed nearly three hundred pounds, Jackie Presser was a pretty good tightrope walker. A fast thinker who never made it past the eighth grade, Jackie balanced his contacts with the Mafia, his informant value to the FBI and his family name to take the reins of the Teamsters and ride them to national influence.

Jackie's father, Bill Presser, was a self-made union leader and organizer. Bill started a window cleaning business. He and partner Jimmy "The Weasel" Fratianno would advise small shops and taverns how badly they needed their windows cleaned...or else. Bill windexedhis way to thc top union post in the state., powerful enough to get Jackie a job as head of the local restaurant employees union. He was so inept, the rank-and-file kicked him out.

Impulsive and brash, Jackie portrayed himself as a big shot and a rising star in the Teamsters. No one agreed. He was the David Modell of his day.

Given extra chances because of his father, Jackie gained a foothold with the Mafia. They promoted his rise through the Teamster ranks. But loyalty was never Jackie's strong suit. Double-crossing both his fellow union members and his mob pals, Jackie became an FBI informant, starting in 1969. Code named "The Tailor," Presser was so important an informant that he wasn't even indexed in the FBI files for fear of discovery. Over the years, Jackie provided invaluable information about his partners in crime, including the likely principals in the Hoffa murder.

In 1980, Jackie rolled the dice and became the sole labor figure to endorse Ronald Reagan for President. Jackpot! Jackie was named senior advisor to the White House transition team. He was consulted on the choice for Secretary of Labor.

After Teamster president Roy Williams was found guilty of bribing a senator and removed from his post, Jackie Presser was waiting in the wings. His term was notable for the complaints of unbridled corruption at the highest levels of the union. Justice Department crime investigators, unaware of Presser's FBI relationship, targeted Jackie. He was indicted on multiple racketeering charges, then revealed as a double agent, playing all sides against the middle.

But unlike many of his associates, Presser had one last double-cross up his sleeve. He cheated both the government and the Mob of retribution by dying of natural causes while still Teamster President in July of 1988.

58 Sam Sheppard

(1924-1970, Cleveland)

The Fourth of July, 1954.

Overnight sensation on a slow news day, the Sheppard Case had all the ingredients just right---a murdered beauty; a handsome and suspect young doctor, son of a wealthy family; a crusading newspaper editor; a high profile coroner with a sense for drama, and; a lurid mystery for a newspaper and TV audience with time on its hands.

Sam Sheppard was convicted in a spectacular trial, marred by an overzealous press and a cadre of police and court officials too willing to co-operate with the media and public sentiment.

The case wouldn't go away. Ten years later, a celebrated young lawyer named F. Lee Bailey took up the cause and won an acquittal for Sam at the retrial. It was clear by then that there had never been sufficient evidence to convict the doctor. But no new evidence pointed in any other direction and the lack of closure continued to haunt the case. And Sam as well. He resumed his practice only briefly, then stumbled through a few more headlines, with his second marriage and his bizarre pro wrestling career. Broken and dissolute, he died of liver failure in 1970.

Still, it wasn't over. Years passed. The Sheppard's only son, Sam Reese Sheppard, plagued by the unsettled memories and the shadow on his family's honor, took up the cause 20 years later, undertaking an exhaustive review of the case and the evidence. He published his results in 1995, presenting a case for exonerating his father and possibly implicating Richard Eberling, a minor suspect at the time, later convicted of the murder of a woman in a subsequent, unrelated crime. Sam Reese was persuasive enough to have the case re-opened in 1996, with court-ordered blood testing of the imprisoned Eberling and review of all available evidence.

The final verdict remains unrendered. Who killed Marilyn Sheppard? The theories and explanations seem to have grown more focused with the passage of time, but the ultimate answer remains as elusive as ever.

191 Reuben Sturman

(1924- , Cleveland)

The Justice Department Organized Crime Strike Force called it "Operation Roadrunner," the plan to bring down the mastermind of the largest pornography ring in the world, Cleveland's Reuben Sturman.

A Russian immigrant in the 1930s, Reuben set off on a normal career path, operating a small candy and tobacco store on the near East Side. A friend taught him the ropes and Reuben opened a business on the side distributing comic books and magazines. In the late 1950s, Reuben was a respectable small business until Hugh Hefner introduced *Playboy Magazine*. Sturman was one of the first to notice the enhanced profits he accrued from selling a glossy publication that included suggestive pictures of young women. He didn't care one way or another about smut himself, but Reuben couldn't resist the temptation of those obscene profits. He broadened his line to include even racier stuff, then made the final leap to outright pornography. It was the most profitable printed material on the market.

Within a decade, Reuben Sturman was one of the largest distributors of sex magazines, books and films in the country. Adept at financial machinations, he used these talents to further enhance his bottom line and protect himself from the law, building a pyramid of paper companies and dummy transactions to dodge criminal charges and taxes. The feds thought they had him in 1978, charging Sturman on obscenity and organized crime violations. It cost him a fortune in legal fees, but Reuben was acquitted. And expensive as it was, he had the money. Although it was never possible for authorities to ferret out the exact numbers through the Sturman maze, some claimed that, at his peak, Sturman was making over a million dollars a day.

Taking a page from the book of Eliot Ness, the Strike Force changed strategy, redirecting efforts toward income tax evasion. Over more than a decade, with some agents spending a good part of their careers on the case, sufficient evidence was uncovered to indict Sturman for millions in tax fraud. He was convicted in 1989, spent millions on appeals and lost again. In 1992, Reuben spent his first day in prison.

He escaped in December of that same year. It was widely assumed that, with the money and chutzpah Reuben had available, he would never be seen again. A few months later, the same federal agents who had put him away tracked him down and arrested him in Anaheim, California.

Sturman was sent to a secure federal prison and remains there today. Subsequent convictions for jury tampering and attempting to bribe a federal judge have added ten more years to his sentence.

Reuben may be gone, but he's far from forgotten. He was able to finance a broadside counterattack over the years, not against the FBI or Justice Department, but the law itself. Sturman is largely responsible for initiating the drastic changes in obscenity laws over that have resulted in virtual nullification of most statutes prohibiting distribution and sale of patently offensive materials.

Baehr
Bernstein
Bolton
Boyd
Day
Finkle
Fleming
Forbes
Hanna
Herrick
Hopkins
Kucinich
Maschke
Stokes
Voinovich
White
Wood

121 Herman Baehr

(1866-1942, Keokuk, Iowa)

After years of affiliation with the family business, Baehr Brewing Company, Herman Baehr struck up a friendship with Marc Hanna that led to a second career in politics. At Hanna's urging, the unknown Baehr ran for and was elected County Recorder in 1903. Hanna died in 1904, but others picked up the fallen GOP banner and looked to Baehr to carry it against seemingly invincible Tom L. Johnson, Hanna's arch-enemy. With the money and influence of most of Millionaire's Row behind him, and a windfall of votes from a tide of recent German immigrants, Baehr pulled off the biggest upset in the history of Cleveland's mayoral elections (at least until Mike White), unseating Johnson in 1909.

Scorned by the press and Johnson's loyal followers among the working class, Baehr served only one term, but not without distinction, restoring conservative fiscal policies and granting authority to the Planning Commission to oversee downtown development, critical to the city's architectural integrity. Baehr instituted the "three-cent fare" pledged by Johnson, initiated construction of the city's longspan bridges, built public playgrounds and bath houses, expanded the municipal park system, won the fight for lower utility rates and ably led a city with a core population of 560,663 (larger than today).

Although he is remembered as the man who toppled Tom Johnson, Herman Baehr's single term as mayor may have been the most efficient in the city's history.

143 Harry "Czar" Bernstein

(1856-1920, Poland)

They didn't call him The Czar for nothing.

Harry Bernstein came to Cleveland from his Polish home in 1868 at the age of 12. He learned English to survive in the public schools and on the streets of Cleveland, teeming with immigrants, foreign and domestic, as the city churned with thousands of new jobs and millions of fresh dollars from the mushrooming oil business. With a quick mind, sure sense of business and powerful personality, Harry found himself in exactly the right place at exactly the right time. He turned pennies into dollars, dollars into bankrolls and bankrolls into small businesses all over the ethnic inner city---restaurants, bars, pawn shops, junkyards---all no-nonsense moneymakers. He opened a bank and brought in tellers who spoke the languages of the new wave of immigrants and welcomed their modest accounts.

By the late 1880s, Harry Bernstein had caught the eye of Mark Hanna, who saw him as a political diamond in the rough and welcomed him into the inner sanctum of the local Republican party. It was a mutually rewarding alliance, as Hanna went on to become the greatest Republican power broker of them all while Bernstein went on to become the Czar, a dictatorial ward leader who could hand deliver every one of the thousands of votes he guaranteed in any election.

Bernstein ruled Ward 16 with an iron fist until superseded by his own protégé, Maurice Maschke, who rose after the turn of the century to outshine even Harry as a GOP star.

33 Frances Payne Bolton

(1875-1977, Cleveland)

The marriage of Francis Payne Bingham to Chester Bolton in 1907 represented a confluence of blue bloodlines, uniting the Perrys, Paynes, Binghams, Castles and Boltons in holy matrimony. All were proud of Frances, who stepped forward in time of crisis and carried the heralded family colors with merit for thirty years.

Of peerless local heritage, Frances was descendant of the Perry, Payne and Bingham families, all titans of business and real estate, all active in politics, community activities and philanthropy.

After a high-bred education at Hathaway Brown and Miss Spence's, the finishing school for girls in New York, Frances worked as a volunteer nurse in the immigrant ghetto neighborhoods, helping provide medical services to the indigent. It was the beginning of a lifetime of benevolent works.

Frances and Chester Bolton were wed in 1907, a marriage made in aristocrat heaven. His parents were also leading citizens. He was also well schooled, at University and Harvard. And like Frances, he was attracted to public service. After volunteer duty in World War I, Chester entered politics (on the Republican side, of course), first as a city councilman, then state senator. He won election as U. S. Congressman in 1928. Bolton led the effort to land the 1936 Republican convention for Cleveland, the last national political convention hosted by the city.

Returned to Congress in 1938, Bolton died suddenly, less than halfway through his fifth term. Mrs. Frances Payne Bolton was designated to complete the remaining year. She served admirably enough to earn approval from the voters of the 22nd District in the next fourteen consecutive elections. She established herself as a respected and effective civic force, in Cleveland and Washington, nationally and internationally.

Years before, Frances Bolton's humanitarian efforts led to creation of the Army School of Nursing during World War I. In World War II, she wrote and navigated passage of the legislation establishing the Cadet Nurse Corps. Both efforts supplied the needed training and support for thousands of front line nurses in the great global conflicts. Her expertise in foreign affairs led to influential committee posts. In 1947, Frances Bolton was the first Congresswoman to lead a U. S. foreign delegation.

Over the years, the Democrats ran everybody against her but Secretariat. The Lady Republican was invincible. Charles Vanik finally edged her out in 1968 in a hard-fought election. Frances Payne Bolton was 82.

She retired from politics, but not from nursing, continuing to actively support the Bolton School of Nursing at Western Reserve, the Payne Fund for children, and Hawken School in Lyndhurst, built on land donated by Frances and her husband.

95 Albert "Starlight" Boyd

(1871-1921, Oak Grove, Mississippi)

The Boyd family joined the Negro exodus to the north in the mid-1880's, arriving in Cleveland with the bleakest of prospects. Albert, the brightest and most personable of the Boyd children, found employment as a handyman and supported his family from then on.

He honed his reading and mathematical skills, then talked his way into a bookkeeper's position. By 1896, he had saved enough to buy a small tavern on Canal Road, soon a popular local watering hole, with Albert its popular proprietor.

He loved diamonds, and prospered enough to sport large ones in flashy rings worn on both hands and on his gaudy pocket watch, earning him the "Starlight" sobriquet.

When the black community migrated, Starlight moved his place to East 14th and Scovill. The Starlight Cafe was a spacious bar and eatery where patrons could drink and dine, socialize, play cards and shoot pool. It soon became the unofficial headquarters of black power in the city of Cleveland.

Starlight joined the Republican Party and worked his way into an influential position in the overwhelmingly black 1st Ward. He joined forces with Thomas Fleming, the first African American elected to Cleveland city council. The two men forged a powerful coalition, capable of delivering thousands of votes on demand. Come election time, the city's high and mighty came courting at the Starlight Cafe. Hanna, Maschke, Baker---they all knew who to talk to if they wanted a single black vote inside the city limits.

Scolded for playing too fast and loose by the "Blue Vein" Old Guard, Boyd and Fleming still managed to cut a wide swath. Money and patronage were the coin of the realm and the Ward 1 twosome had plenty of both to dole out. After more than a decade of financial and political prosperity, the Boyd-Fleming duo had grown powerful enough to warrant the attention of higher forces.

With the support of both white and black reform groups, an attempt was made in the 1920 election to oust Fleming from his seat in Council and strip Boyd of his political clout. Harry Clay Smith, a respected former state legislator, launched a vigorous campaign that threatened to end Fleming's career. It took all the strength and savvy Starlight Boyd could muster to defend against the onslaught. He pulled in every IOU he had on the streets of Ward 1 and put out a king's ransom in gifts, favors and cash on behalf of Fleming. With the election in doubt to the final day, Boyd's herculean effort made the difference. Fleming held his seat by a few hundred votes, in spite of claims of ballot shenanigans that were most likely true, some added insurance provided by Starlight.

Fleming was never seriously challenged again. His power continued to swell for another decade, until an influence peddling scandal culminated with his conviction for bribery and ended his political career. For Starlight, the cost of victory in 1920 was extreme. Completely exhausted by the pace of the campaign, he took ill shortly after the election and never recovered, passing away at 40. His death marked the end of the first era of African-American influence in city politics.

63 William Howard Day

(1825-1900, New York, New York)

Along with Cleveland compatriot John Malvin, William Day led the 19th century abolitionist crusade as a courageous civic leader, editor and publisher. Day graduated from Oberlin College, the only U. S. college open to Negro students, in 1847. He moved to Cleveland and immediately initiated a campaign to repeal the Black Laws, the oppressive state statutes. In 1848, he co-sponsored a convention of leading Negroes in Cleveland to develop strategies for abolishing slavery, hosting the event with John Malvin and Frederick Douglass. It was the first such national event in American history and subsequently led to the National Convention of Colored Men, the Afro-American Council, the Niagara Movement and the NAACP.

He continued his civil rights efforts, joined in 1852 by his wife, Lucy Stanton Day, the first black woman graduate of Oberlin. In 1853, with Lucy's help, Day began publication of *The Aliened American*, the city's first black newspaper. He was also Cleveland's first black librarian, and first black professor, teaching math and linguistics.

Allied with John Brown of Harper's Ferry notoriety, Day printed the radical "Provisional Constitution" for the new government Brown and his followers planned to establish.

Along with Father John Malvin, founder of the first black church and school in the area, William Howard Day was the leading pioneer of the African American community in Cleveland and a major contributor to international efforts to forever end the enslavement of black people.

156 Herman Finkle

(1891-1952, Detroit, Michigan)

The "Little Napoleon of Ward 12" served a record 35 years as Cleveland city councilman, ruling his ward like a feudal lord and climbing to the top ranks of the local Republican machine. His first election required only one vote. His marriage to the sister of GOP strongman Alex Bernstein opened political doors. With the blessing of Bernstein and the party regulars, he was handily elected to the 12th ward post in 1912.

In the intervening years, Herman Finkle went through an extraordinary metamorphosis. A ferocious political in-fighter and unswerving party loyalist in his early years, Finkle was reviled by his Democratic opponents as the most ruthless and unscrupulous of partisans. He was repeatedly accused of shady election capers, council double-crosses and underhanded dealings. Most of the city's reputable citizens' groups lobbied hard to rid council of his noxious influence. Finkle disdained them, entrenched and impervious.

In 1934, his daughter's sudden death dealt him a crushing personal blow, and changed his public life. He emerged from a lengthy period of mourning and soul-searching a different man, more compassionate and humane. In a paradigm shift, he refocused his interests on the common good and abandoned his interests in partisan squabbles, fighting just as hard for better services and minority rights as he had for the party. In his twilight years in council, he was hailed as a benevolent leader and honored as an accomplished legislator devoted to the people.

115 Thomas & Letitia Fleming

THOMAS (1874-1948, Mercer County, Pennsylvania)
LETITIA COUSINS (187601963, Tazewell, Virginia)

The foremost couple in the early annals of Cleveland's black political history, Thomas and Letitia Fleming overcame ferocious opposition, controversy and personal tragedy to make lasting contributions to politics, business, women and minority rights and civic affairs.

Thomas Fleming started as a barber, but soon found politics more to his liking. The hours and the profits were better, and he didn't have to sweep up all that hair at the ned of the day. Fleming joined the local Republican ward club (still the overwhelming party of choice of black Americans at the turn of the century). In less than a year, he became the leader and spokesman for a new generation of black men who would not settle for the passive philosophy of the Old Guard Negroes who counseled patience and restraint in dealing with the inequities of society. For the next 30 years, Fleming was the leading social and political activist and leading of the black community.

He founded one of the nation's early Negro newspapers, *The Cleveland Journal*, in 1903. In 1906, he graduated from Cleveland Law School and was admitted to the bar. Seizing on the opportunity provided by Cleveland's growing black population, he ran for City Council in 1907, but was soundly defeated. Undismayed, he ran again in 1909, this time with the support of the party, and became the first African American elected to office in the city of Cleveland.

In the next few years, he formed a powerful alliance with Starlight Boyd, a successful local entrepreneur, and married Letitia Cousins, a dynamic teacher and women's rights activist newly arrived in Cleveland from West Virginia. This threesome formed the nexus of black power in Cleveland for a generation. Together, they changed the political landscape.

With the support of Starlight and Letitia, Thomas Fleming ran off a string of impressive successes. While serving in Council, he acquired impressive business holdings with Boyd as his partner. The two opened a realty company, building homes and businesses on the near east side. Barber shops, taverns, drug stores and clothing stores added to the profits. By the end of the decade, they were very wealthy men. In an era without government programs and meager services for Negroes from white charities, the Flemings' generosity and concern for their community filled the void. They provided food, shelter, care and comfort for the needy and destitute with their own funds.

Thomas Fleming was a co-founder of the Cleveland Board of Trade (a black business cooperative) and the Association of Colored Men. He established the first black Elks Club in the city and successfully lobbied for the first employment of Negroes in municipal posts and in white collar positions in the oil, insurance and utility industries. He fought for passage of legislation that provided playgrounds and swimming pools in the Negro districts and defied the Ku Klux Klan at the height of their power in 1910, successfully obstructing the establishment of a Cleveland chapter of the racist organization.

Often challenged for his Council post by both resentful blacks and establishment whites, he was continuously re-elected, vanquishing all opponents. Even after Starlight's death in 1921, Fleming's wealth and political might continued to expand. By the late 1920s, he was not only respected, but feared by the high and mighty. He claimed to control more votes than any other man in the state of Ohio and few doubted his boast. The fact that a Negro had gained such influence did not sit well in all quarters.

In 1929, steps were taken to rectify the situation. Fleming was indicted on bribery charges for supposedly accepting a paltry $200 to secure passage of a special ordinance. In spite of flimsy evidence, the wheels of justice moved with lightning speed. He was accused on January 21st and indicted the following day. The trial began in less than two weeks and ended four days later, with an all-white jury returning a guilty verdict after brief deliberations.

Several appeals failed and Fleming was packed off to prison, serving more than two years. In his absence, Letitia made a valiant effort to hold the fort, announcing as a candidate for his vacated seat in council. Again, higher powers intervened, throwing their support behind her opponent. Lawrence Payne was elected councilman and moved quickly to replace Fleming's supporters in ward and precinct positions. The Fleming-Boyd era had come to an abrupt end.

After his release, Fleming withdrew to private life, but Letitia remained as active as ever on behalf of women's and minority causes. She organized the National Association of Republican Women, chaired the Negro women's campaign for four presidential candidates, led the campaign for appointment of a Negro to the Cleveland School Board and helped direct the activities of the County Welfare Board for more than 20 years.

Letitia Fleming lived to see passage of the federal laws and Supreme Court decisions that mandated equal rights and integration. She saw the March on Washington, the days of Martin Luther King and Malcolm X. She passed away in 1963 at 86.

171 George Forbes

(1931- , Memphis, Tennessee)

A young city councilman when the black community still had little more than token representation in city government, George Forbes rode the Sixties tide of civil rights and black pride to the heights of political power and influence in Cleveland.

A surprise election victor from Ward 27 in 1963, Forbes was a presence in City Council right from the start. With the addition of Forbes and George White, blacks held ten of thirty seats in council. According to the census, ten of every thirty Clevelanders were black. An era of equitable representation had begun. Forbes and the Stokes brothers were among the first to realize black power was there for the taking.

Forbes' critics complain that he learned the lessons of insider politics all too well. Indicted but acquitted on charges related to unusual record keeping and curious expenditures in the 70s, Forbes scoffed at the allegations and continued to boraden his philosophy of correlating politics and business. His law practice and private interests thrived as he became more entrenched as council president.

Forbes was one of the villains in the Kucinich version of the city's ignominious default in 1978. The council president sided with the unyielding banking interests against the Boy Mayor when the clock struck midnight and the city's fate was sealed.

The election of George Voinovich as mayor in 1979 heralded a new era for Cleveland and the pinnacle of power for George Forbes. These two men, of variant parties, races, backgrounds and ideas, shared a common belief: local government, business and financial communities had to co-operate in the mutual interests of survival. The Great Compromise---with Forbes handling the patronage and Voinovich getting needed support for his plans---led to an era of good will and a concerted effort to rehabilitate the city.

Tall and impressive, upright as a preacher, dressed like a banker, voice like rolling thunder---George Forbes has an icy stare and a smile warm as fire. Sometimes, he can go from one to the other in the flash of dark eyes. His friends claim there is none better and his enemies swear there is none worse.

Making no bones about the benefits of favoritism, Forbes used his control on the purse strings to whip his legislative peers into line. Occasionally, when conciliation didn't work, fiscal intimidation came in handy. He could usually win over even the most recalcitrant councilman one way or another. The only group he never made headway with was the media. For some reason, they insisted on depicting him as a ruthless, arrogant, difficult, self-serving sourpuss with a terrible temper. Maybe it was the time he threw the chair, or threw the reporter. Maybe it was the water pitcher smashed on the table or the smashed lights and camera. Maybe it was all that foul language, or the shouting and scuffles at City Hall. Whatever. It didn't diminish anything but his mood. By the end of the decade, he was recognized as the implicit co-mayor, with cumulative powers invested in the city council leader unprecedented in the city politics.

In 1990, the media finally got a clear shot at him. With Voinovich stepping up to governor, the door was open for George to realize the dream he had since the day he watched Carl Stokes take the oath of office. He wanted to be mayor of Cleveland. Days before announcing his candidacy, he laid out the strategic numbers in a private conversation:

> *The registered voters in this damn city are 55% black and 45% white. For every four white people that vote, five black people will vote. That's a fact. I don't give a damn who they run---Hagan, Gaul, Feighan, Garofoli, Carney, I don't care if they run George Washington. The next mayor of this town is going to be a black man. And that man is going to be me.*

He was right about everything but that very last thought. Overconfident and slow out of the gate, he was mauled by the press and out-hustled by young black opponent, Mike White. The surprise endorsement of White by the *Plain Dealer* and breaking ranks on the east side sealed his fate. He was left on the sidelines when White was swept into office in November.

Forbes was gracious in defeat. In spite of the bitter contest, he pledged to support White and bowed out of active politics, returning to private practice. In 1992, he surprised some by returning to the public scene, seeking the presidency of the local NAACP. Controversy followed---it always does with George---as Forbes was narrowly elected. He remains in the post today, a blunt and forceful spokesman for the organization.

6 Marc Hanna

(1837-1904, New Lisbon, Ohio)

A man with rare appreciation for theatrics, both in politics and life, Marcus Alonzo Hanna was one of Cleveland's greatest patron of the arts, with special emphasis on theater. He owned the Euclid Avenue Opera House and the Hanna Theater. Once, he even starred in a play himself, playing the comedy lead in *Mr. Pickwick and His Friends* in 1873.

On a more serious note, he was, in the words of no less an authority than Theodore Roosevelt, "the most influential man of politics this nation has ever known."

Marcus Alonzo Hanna was from a solid but hardly wcalthy family. Hc attended public Central High School. Classmate Johnny Rockefeller was his closest friend. (Good choice, Marc.) Hanna attended college briefly at Western Reserve. Restless, he quit school to work for his family's wholesale grocery store. At the same time, Cleveland was making its presence felt in the national halls of power, flexing its muscles of extraordinary new wealth and corporate influence. Hanna took interest in the new politics, joined the 19th century version of the Young Republicans, and became active in the party. The GOP was on the rise. Hanna vigorously supported its policies and enjoyed the action.

In the meantime, he married Charlotte Rhodes, daughter of Daniel Rhodes, the city's leading mining mogul. Marc had a great sense of who to hang around with.

Things were a little tense at first because Papa Rhodes was a staunch Democrat, but Marc was a charmer. Before long, the two of them were getting along famously. Hanna was offered a position at Rhodes & Company. He must have been a particularly excellent employee, because they ended up calling the place M. A. Hanna & Company with Marc replacing Pops as primary owner.

Hanna was an excellent businessman himself, and he had the right friends in all the right places. For example, it made it a lot easier for Hanna to do business with Standard Oil when he was playing golf with John D. Rockefeller twice a week.

In 1880, Hanna turned his main focus from business to politics and seized his first real opportunity to get involved on a national level when fellow local James A. Garfield made a run for the presidency. Garfield came to him for financial support, but Hanna did much more than that. He changed the style of American elections.

Hanna came up with the idea of the Cleveland Business Man's Marching Club. It was the country's first political action committee. Leaders of industry and finance donated free advice and free skills to the campaign, and lots of free money. It was restricted to Cleveland that year, but soon spread as other metropolitan power centers realized the potential. It permeates the nation's political system today.

Word of Hanna's skills spread as well. He was welcomed into high party councils. As his political circle widened, he struck up yet another serendipitous friendship, this time with William McKinley, the robust congressman from Canton. Hanna considered McKinley presidential timber and named himself the logger who would haul the big guy to the White House.

Eschewing the tradition of dignified politicking, Hanna introduced entertainment to the presidential contest in 1896. Exciting rallies, giveaways and back room promises superseded party platforms and personal philosophies as campaign priorities.

McKinley won the election and was returned to office in 1900, again with Hanna calling the shots. As the president's largest contributor and closest confidante, Hanna benefited in myriad ways. His businesses thrived, his stature was immense and he was even able to achieve high office himself, without the cumbersome necessity of campaigning before the public. In 1897, he was appointed to fill the Ohio senate seat left vacant by the death of John Sherman. The following year, he was re-elected senator in a close vote in the Ohio legislature.

Hanna retained his singularly powerful position on the national level, even after the assassination of his friend McKinley in 1901. But McKinley's sudden death stunned him, sapping his strength and enthusiasm. The loss of control of his hometown stronghold to Tom L. Johnson and his new Progressives was another blow to his ego and another indication that his power days were numbered.

Marc Hanna was re-elected to a second full term in the U. S. Senate in 1904, but did not serve. He died after a brief illness in February of that year. The Hanna name remains omnipresent in Cleveland and the Hanna methods are still employed in political campaigns across the nation, but there has never been another like him. He was the Boss of Bosses.

114 Myron T. Herrick

(1854-1929, Huntington, Lorain County, Ohio)

Another of the late 19th century wonder boys, Myron Herrick came to Cleveland to practice law, changed his focus to banking, then used his profits and experience to plunge into diverse industries. He was one of the partners in the National Carbon Company (later Union Carbide), a derivative of Brush Electric's phenomenal success. At the same time, he underwrote construction of the Cleveland Arcade and other landmarks. Myron helped organize CEI to generate the area's power needs and generate another fortune for Myron.

The rewards were gratifying, but business was just another vehicle to his most prominent career in politics. Endeared to fellow Clevelander and political mogul, Marc Hanna, he had full Republican support in his winning bid for City Council in 1884. In 1903, he was the point man in the last classic battle between Hanna and Tom L. Johnson.

After serving as Hanna's political lieutenant for a decade, Herrick was hand-picked to take on Johnson in the 1903 race for Governor. In spite of Hanna's unsurpassed national influence, Johnson had already bested him in the struggle for the city's transit system, then trounced him again by winning election as mayor in Hanna's home town. The 1903 gubernatorial race would determine if Johnson's Progressive Democrat agenda would play across the state, and maybe the nation. Johnson was a peerless campaigner, but Hanna's clout and Herrick's character carried the day, overcoming Johnson's dynamic barnstorming with just as much energy and a lot more money. It was a monumental defeat for the populist forces. They retreated to their Cleveland enclave, never to recover the momentum of Johnson's early years.

In the twilight of his career, Myron Herrick rose above politics to become a distinguished diplomat and statesman. Ambassador to France when the World War broke out, Herrick risked his life to help evacuate Americans, then remained behind to assist the French in war relief efforts. He returned as U. S. Ambassador to France in 1921 and worked diligently to restore relations between the two countries which had deteriorated in the aftermath of the war.

Herrick is credited with one of great public relations efforts of his era. Drawing on years of experience with world-class showmen like Hanna and Johnson, Herrick spurred French interest in Lindbergh's transatlantic flight and orchestrated the French reception for the heroic aviator. The palpable bonhomie generated by Lindbergh's touchdown at Orly before a delirious crowd of Parisians was worth more than any treaty. The first man to greet Charles Lindbergh on the ground, the one in all the historic photographs, is Myron T. Herrick of Cleveland, Ohio.

54 William Hopkins

(1869-1961, Johnstown, Pennsylvania)

He came to Cleveland in 1874 and spent more than 85 years here, leaving his mark in the history books, on the city and its skyline, and his name on the airport.

After voters approved the noble experiment to try to extricate municipal government from the clutches of party politics, William R. Hopkins was selected as the first City Manager in Cleveland's history. Intended to balance a strong central administrator with the collective oversight of a vigorous city council, the plan failed primarily because of Hopkins' efficiency. His take-charge attitude diminished Council's role to near irrelevance. His opponents finally managed to have him replaced as City Manager in 1929, and the system abolished altogether in 1931.

But while Hopkins was in charge, things happened. He initiated an ambitious parks program, revitalized the city's welfare institutions and approved construction of the massive Public Auditorium. Without waiting for Council's approval, he optioned a thousand acres of land to the Southwest, approved the plans, secured the funds and built the first municipal airport in the nation, with the first control tower. Critics said that it was too far from downtown to be of much use. Far-sighted William knew better. Today, it's the closest primary airport to a top-20 American city and the only one never to have suffered a major air disaster.

Why do you think they call it Hopkins?

154 Dennis Kucinich

(1946- , Cleveland)

Boy Wonder to some, Dennis the Menace to others, little Dennis Kucinich had the guts to grab the throttle at City Hall in the 1970s and took the whole city on a wild and unforgettable ride through the politics of the New Progressives, defying the old bosses, tangling with the captains of industry, seeing villains behind every tree and bringing the city to the brink of financial chaos.

That he ever got there in the first place was a testament to his amazing tenacity. Oldest son in a chronically poor family, Dennis scrubbed floors and worked night shifts before he was fourteen to pay for his siblings' parochial schooling and put food on the table. There was a time when he wore the same pair of pants for ten months. Less than 20 years later, this forlorn little boy was the mayor of one of the largest cities in America.

Elected to city council after a door-to-door campaign in 1969, Kucinich garnered media attention for his espousal of populist causes and used it to win the clerk of courts post in 1975. With the city floundering under lackluster leadership, Dennis entered the non-partisan mayoral primary in 1977. An aggressive campaign waged on a grass roots level---already a Kucinich trademark---ousted incumbent mayor Ralph Perk and led to a one-on-one battle with Ed Feighan in the November finals. The electorate chose Dennis over the soft-spoken Feighan, making him the youngest big city mayor in the country.

Saddled with debt, plagued by controversy and confronted by a hostile council and a wary business establishment, the Kucinich Administration never got off the ground. While Dennis himself remained a well-intentioned voice of the working class, his staff came across as belligerent and inexperienced in dealings with the public and the press. Bob Weismann and the Grdina sisters came to personify a bunker mentality at City Hall. Kucinich's refusal to sell Muny Light to CEI led to an orchestrated counter-attack by powerful forces, led by Brock Weir of Ameritrust, who refused to roll over the city's short term notes unless Dennis capitulated. The stalemate cast Cleveland into default, the first major municipal financial collapse since the depression.

The abrupt firing of police chief Richard Hongisto on live television exacerbated a bad situation. Petitions were circulated and Dennis Kucinich was forced to face Cleveland's first recall election in 1978. He retained office by a minuscule 236 votes out of over 120,000 cast. Weary and dispirited, he was easily defeated for re-election in 1979 by George Voinovich.

As the years wore on, Kucinich repeatedly tried to win back elected office. He was rejected in a bid for state auditor, badly beaten in a run for Congress and embarrassed in an abortive race for governor in 1986. Finally, in 1994, he upset Anthony Sinagra to win a seat in the Ohio Senate. Against the tide as usual, he was the only Democrat to unseat a Republican incumbent in Ohio that GOP landslide year, and one of the few in the nation.

The emergence of Cleveland Public Power as a thriving municipal utility and the consensus among modern historians that Kucinich had been a whipping boy for self-serving business interests in the 70s has helped rehabilitate his reputation. The "new" Dennis, at 49, may be on the brink of a second career in the upper echelon of local politics.

Still an unapologetic populist and a champion of environmental causes, he handily won the Democratic nomination for Congress and is poised to take on Martin Hoke in November, 1996, a heavyweight battle that many experts expect to be the most interesting and hardest fought local contest in years.

141 Maurice Maschke

(1868-1936, Cleveland)

Born two years after his German parents immigrated here, Maurice Maschke grew to become the most influential ethnic American in a swarm of Cleveland WASPs, leader of the county Republican Party for more than 30 years. Another Central High School grad, he earned a degree at Harvard and returned here to practice law. Appointed county recorder in 1897, he had an innate sense of the machinations of politics and moved up rapidly through the ranks, forging alliances with those in power as well as those ascendant to it. He moved easily in many circles, at formal dinners with Marc Hanna, hoisting steins at German picnics with Herman Baehr or playing cards in the back room of a saloon with Negro ward broker, Starlight Boyd.

By 1900, he ranked among the most influential of politicians. His name never appeared on a ballot. With McKinley's death in 1901 and Hanna's in 1904, Maurice Maschke assumed the mantle of leader of the Ohio Republicans. He held the chairman's post until 1933, when the Democrats, behind the popularity of FDR, took the upper hand.

In an era of political giants, no one wielded more clout than Maschke. He was influential on the floor of four national conventions, with Teddy Roosevelt, William Howard Taft and Warren G. Harding among those in his debt. It was Maschke who found a way to bring an end to the career of Tom Johnson, a painful thorn in side of Republicans for two decades. Maschke trotted out Herman Baehr, a presentable but unknown GOP bureaucrat, to take on Johnson in 1909. While Democrats scoffed, Maschke had done his homework. Twenty years of German migration had swelled the city's population by more than 50,000 Teutonic loyalists. In November, the polling booths were swarming with liederhosen. Election night was like one big Oktoberfest as Baehr shocked Johnson and ended an era.

Uncompromising for his party, in his private life Maurice Maschke was a gregarious man of many passions, an expert on the theater, stalwart Harvard alumnus, avid golfer and national champion card player. He could quote whole passages from Shakespeare and discourse at length on science and philosophy. He was a recognized authority on diverse subjects, from roses to tournament bridge.

20 The Stokes Brothers

CARL STOKES (1927-1996 , Cleveland)
LOUIS STOKES (1929- , Cleveland)

The first black mayor of a major American city, Carl Stokes was swept into office in 1967 on a wave of civic goodwill and personal charisma. Speaking in an eloquent cadence that echoed Martin Luther King, Jr., Stokes exuded confidence and charm, inspired hope and pride among black voters and admiration among whites.

A high school dropout, Stokes returned to Cleveland after army service and resumed his education, obtaining his degree in law. Elected to the state legislature in 1962, he established himself as a fine orator and able organizer. In 1965, in the midst of a seething era of racial turmoil, he decided on a bold run for the city's highest office. Ignoring the Democratic primary against incumbent Ralph Locher, Stokes won a place on the November ballot as an independent. Campaigning courageously on both sides of town, he threw the gauntlet down to white voters, daring them to overcome divisive racism and support the one man who could unify the city. He was defeated by less than 1% of the vote and immediately vowed to make up the difference in his next outing.

In 1967, marshaling the forces he had gathered for two years, Stokes ousted Locher in the primary, then faced off against Seth Taft, heir apparent of one of America's most respected political families. The symbolism of the campaign was apparent: great grandson of a slave pitted against the grandson of a U. S. President. 80% of Negro voters and 72% of whites turned out to cast ballots. All of them counted. When the dust settled, Carl Stokes had one by a margin of less than one-half of one percent.

The Stokes administration met with mixed success. Eagerly supported with federal funds by Democrats in Washington, Stokes' programs met stiff resistance at home, especially from an entrenched police department opposed to many of his reforms and a suspicious white community, uneasy in a new era of shared power. The shock of the Glenville Incident, a violent but brief exchange that raised the specter of the devastating 1966 Hough Riots, further diminished the hope that the election of a black mayor would act as a panacea for the city's racial ills. The city's industrial base continued to dwindle and white flight to the suburbs accelerated.

In spite of the complex problems, Stokes could cite many successes. The city made important progress in public housing and revitalization. The first steps were taken to deal with water pollution. Spending on schools, streets and services increased dramatically. Racism and discrimination were deep rooted, but Stokes can be credited with initiating the first meaningful dialogue between local white and black cultures.

Carl Stokes was re-elected in 1969 by another razor-thin margin. In 1971, frustrated with his failure to overcome resistance in the city service departments, he declined to seek a third term, accepting a broadcasting position in New York. He returned to Cleveland to practice law in 1980 and was elected municipal court judge a few years later. A subsequent appointment as a U. S. ambassador rounded out his public career.

The legacy of the Stokes years can be found more on the human side of the ledger than any lasting program or monument. He shattered the barriers to public office and forever destroyed the perception that the black disadvantage in municipal elections was insurmountable. Following his lead, a generation of African Americans emerged as civic leaders---Louis Stokes, George Forbes, Arnold Pinkney, Morris Jackson, Fannie Lewis, Jeffrey Johnson, Stephanie Tubbs-Jones and current mayor Mike White---all indebted to Carl Stokes' spirited example.

In the Sixties, it was Carl Stokes who dominated the news and local politics. In the Nineties, it was Louis Stokes who had become the personification of black political achievement and endurance.

Side by side with his brother, Louis Stokes was a savvy political operator who helped carve out a winnable congressional district by bringing a successful lawsuit that changed the way the districts were drawn. Soon after Carl was elected mayor, Louis ran for Congress. Successful in 1968, he has been re-elected thirteen times. Active at first as a rebellious member of the black caucus, Louis Stokes rose in rank and seniority as the years passed to become one of the most powerful members of the House.

He headed the Select Committee on Assassinations in 1977, signing off on the shocking conclusion that President John Kennedy "...was probably assassinated as a result of a conspiracy." In 1980, he led the House Ethics Committee and chaired an important appropriations subcommittee for years. A consistent liberal and unapologetic standard bearer for African American causes, Louis Stokes' star continues to shine, bright as ever after thirty years while the blazing comet of Carl Stokes shot across the political heavens in less than six. His 19th District remains one of a handful of fully operating political machines left in this country.

148 George Voinovich

(1936- , Cleveland)

The Un-politician who does not like to glad-hand, shuns social engagements and is not known for stirring oratory or personal charisma, George Victor Voinovich emerged from a series of political defeats in the 1970s to become the most successful political figure in modern Cleveland history.

Following the tumultuous term of his predecessor, Dennis Kucinich, Voinovich ran on a "return to normalcy" platform and easily won election as mayor in 1979. In 1980, the term of office was increased from 2 to 4 years. Voinovich was re-elected in 1981 and 1985, leaving office in 1989 for a successful run for governor.

His tenure at City Hall was notable for its serenity. After a decade of crisis, consternation and confrontation with Stokes, Perk and Kucinich, the citizens seemed to welcome the respite provided by the reasoned voice, fiscal conservatism and conciliatory attitude of George the Peacemaker. He brought the city back from default, reorganizing municipal departments and instituting sound financial policies. He re-established good relations with the corporate power brokers and won back the confidence of the banks. The long overdue revitalization of the downtown area became a reality under Voinovich, as builders and investors flocked to take advantage of the tempting tax abatements and amicable terms dangled by the city.

By the mid-80s, Cleveland was the "Comeback City," with new skyscrapers and bustling developments bringing the Flats back to life as an entertainment district. The renaissance was not all roses and ribbon cuttings. The decline of residential areas, poverty, crime and the school system's free fall remained unresolved problems.

George Voinovich's most successful---and most controversial---alliance was the bond he forged with powerful city council president, George Forbes. Voinovich ended decades of feuding between the mayor and council by simply acquiescing to most of Forbes' demands. In return for transferring control of the local patronage system to Forbes, the mayor won prompt approval from council for critical elements of his plans. Through the 80s, George and George ruled like mayoral partners.

To his credit, the one volatile issue Voinovich refused to budge on was Muny Light. Expected to bow to corporate pressure and sell to CEI, the mayor became the surprise white knight of the Kucinich crusade, retaining the power plant, making necessary improvements and giving life to a reborn Cleveland Public Power, which has served the area well (and profitably) ever since.

As Governor of Ohio since 1990, Voinovich has applied the same principles, accruing a record surplus of state funds, avoiding scandals and controversies, and winning re-election in 1994 by the largest plurality in modern times.

176 Mike White

(1952- , Cleveland)

Cleveland's second African American mayor and second youngest mayor is first in force of personality, confidence and motivation. Whether campaigning for election, the schools or the football franchise, Mike White is always on the stump, rallying others to the cause.

Raised in Glenville and educated in the public schools, Mike White's first serious lesson in power politics came during his years at Ohio State. He led a protest against the discriminatory policies of the Columbus public bus system and was promptly arrested. He ran a bold campaign the following year for Student Union President and won election as the first black student body leader in OSU history. Contentious when required, he also displayed a deft talent for conciliation at critical times. In the tense days after campus protests turned to riots in the early 70s, he stood shoulder to shoulder on the campus oval with Woody Hayes, urging students to keep the peace.

Back in Cleveland after college and a stint as the mayor's aide in Columbus, White won election to city council. He was the brightest protégé of George Forbes before moving on to the state senate. In 1989, he threw his hat into the crowded ring with a cluster of big political names vying to replace departing Mayor Voinovich. The dark horse in a field that included a county commissioner, the county recorder, a former mayor's son and heavy favorite Forbes, Mike White made it to the two-man finals with the help of a surprise endorsement from the *Plain Dealer*, then completed the stunning upset by besting his old mentor in the runoff.

A natural born populist, White was pragmatic enough to put some of his agenda on hold while completing the work of his predecessor, presiding over the completion of the downtown revival that had been a decade in the making. The dream became reality as Gateway, Society Center, the Rock and Roll Hall of Fame and the Great Lakes Science Center rose from the ground, flanked by dozens of new restaurants, shops and offices. Time and again through the early 90s, the nation has marveled at Cleveland's renaissance.

Re-elected by the largest margin in the city's history, White's ambition didn't diminish. He fulfilled his pledge to make the city safer, putting over 1,500 more police on the streets.

At the same time, he didn't forget his commitment to the city's residents. The long disparaged Hough area has become a model for revitalized housing. Downtown living space, almost nonexistent for decades, is back in vogue.

White's most dramatic struggle in six years as mayor was about football. When Browns' owner Art Modell shocked the city by revealing a secret agreement to move the team to Baltimore, the mayor launched a counterattack that left Modell and the NFL gasping for air, including mass protests and a legal barrage. The national outpouring of sympathy for Cleveland and scorn for Modell added to the pressure. When the dust settled, the city won the rights to a new franchise and kept the cherished Browns' name and colors.

Still, it's never easy. In spite of his best efforts, the school system remains in critical condition, wallowing in red ink, hobbled by years of dubious court remedies and inept management. Police chiefs come and go faster than Indians' managers in the old days. Council-mayor relations are cool in the best of times, glacial in the worst. Ill-timed criticism of collective bargaining laws precipitated the biggest protest demonstration in decades (Mikey forgot there was a labor convention in town). Through it all, Mike White "keeps keepin' on."

Mike White has already left his brand on Cleveland and early indications are that he will easily win re-election to a third term and become the longest-serving mayor ever. Only time will tell how high he will climb among the ranks of Cleveland leaders. And beyond. Now if he can just find that $300 million for a new stadium...

72 Reuben Wood

(1792-1864, Middletown, Vermont)

One of the area's most prominent early arrivals, Reuben Wood served the city, state and nation with distinction. The most fascinating footnote to the career of this fine man, now all but forgotten to history, is that he came within a single vote of becoming president of the United States.

Reuben Wood served in the War of 1812, then decided to make Cleveland his home. He arrived here with his family on Walk-in-the-Water, the Great Lakes' first steamship. Educated in the law, he was the third practicing attorney to take up residence (the legal field was already getting crowded). His natural talents for leadership and organization were quickly recognized and he was elected president of the village in 1921, then served in the Ohio Senate. Appointed to the district bench, he was later elected chief justice of the state supreme court. In 1850, Reuben Wood was elected governor of Ohio, the first from Cleveland. He presided during the adoption of Ohio's state constitution.

Governor Wood was an outspoken abolitionist and advocate of civil rights. He opposed the repressive Black Laws and the federal Fugitive Slave Law, promoted progressive Free Soil legislation and supported the Underground Railroad, helping to make Ohio the land of freedom for many escaped Southern slaves.

In 1852, Wood was poised to become the Democrat candidate for president when a convention deadlock opened the door to his nomination. The overwhelming Democrat advantage virtually assured their candidate of election in November. Party leaders counted heads. Assured the votes were there, they called for a ballot to confirm Reuben Wood as the Democrat standard-bearer.

At the last moment, he was derailed by one of his own. The chairman of his home state delegation was none other than J. W. Gray, cantankerous publisher and editor of the *Plain Dealer*. A fellow Clevelander, and fellow Vermont native, he adamantly opposed the governor's "Hunker Democrat" conservative fiscal policies, and refused to deliver Ohio's votes. Shocked by the break in ranks in his own backyard, the convention balked, then turned to Franklin Pierce of New Hampshire as a last-minute alternate. Pierce was nominated and elected to the Presidency.

A bitterly disappointed Reuben Wood retired from politics soon after, returned to his Cleveland home to practice law, and canceled his subscription to the *Plain Dealer*.

Ackley
Andrews
Begun
Biggar
Brush
Crile
Cushing
Glaser
Hulett
King
Masters
Miller
Merrick
Morgan
Morley
Stone
Whittlesey
Winton

Science & Technology

99 Horace Ackley

(1815-1859, Genessee County, New York)

The seeds were planted for Cleveland's later reputation as one of the foremost medical centers of the world by men like Horace Ackley, an eminent doctor, surgeon, professor and researcher who never graduated from a medical school.

Ackley studied in Rochester and attended a state medical college in New York, but he passed all tests in 1834 and won his license to practice, without a degree. He never returned to school.

After years spent developing expertise in anatomy, Ackley came to Cleveland in 1839. He quickly established a reputation as the finest surgeon in the Western Reserve. In the 1840s, he introduced ether as an anesthetic in his surgical procedures, only months after the technique was first tested.

Dr. Ackley was a co-founder of the Cleveland Medical College, which continues to thrive 150 years later as the Case Western Reserve University School of Medicine and its affiliate, University Hospital, both internationally prominent institutions. Earlier, the good doctor was a prominent member of the staff at Willoughby Medical School. The impetus for his move to Cleveland is the stuff of medical legend.

Early in the nineteenth century, medical study was severely hampered by perceived religious and ethical restraints which discouraged the use of human corpses for medical research. Ackley and others dedicated to furthering the study of anatomy were forced to resort to clandestine tactics to obtain the cadavers required for dissection and analysis. Ackley, his associates and students considered it their solemn duty to procure subjects by whatever means necessary in the interests of advancing medical science. Some Willoughby citizens considered their tactics illegal, immoral and blasphemous. "A cretinous bunch of body-snatchers" is what one irate neighbor called them. After one popular and recently deceased local was removed from his not-so-final resting place in a nearby cemetery, a confrontation ensued at the college, with guns brandished and harsh threats exchanged between the collegians and citizenry.

Ackley defused the situation by personally promising to end the staff's late night sojourns. A short time later, he moved on to Cleveland, where the residents were apparently less sensitive about the unspoken requirements of medical research.

Horace Ackley also founded the Northern Ohio Insane Asylum in 1851. Little did he know what an important contribution that would turn out to be in the years to come.

107 Samuel Andrews

(1836-1904. Oaksey, England)

The Wizard of Standard Oil, Samuel Andrews can claim as much credit as John D. Rockefeller for the creation of the heavyweight champion of the industrial revolution. If it wasn't for Sammy, the Rockefellers would still be scurrying around on the floor of the futures market, bidding on bushels of soybeans.

Andrews arrived in the U. S. with a solid work ethic and a talent for making candles. Petroleum was an still an unknown commodity in the 1850's. Sam was expert at refining the few available fuel oils---lard and coal---and immediately recognized the potential of the new "black gold" when it was introduced in 1859. He managed to convince his friend and fellow Englishman, Maurice Clark, to invest in his first refinery. Clark brought in the partner from his small brokerage firm to handle the books, young Johnny Rockefeller.

It's fair to say the new enterprise did not disappoint the stockholders. Andrews' refining techniques were years ahead of the competition, enabling the fledgling company to quickly dominate the new industry. In 1870, the company changed its name to Standard Oil.

Sam's technical knowledge and hands-on skills were superior. His corporate savvy left a lot to be desired. Years of success did not stop him from second-guessing what he perceived as Rockefeller's reckless schemes and furious expansion. Andrews saw the inevitability of Standard's collapse and was happy to sell his interests to Rocky in 1874 before it happened. Not his best decision. It hasn't happened yet.

Retiring as a millionaire before the age of 40, he spent the rest of his life catering to the whims of his eccentric wife, Mary, and as a generous philanthropist on the local scene, donating hefty sums to educational institutions.

He is best remembered today not as the working nexus of the Standard Oil fortune but as the millionaire buffoon responsible for Andrews' Folly, the stone white elephant of Millionaire's Row. At the urging of Mary, who aspired to have Queen Victoria herself as a house guest, Sam opened the floodgates of his wealth, spilling a fortune onto the Euclid Avenue property that soaked it up and thirsted for more.

Finally completed in 1885, it was the family home only briefly before Mrs. Andrews realized that waiting for Her Majesty was like waiting for Godot. Queen Vicky would not only never make it to Cleveland, she never set foot in the U. S., never even left jolly old England, and hardly ventured beyond the castle in her dotage. Sam and Mary moved to Washington and the 100-room money pit stood vacant for years. The largest residence ever built in Cleveland was unceremoniously demolished in 1923.

152 Edwin Beeman

(1839-1906. LaGrange, Ohio)

Chew on this one---Ed Beeman was a moderately successful medical researcher until he stumbled across a strange compound ingredient found only in pork bellies. What the good doctor was doing tinkering around in the lab with pig leftovers has never been reported.

At any rate, Doc Beeman discovered through further research that the new compound he called "pepsin" aided digestion and provided relief for minor stomach disorders. Again, there is no information available about just how the doctor managed to get his patients to try the mysterious elixir that had been, until recently, sloshing around in the intestines of some hog.

Pepsin became all the rage and Beeman set aside his practice to begin bottling and selling the stuff himself. Good thing for him the FDA didn't exist yet or he probably would have ended up in the slammer.

By 1890, he had formed the Beeman Chemical Company along with a few financial partners. It was then that Doc Beeman took one giant leap for pork bellies when his trusted bookkeeper, Nellie, suggested that he mix pepsin with the other hot new fad, chewing gum, another Cleveland innovation that was taking the country by storm.

Within months, the Doc was selling Beeman's Pepsin Gum. Sales boomed for a decade. Beeman Chemical was sold to the American Chicle Company in 1900. Beeman retired a millionaire. And the moral of the story is, if you're on to something good, stick to it.

60 Semi Begun

(1905 - 1995, Gdansk, Poland)

The tale of the tape...and the floppy disk, and the VCR, and the Black Box and all kinds of other landmark inventions of modern communications technology owe their creation or their form to Dr. Semi Begun. Slip in a cassette and begin the Begun.

After earning his engineering *bona fides* in Berlin, Semi began working on magnetic recording techniques for the Lorenz company in Germany. Magnetic recording had been demonstrated at the 1900 World's Fair in Paris, but it was crude and impractical. The impediments were deemed so insurmountable that little development was undertaken for more than twenty years. But Semi was able to design the "Dailygraph," a dictating machine used throughout Europe in the 1930s. Later, he developed the first tape recorder, which was utilized for remote broadcasts in Germany.

Working in Germany in the 1930s, Begun witnessed the ominous shift toward military applications and decided to take his leave, certain that Europe was headed for conflagration. He came to New York in 1935, started his own company , and tried to market his "Soundmirror," tape recorder to government and industry. The response was a collective yawn. Sales were dismal. One of the few sold was used by the city to provide repetitive announcements of traffic conditions for motorists on the George Washington Bridge.

In 1938, his business closed for lack of funds, Semi was hired by Brush Development in Cleveland, a small, innovative electronics company started by the heirs of electricity scion Charles Brush in the garage of the Brush mansion. The company had developed a process for artificial production of crystals and was interested in expanding their uses. Semi had some good ideas.

With Brush, Semi Begun developed a practical magnetic tape. First utilized for the "Black Box" in military aircraft, it later became the foundation of a multi-billion-dollar consumer industry of its own. Audiotape, videotape, magnetic data tape, music cassettes, computer cassettes, VCRs---Semi Begun provided the world with the primary medium for the most precious commodity of modern man: information.

He also developed torpedoes with sonar homing capabilities, another military application, this one not adaptable for consumers. At least not yet.

In 1947, Semi introduced an improved Soundmirror for home recording. It was popular, but competitor companies, better adapted for mass production, seized control of the market with hastily produced imitations. Semi shrugged and veered off in a different direction. Realizing the need for protective casing of the fragile tape, Begun sought assistance in finding proper design and materials. The 3M company responded with a viable plastic solution and the massive cassette and videotape business became an instantaneous reality. Among Semi's other inventions was the "Mail-a-Voice," the first erasable paper disc. This was also the first floppy disc, later an essential component of computer evolution.

The children and grandchildren of Semi Begun's creations are countless---voice mail, answering machines, karaoke, wiretapping, beepers, message systems, video cameras, boom boxes, and more permutations every year.

He even made an important contribution to meteorology. He was approached by Bell Telephone, in search of a way to repeat a recording that needed updating every day for thousands of callers. For over forty years, the 24-hour call-in weather report has been brought to you by...Semi Begun.

This is a recording.

177 Hamilton F. Biggar

(1839-1919, Oakville, Upper Canada)

From a family that traces their roots back to Robert of Biggarstown, Dumfries, Scotland, a 16th century Canadian immigrant, Hamilton F. Biggar studied law and passed the bar before deciding on a career in medicine. He came to Cleveland to attend the Homeopathic College. Biggar spent years as a resident at hospitals in Philadelphia and New York, then returned to Cleveland and opened his practice.

Homeopathic medicine reached its peak during the mid-19th century, then gradually declined. The reversal of fortune didn't effect Biggar. His practice was supported by patients like John D. Rockefeller. He helped establish the Cleveland Homeopathic Medical College in 1850 and served as professor of surgery while earning a reputation as a noted lecturer and a crusader for progressive patient care.

When the Cleveland Workhouse opened for business in the 1890s, Dr. Biggar assumed the role of Director of Medicine, a daunting task at an overcrowded institution with meager interests in the health of its inmates. His genuine concern and efficient methods led to the workhouse's standing as a model for municipal prison health care.

Biggar's children, grandchildren and great-grandchildren are Clevelanders, many conspicuous achievers in local business and civic activities.

8 Charles Brush

(1849-1929, Euclid, Ohio)

If you are reading this at night, you can thank two men: Thomas Edison and Charles Brush. Old Tom hailed from just down the road in Milan, a stone's throw beyond the qualifying perimeter for inclusion in the *Cleveland 200* rankings. Lord knows, we'd love to have him, but we can't include Abraham Lincoln just because his funeral train stopped on Public Square and we can't include Edison just because he's close.

There's no question about Charles Brush. A local boy, born and raised, Brush attended public schools and earned a degree in mining engineering at the University of Michigan. Frustrated by a lack of work in his field, he formed a company of his own, with financing help from Charles Bingham, hoping to improve on the technology for the telegraph industry.

His expertise in chemistry and research into the embryonic field of electricity led him to a series of experiments that culminated with his invention of an open-coil dynamo in 1876. It proved to be one of the most important breakthroughs of the century---a safe, inexpensive source of power. Power for machinery and equipment. Power for transportation. Power for light.

It was God Who said, "Let there be light," but it was Charles Brush who said, "Let there be light at night." In 1878, Brush invented the arc light, powered by his own dynamo and capable of generating thousands of watts of illumination for extended periods, an innovation so astounding as to be completely incredible to the citizens of the day. With the permission of the city, he decided to demonstrate his new product in a most dramatic fashion. Brush erected huge arc lights on 150-foot poles around Cleveland's Public Square. Weeks of publicity lured crowds as tens of thousands of local residents were joined by the curious from throughout the Midwest to witness Brush's attempt to make history by being the first to light up a city with electricity (Thomas Edison was still months away from perfecting his tiny light bulb).

Shortly after dark on April 29th, 1879, the switch was thrown. One towering arc lamp came alive with a purplish glow, then another, and another. In a few minutes, the purple haze gave way to a pure, white light and the entire square was bathed in artificial sunshine. The crowd roared, cannons boomed in salute and the Cleveland Grays" Marching Band paraded through well lit square with a musical fanfare. Headlines across the nation and the world proclaimed the dawn of a new era. Brush was hailed as a genius and Cleveland acclaimed as host of one of the most prestigious events in the history of technology. It was one of the city's shining moments.

Permanent arc lights were erected on Public Square and adjoining downtown streets. Other cities followed in short order. By the mid-1880's, arc lights illuminated the night skies over most of the larger U. S. cities as well as many of the world's great metropolises: London, Paris, Tokyo, Montreal, Mexico City and more.

Brush Electric Company joined the front ranks of industry. Through a series of mergers that ultimately united the concepts and products of Brush and Edison, the General Electric Company was born. Inspired by Brush, another group of engineers and investors started another little electric company in Cleveland in 1886. This one was led by young George Westinghouse. If it weren't for Cleveland, nothing would happen when you flick that switch on the wall. Is this a great town or what?

Charles Brush didn't rest on his laurels. When he wasn't being feted at testimonial dinners, picking up medals from European royalty or receiving honorary degrees, he was back at work. In 1892, he helped establish Cleveland Electric Company (later CEI), assuring his home town of adequate electric power for more than a century.

His chemical background led him into other fields. He founded what would become the Medusa Cement Company and the Linde Air Products Company. His son, Charles, Jr., kept up the good work by starting Brush Laboratories, which evolved into Brush-Wellman, the world's largest beryllium company. You may not use much beryllium yourself, but NASA does. It's the primary component of the heat-shields that keep space vehicles from returning as toast.

Brush was just as active in community affairs. He was a co-founder of the Case School of Applied Science, president of Euclid National Bank, director of the Cleveland School of Art, president of the Cleveland Arcade Company and trustee of Western Reserve University. He established the Brush Foundation shortly before his death.

Brush High School is named in honor of the great inventor, industrialist and philanthropist. For years, the schools sports teams have bewildered opponents with their nickname, the "Arcs." The Arcs? Why the Arcs? Now you know.

17 George Crile & Family

(1864-1943, Chili, Ohio)

A courageous and creative medical practitioner, Dr. George Crile was a highly regarded surgeon and expert in battlefield techniques, a veteran of the Spanish-American War. Returning home, he was active as a surgeon and researcher at many leading hospitals.

In 1915, he again volunteered for military service as commander of one of the largest hospital units on the French front years before American entry into the hostilities. He remained on active duty throughout the war. His efforts as both surgeon and administrator are credited with saving hundreds of lives and revolutionizing battlefront medical techniques. New weapons of mass destruction produced overwhelming new problems---instantaneous casualties in unprecedented numbers. Crile responded by streamlining field triage and assembling medical personnel in precision teams to accelerate life-saving treatment and vastly increase the number of injured who could be treated in critical time.

Back in Cleveland again after the war, Crile applied his wartime experience to civilian practice, convincing his longtime associate, Dr. Francis Bunts, and several other of his most respected peers that the doctor and staff format was a thing of the past: complex, state-of-the-art surgery required a team of specialists, each adept in their respected fields. With this philosophy in mind, Crile, Bunts, Dr. William Lower and Dr. John Phillips founded the Cleveland Clinic in 1921, with the specific goal of making it one of the nation's foremost medical centers.

It didn't take long. The Clinic's modest facilities at East 95th and Euclid were rapidly expanded as its reputation grew. Crile was first president of the institution while continuing his medical practice and research. He introduced several breakthroughs in surgical techniques and blood transfusion processes and authored over a dozen respected medical books along with numerous essays and articles on a wide variety of subjects, from goiter disease to the components of human intelligence. Dr. Crile was world renown in medicine, recipient of numerous awards and honorary degrees and a co-founder of the American College of Surgeons.

In spite of all the honors and accolades, Dr. Crile once said that the most vivid memory of his medical career was its greatest disaster. In May of 1929, x-ray film caught fire in a storage room at the Clinic, releasing deadly phosgene gases that killed 123 people. Crile was on the scene, witnessed the horror first hand and assisted in treating the victims. His friend and partner, John Phillips, was among the casualties.

The Clinic had been in existence less than ten years and it was widely believed that the disaster would mean the end of the promising facility. Crile wouldn't let it happen. In subsequent investigations, the Clinic was cleared of responsibility for the tragedy. Crile and his fellow doctors rebuilt the Cleveland Clinic, instituted strict safety standards and evacuation procedures that were later adopted by other hospitals, and persevered.

It remains at the same location today, but the physical plant now approaches the size of a major university, with over 600 affiliated doctors and 2,000 nurses, technicians and other support staff providing world class care for more than 12,000 patients annually. The Cleveland Clinic is universally recognized as one of the finest medical facilities in the world.

George Crile, Jr. followed in his father's giant footsteps. An equally disinguished physician and Cleveland Clinic administrator, he also pursued a wide range of other interests and was highly respected as an author. He led the efforts to maintain the highest standards for excellence at the Clinic after his father's death in 1943. Crile, Jr. was a world traveler and lecturer and an important factor in the Cleveland community.

In 1963, George Crile, Jr. married Helga Sandburg. The union instantly created one of the most fascinating and popular couples ever to grace the Cleveland scene. George was in his prime as the standard bearer of the nation's most prestigious medical family. Helga was the daughter of America's most beloved poet, Carl Sandburg. Her uncle was Edward Steichen, the country's most celebrated photographer. Helga was an accomplished author and poet herself, with several published books and collections of verse to her credit. Their whirlwind romance lasted for 25 years, until George's death in 1989, adding a welcome touch of class to the local scene.

They married late and had no children. Too bad. With bloodlines like that, Cleveland could have had a human version of Secretariat.

123 Harvey Cushing

(1869-1939, Cleveland)

Another of the countless graduates of Central High School to achieve prominence in a wide array of endeavors, Harvey Cushing went on to graduate from Harvard Medical School and post-graduate study in Europe. As a master surgeon, he introduced many advanced techniques that remain cornerstones of modern surgical procedures. His academic career was equally impressive. Cushing was a distinguished professor of surgery , first at Johns Hopkins, then Harvard and Yale.

Dr. Harvey Cushing became the first neurosurgeon in the United States. His remarkable successes in operations on the brain and neurological system spawned rapid advances in surgery, medical research and technology.

In 1926, at the height of his illustrious career, Dr. Cushing found time to write an incisive and informative biography of his mentor, Sir William Osler, and won the Pulitzer Prize.

174 Theodatus Garlick

(1805-1884, Middleburg, Vermont)

Some achievers are mistreated by history for no apparent reason. Theodatus Garlick ranks high among Cleveland's least remembered heroes.

Born in Vermont, he came to Cleveland in 1818 to join his brother Abel as a blacksmith, stonecutter and carver. Two years later, Theodatus and Abel laid claim to the title of Cleveland's first archaeologists when they undertook excavation of an Indian mound at Euclid and Erie Streets, uncovering a number of centuries old artifacts.

Garlick saved enough money to attend medical school in Baltimore and became a surgeon, combining his craftsmanship and medical knowledge to become one of the nation's first plastic surgeons.

His remarkably varied and auspicious career had hardly begun. A voracious reader and researcher, Garlick studied the writings of Da Guerre and built his own camera, taking the first photographs ever in the Western Reserve in 1839, the same year the first cameras were imported from Europe to the U. S. east coast.

History tells us the first American photographs were taken in Boston late that year but Garlick's may have actually pre-dated them.

Years later, after reading of European experiments in fish breeding, Garlick again set out in an entirely new field on his own. He built the first fish hatchery in America on Dr. Horace Ackley's farm in Cleveland in 1854 and became the first American to breed fish artificially.

Never completely abandoning his first career, Garlick somehow found the time to become the area's best known sculptor. Artist, mason, surgeon, inventor, archaeologist, philanthropist and author, Dr. Theodatus Garlick deserves credit as one of Cleveland's most productive citizens.

193 Donald Glaser

(1926- , Cleveland)

You probably don't recall the name of Donald Glaser, and that's understandable if you're not familiar with his work in the field of theoretical physics devoted to the study of high-energy particles. Your probably didn't even know that Don invented the vacuum-sealed bubble chamber. It sounds like a toy, but it’s not. The bubble chamber facilitated the vast expansion of this entire field of important work in advanced physics.

You should know that his work was extraordinary enough to win the most cherished international award for scientific achievement in the world in 1960, making Donald Glaser the first native-born Clevelander to win a Nobel Prize.

50 George Hulett

(1846-1923, Conneaut, Ohio)

In 1903, working as a construction engineer with McMyler Manufacturing Company, George Hulett designed the Hulett Unloader that revolutionized loading and transport systems. Their component parts were elemental, but the scale and articulation unprecedented. The Unloaders were simple but massive mechanical giants, each capable of outperforming fifty longshoremen.

The Hulett Unloaders were duplicated throughout the Great Lakes and across the oceans. Historians and economists cite Hulett's major impact on the American economy. It meant more ore, more oil, more ships. Faster and cheaper. It changed the pace of heavy industry and entrenched Cleveland as an innovative industrial center.

Four of the Unloaders remain on the Cleveland lakefront today, standing shoulder to shoulder on the shore, west of Edgewater Park, mute testament to Cleveland's glory days of dominance in shipping, mining and metal.

138 Zenas King

(1818-1892, Kingston, Vermont)

Long known as the City of Bridges, an aerial view of Cleveland reveals the incredible network of massive iron and steel tendons that span the web of waterways and link patches of land into a working metropolis. Much credit for this industrial age marvel goes to Zenas King.

Hailing from colonial Vermont stock, Zenas King arrived in Cleveland at 21 to ply his trade as a merchant. In spite of a lack of formal training, he displayed an uncanny mechanical ability and earned extra money as a contractor on small projects for the locals. Ill health forced him to give up his partnership in a general store near Milan. During a lengthy convalescence, King studied heavy engineering theories and practices. In the late 1850's, he returned to work, this time with the Mosley Bridge Company of Cleveland. He was the catalyst of the company's success and owner of a number of new patents for iron bridge building.

Establishing his own contracting firm in 1863, Zenas King went on to become the leading builder of monumental bridges in the nation, erecting over 150 miles of longspan bridges in the next twenty-five years, including many that remain Cleveland landmarks today.

181 William Masters

(1915- , Cleveland)

A trained physician and educator, Dr. William H. Masters enjoyed a respectable but relatively obscure career until 1966, when he published the meticulous results of years of first hand observations and recorded data accrued from observing volunteer individuals and couples who performed sexual acts in the "laboratory" of Masters and Dr. Virginia E. Johnson, his wife and research partner.

Their observations and conclusions were published in an erudite tome, *Human Sexual Response*. The book was an instant best seller as Americans suddenly found an interest medical research papers. There was controversy regarding Masters & Johnson's methods, results and the ethics of the experiments themselves. How could they scrutinize sexual activities between people in a laboratory format like cells on a glass slide? Where did they get the volunteers for these suspicious experiments? Where there any pictures in the book?

The authors responded with an impressive showing, appearing serious and credible in the media. The pair came to be recognized as therapeutical gurus of the New Age of sex and morality. More best-sellers followed: *Human Sexual Inadequacy* (1970), *The Pleasure Bond* (1975), *Homosexuality in Perspective* (1979) and *Human Sexuality* (1982).

The good doctors appeared often on radio and television, and granted frequent lengthy interviews to explain their intriguing results and provide assurances of their objectivity and responsibility.

At the same time, a muted backlash suggested that the whole project was a formal exercise in voyeurism, that Masters was little more than an Emperor Peeping Tom, and that he, like his subjects, had no clothes.

The most famous practitioners of sex therapy since Sigmund Freud were divorced in the 80s. Press reports confirmed that the reasons were personal, but certainly not related to any sexual dysfunction.

104 Myra King Merrick

(1825-1899, Leicestershire, England)

Myra King Merrick had an unfortunate beginning to her medical career. Shortly after her marriage to Charles Merrick, her husband became seriously ill. Standard treatment had no effect. Myra refused to accept the dismal prognosis offered by doctors and initiated her own research into the problem. She read medical tomes, attended lectures and corresponded with experts. Finally, she attended school and became a licensed physician herself. She restored her husband to good health, then moved with her family to Cleveland to open her own practice.

A practitioner of homeopathy, Dr. Merrick soon developed and extensive and impressive client list, including the Rockefeller family and several other of Cleveland's eminent citizens. She helped establish the first medical school for women in the area and served as its president and professor of obstetrics for many years. Merrick also founded a hospital to serve the special needs of women and children. The Women's and Children's Free Medical and Surgical Dispensary became Woman's Hospital and served the Greater Cleveland area for more than a century.

Myra King Merrick was the first woman doctor in Cleveland, first in Ohio, and among the first in the United States.

182 Dayton Miller

(1866-1941, Painesville)

The chairman of the physics department at Case Institute of Technology for 47 years, Dayton Miller was one of the most innovative thinkers and cutting edge scientists in the area's history. Miller's biography features a long list of lasting accomplishments...and some of the most interesting and productive mistakes on record.

Miller's specialty was sound and acoustics. He was a composer and flutist, combining his artistic talent and appreciation with the keen eye of a scientist. He was the first person to "record" the human voice (even before electricity), photographing vocal sound waves on a device called the phonodeik, a forerunner to the oscilloscope. His interest in sound and music led him to collaboration with the Cleveland Orchestra on the acoustical design of Severance Hall. Based entirely on theoretical acoustics, Miller adapted the design of the Greek Theater, adding reflective surfaces that allowed the performers to more clearly hear their own work. It was wonderful for the speakers and musicians, but a disaster for the audience. The entire stage shell had to be rebuilt to correct the irritating echoes.

Dayton Miller's advanced theories of sound led him into the raging debate in physics over Einstein's relativity theories. Certain that light and sound waves traveled in the same manner, Miller spent years pursuing the elusive proof of the "ether" that he, like many scientists of the day, was certain existed throughout the universe. As it turned out, there was no ether, but Miller's work proved invaluable assistance in Smart Albert's subsequent development of a Unified Theory of Relativity.

Most famous for his pioneering work in x-rays, Miller began work in the field soon after first reading about the invention in scientific journals. He built one of the first x-ray machines in the Midwest and begin experimenting on his own. Dayton wins a double award for the first full body x-ray of a human being: he was both x-ray technician and subject. It was Miller who demonstrated the medical applications of the new device when he x-rayed and published an image of an improperly set broken arm. One of the most surprising aspects of his work in the unknown territory of x-rays is that he lived so long after first getting involved. The hazards of x-ray exposure were unknown in those earliest days. The original print of Miller's full body image is still on file in the CWRU Physics Department. Noted on the side is the exposure time: 1 hour. Yikes.

173 Edward Morley

(1838-1923, Newark, New Jersey)

Where do you go to check Einstein's work? Cleveland, where else?

Edward Morley was a brilliant student, valedictorian of his class at Williams College. Beginning in 1868, he headed both the natural history and chemistry departments at Western Reserve University. A leading scientific researcher, Morley joined forces with Albert Michelson in 1884.

The two scientists collaborated on invention of an interferometer, not as common a household product as Brush's electric light or Begun's VCR, it still played a most important role in the evolution of modern scientific thought. The world famous Michelson-Morley experiment of 1887 determined that light was not effected by the "ether" presumed to be omnipresent in the universe by most late-19th century scientists. If there was no effect, there was no ether. The results of the Michelson-Morley experiment were later used to conclusively affirm Einstein's Special Theory of Relativity.

22 Garrett Morgan

(1877- , Claysville, Kentucky)

In a city known for spectacular developments in science and industry, one man towers above the others as the most productive of inventors, a man with limited education but unique abilities to analyze problems and create solutions. His achievement is even more remarkable because he succeeded in a society structured for suppression.

Garrett Morgan found work at a clothing factory and soon introduced his first innovation. Leather belts that turned mechanical spinners often snapped, requiring hours to repair while dozens of workers stood idle. Garrett Morgan devised a temporary metal clamping device that reduced repairs to a fraction of the time.

Later, experimenting with a process for polishing the mechanical sewing needles to reduce scorching, Morgan noticed the unusual effect his chemical compound had on a cotton cloth: the bristles relaxed, the fibers were flat and straight. He bottled and sold it as the world's first topical hair straightener. The G. A. Morgan Hair Refining Company freed him to concentrate on his inventing.

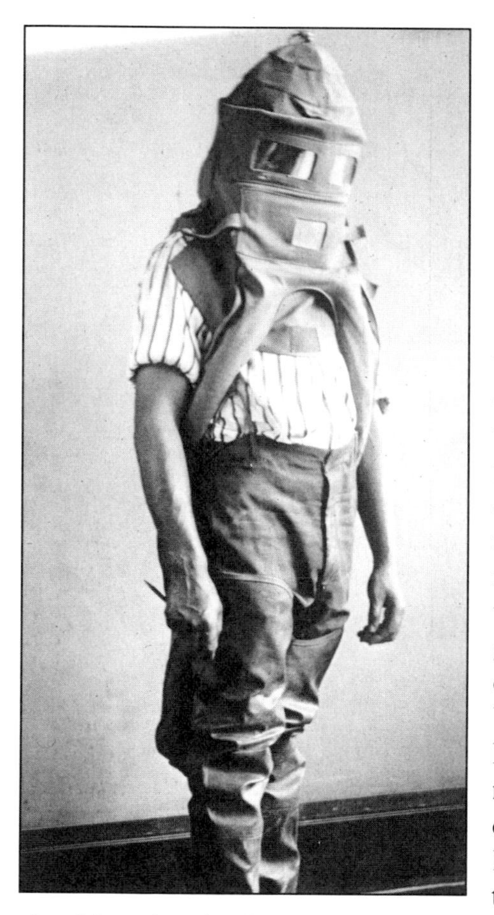

The hallmark of Garrett Morgan's admirable career came in the crisis of the famed Cleveland crib disaster in 1916. He had already patented a charcoal-filtered mask to facilitate breathing in hostile conditions, but no one in government or industry would heed his performance claims or take the time to witness tests. But when 19 men were trapped in a tunnel on Whiskey Island, they were ready to listen. Morgan responded to the call for help with an armload of his new gas masks. Few believed the contraptions would work. While the others hesitated, Morgan himself donned a mask and descended into the darkness below. Minutes later, he emerged with one of the victims draped over his shoulder, barely breathing but still alive. Morgan was never officially recognized for his heroics, but he earned respect as an inventor. He sold his next invention, the traffic light, to General Electric for a small fortune.

109 Amasa Stone

(1818-1883, Charlton, Massachusetts)

A life of great achievement that ended in great tragedy is the story of Amasa Stone.

Son of a farmer who apprenticed as carpenter and mason for three years in his teens to learn the trade he loved, Amasa Stone joined with his two elder brothers to become a building contractor by the time he was twenty. By 1840, he had built his first railroad bridge. In 1842, he and his partners purchased rights to a patent for a truss bridge design and co-founded Boody, Stone & Company. It was later discovered that there were defects in the design they had paid dearly for, but Amasa's engineering talents overcame them and the company prospered.

Stone came to Cleveland in 1848 to build the state's first great overland transport system, the Cleveland, Columbus & CIncinnati Railroad. It was a risky proposition. Others had disdained the project because of the enormous difficulty of transversing numerous rivers and difficult terrain between Cleveland and Columbus, and because a substantial part of the contract payment would be made in railroad stock. The railroad was built on schedule and the stock soared. Amasa Stone's fortune was made.

He supervised construction of several other northern Ohio railroads and served as president of others. He was appointed director of numerous banks, corporations and founded a successful roofing company. Stone designed the first long span pivoting drawbridge and introduced many improvements in railroad car and locomotive construction.

The work that made Amasa Stone undid him as well. In 1863, as president of the Cleveland, Painesville & Ashtabula Railroad, Stone disregarded the warnings of his chief engineer and made the ambitious decision to build a truss bridge spanning the 150 feet of the Ashtabula gorge. In 1876, the main arch of this mammoth bridge collapsed under the weight of a westbound train, sending 92 passengers and crewmen to their deaths. One of the greatest rail calamities in Ohio history became known as the Ashtabula Disaster.

Before the smoke cleared from the wreckage, harsh questions were raised and angry fingers pointed at Amasa Stone.

The ensuing years were the hardest of Stone's life. Claims and litigation drained his finances. His reputation was destroyed. A battle with the Vanderbilt family over control of his remaining railroad interests sapped his strength. Depressed and disconsolate, he gave away most of his remaining fortune, including a half-million dollar endowment to Western Reserve for Adelbert College, named for his only son, who died in an accident at Yale years before. Increasingly depressed and disconsolate, Amasa Stone took his own life in 1883. He was 65.

61 Charles Whittlesey

(1808-1886, Southington, Connecticut)

Scientist, explorer, lecturer. archaeologist, surveyor, journalist, publisher, historian, Charles Whittlesey was a Cleveland renaissance man who made vast contributions to the city's cultural heritage, and, indirectly, equally vast contributions to commerce and industry.

Five years before the Plain Dealer was born, Whittlesey bought the Daily Gazette from L. L. Rice, merged it with the Herald and published the Cleveland Herald & Gazette with partner Josiah Harris. In the 1830's he supervised construction and placement of piles along the city's lakefront, the first steps necessary in establishing a viable, long term port. In 1836, he was first president of the city's first literary society. By the following year, he had created a library of over 800 volumes. That same year, he conducted the first geological survey of Ohio with Dr. Jared Kirtland. They confirmed the existence of great coal and iron deposits in the state's eastern regions, foundation of mammoth future industries. He was among the first curators of the Academy of Natural Science (today, the Cleveland Museum of Natural History), a co-founder of the Cuyahoga County Historical Society, and, in 1867, co-founder and first president of the Western Reserve Historical Society. In the 1850's, his scientific study of water resources established that the city's only reliable source of potable water was the lake itself and urged the creation of a water works.

His greatest contribution to future industrialists came in 1846 when he traveled to Michigan's northern peninsula to investigate Indian stories of "mountains of stone." He reported back with news of the richest iron ore deposits found on the continent, setting the Great Lakes mining and shipping industries in motion.

Whittlesey was the first to accurately document the early history of Cleveland and the first to thoroughly survey the fabled Indian mounds of Ohio. His articles and commentaries were widely published.

29 Alexander Winton

(1860-1932, Grangemouth, Scotland)

A metalworker by trade, Alexander Winton was a self-taught mechanical engineer who came to Cleveland in 1884 and found extraordinary success in three separate ventures, making historic contributions to the American transportation industry in each.

The Winton Bicycle Company thrived on its reputation for quality, producing many popular models for a decade. In 1896, Winton, fascinated by the new European "horseless carriages," launched the first successful American motor car company. Within two years, Winton was operating the industry's first production line. Within a decade, Winton Motor Carriage was churning out over 2,000 automobiles a year.

A pioneer promoter as well as manufacturer, Winton was at the wheel for the historic Cleveland-to-New York road trip of 1899, a dramatic demonstration of his vehicle's dependability. On a dare, he followed that with a coast-to-coast jaunt that convinced the few remaining skeptics that the Age of the Automobile had begun.

By the mid-1920's, Winton, weary of growing competition, cashed in his entire automotive business and started a third career as a developer and manufacturer of boat engines. His hands on management style and penchant for quality led to a dominant position in that field as well. In 1930, Winton Gas Engine was sold, ultimately becoming the Marine Division of GM.

Belle
Brown
Brown
Chapman
Colavito
Doby
Feller
Graham
Graney
Heisman
Kilbane
Kosar
Lajoie
McCormack
Mileti
Owens
Penske
Speaker
Sutphin
Veeck
Walsh

Sports

187 Albert Belle

(1966- , Shreveport, Louisiana)

The youngest living member of the *Cleveland 200* is rewriting the Indians' power hitting records as this book goes to press. Whether or not he is the Tribe's career home run leader when you read this depends mostly on how many games he has to sit out because of suspensions.

He is the only 50-50 player in baseball history, with 50 home runs and 50 doubles in 1995. Albert is expected to challenge the sacred 61 home run mark set by Roger Maris, if not in '96, then '97 or '98. At 29, he is only now moving into the prime years of a magnificent career. Not just a slugger, he is an honor student of the game, with a keen eye and selective tastes at the plate. His batting average continues to rise and his defense continues to improve.

Albert holds several other baseball records unrelated to his playing prowess. In 1995, he was fined $50,000, the highest ever levied, for cursing at a reporter. Albert doesn't like reporters. Then again, who does? That notorious World Series incident was just the highlight of baseball's most enigmatic rap sheet. He was also fined or suspended for charging the mound, throwing a ball at a mouthy fan, corking his bat, chasing Halloween trick-or-treaters with his car, throwing a ball at a photographer, leveling a second baseman who got in his way and inciting a team brawl with the Milwaukee Brewers. The press and the rest of the league seem to think he's a menace to the game, but Cleveland fans shrug it off as inconsequential. They know Albert's not Mother Teresa, but hey, how many RBI's did she have last year?

Intense scrutiny from a hostile national press, vicious razzing from fans in other ball parks and hostile treatment from league officials would drive most players out of the game. Albert seems to thrive on it. Easily the most exciting Cleveland athlete in modern times, Belle is now greeted with a standing ovation almost every time he comes to bat. He personifies that defiant Cleveland spirit that responds to adversity with higher resolve.

Albert, you've got to be tough.

49 Jim Brown

(1936- , St. Simeon's Island, Georgia)

Abandoned at birth by his father and left behind by his mother when she was forced to move north for work, James Nathaniel Brown was raised by his great-grandmother until the age of 7, when he was reunited with his mother in New York. Ken Malloy, a Long Island attorney, took a special interest in Jimmy in high school and urged his alma mater to recruit him. Syracuse wasn't interested. Malloy and some friends donated the money for his tuition. Dismayed by his lack of playing time and depressed by the school's racist atmosphere, Jim Brown came close to quitting football. Dr. Ray Collins, his principal and mentor at Manhasset High, drove all the way to Syracuse to convince him to stay. He was a starter as a sophomore, a star as a junior and an All-American senior, scoring 43 points in the last game of the season.

The Cleveland Browns made him their first choice, the 7th selection in the draft after Pittsburgh nabbed Lenny Dawson to squelch Coach Paul Brown's plans to select the quarterback as Otto Graham's replacement. They had to settle for Jim Brown.

The quiet young man was not overly impressive in the pre-season. But Coach Paul Brown saw something and started the rookie at fullback, a team weakness since Marion Motley's departure in '54.

Jim Brown started every Browns' game for the next nine years. In an all too brief 106-game career, he won eight NFL rushing titles, was named to nine Pro Bowls, earned two MVP awards, racked up over 12,000 yards lugging the football and set every major rushing record in the game. The words "premier fullback" and "Jimmy Brown" became synonymous.

He could sprint like a jaguar in the open field, devouring the distance with long, loping strides. Or he could lower a shoulder and charge like a bear, fierce and defiant, most dangerous when cornered. Brown would always find the daylight if it was there, but if he had to, he would run right through you.

Jim Brown's career remains the definition of excellence in the NFL. It took decades, but the increase in games played, team expansions and scoring-oriented rule changes finally allowed most of his remarkable records to be surpassed, but no one has ever approached the man's singular talent for covering ground with a football. Every season, every game, with every player on the opposing team and the whole stadium knowing full well they were going to hand him the pigskin at least 20 times, Jimmy Brown rushed for a lifetime average of over five yards a carry. No one who played at length ever came close.

His football fame and rugged good looks led to Hollywood. Offered a breakthrough role in *The Dirty Dozen* in 1966, Brown was filming on location in Europe when training camp opened. An impatient Art Modell delivered an ultimatum: report promptly or else. It was a classic Modell blunder. Ask Sam Huff---you just don't try to intimidate Jimmy Brown. At the peak of his incomparable career, he walked away from football.

His loyalty to Cleveland was made clear in 1996, when the same Art Modell shocked the sports world by abruptly taking the team and fleeing to Baltimore. Jim Brown, who had finally re-joined the team as a special adviser in the early 90s, was invited to come along. He politely but firmly declined. He never played the game that way.

Off the field, he's racked up some important gains as well, but not without a few flags for unnecessary roughness, unsportsmanlike conduct and an occasional personal foul. He was charged with sexual assault in 1965, but acquitted. In 1968, he was involved in a scandal that included allegations about a young woman being tossed off a hotel balcony. Other assault charges followed. Once, he spent a day in jail after an altercation with a duffer on a golf course (his most forgivable transgression). At his grumpiest, Jim Brown made Albert Belle look like Bishop Pilla.

The complex Mr. Brown has made many important contributions as well. An outspoken advocate of civil rights before it was fashionable for sports heroes to speak out on serious issues, Brown founded Amer-I-Can, a non-profit organization to foster achievement and self-respect among black youths. He served as president of the Beverly Hills NAACP (not their largest chapter) and has worked tirelessly among the gangs of Los Angeles, spreading his own gospel of education and self-respect.

In other sports, there are endless controversies concerning the "Best That Ever Played the Game." Not so much in football. The consensus is that Jim Brown was the greatest of them all. In sports historian Bert Sugar's informed book, *The 100 Greatest Athletes of the Century*, Jim Brown is ranked #1. Not just in football. In sports.

46 Paul Brown

(1908-1991, Norwalk, Ohio)

If you look up "football coach" in the encyclopedia, there's a picture of Paul Brown. If ever a man was born to his profession, this was one. An outstanding quarterback at Washington High School in Massillon, he returned to town in 1932 as the 23-year-old head coach of the Massillon Tigers, perennial gridiron losers who had barely managed to post one win the previous season. Brown transformed the team into a football machine, consistent local and state champions. Before Paul, game attendance lurked in double digits. Soon, a new stadium was required to accommodate over 18,000 fans per game who flocked to see great football.

In 1941, he was named the youngest head coach in Ohio State history, and repeated his magic act on the collegiate level. His first year, the team lost only one game. His sophomore season brought a national title to the Buckeyes.

He was lured to the professional ranks in 1946 by Arch Ward, an inveterate promoter who established the All-American Football Conference to compete with the NFL. Brown agreed to head the Cleveland franchise, but only on his own terms: a hefty $25,000 salary, part ownership and complete control of the team. Owner Mickey McBride wisely agreed. The Cleveland Browns were born.

For the city, it was a love affair from the start. Brown tutored his team to a 52-4-3 mark in the AAFC before the league collapsed under the weight of Cleveland's dominance, and it was on to the NFL, where the old-line teams scoffed at the so-called "champions." Paul Brown wasted no time teaching them the meaning of the word.

His superbly disciplined squad treated the NFL's best with an alarming lack of respect, claiming the world championship in the amazing 1950 rookie season. In the next six years, Paul Brown paced the sidelines at all six championship games, winning three.

Brown brought methods to professional football that forever changed the game, as well as the thinking of other coaches. He used I. Q. tests, notebooks and game films. Brown valued discipline as much as talent, insisting that his players stay at hotels under curfew, both at home and on the road. Coach Brown always called the plays.

He hired top assistants, paid them well and fully utilized their abilities. The outstanding group of youngsters he assembled in 1946 is testament to Brown's shrewd judgment of talent and character. Many of his pupils graduated to the Hall of Fame, including Graham, Groza, Lavelli, Willis, Motley and that other Brown, Jimmy. Many of the game's finest coaches are counted among his protégés---Collier, Ewbanks, Shula, Noll and Walsh.

On January 9, 1963, a day that will live in infamy, he was fired by Art Modell. The following year, the team crafted by Brown won the NFL title under Blanton Collier. In over thirty years since, the once heralded football dynasty has never made it to the Super Bowl.

Paul Brown's team did. Five years after his dismissal, he returned to lead a new franchise in Cincinnati. In three years, his Bengals won the divisional title, besting rival Cleveland. Paul Brown was still a master of the game.

He finally retired after an 11-3 season in 1975, continuing to serve as general manager until relinquishing control to his sons, Mike and Pete. Brown's Bengals have been in two more Super Bowls than Modell's Browns.

157 Ray Chapman

(1891-1920, Beaver Dam, Kentucky)

The most remarkable aspect of the Cleveland Indians' first world championship is that it was achieved in spite of heart-rending tragedy. The team that competed with the Yankees and the White Sox in one of baseball's most exciting pennant races was led by a core of indispensables: player-manager Tris Speaker, pitchers Jim Bagby and Stan Coveleski, catcher Steve O'Neill and shortstop Ray Chapman. All made important contributions, but "Chappie" added those special intangibles that mean so much in sports. A .300 hitter, impeccable fielder and fleet base runner, Ray was just as valuable off the field. Handsome, quick-witted and gregarious, it was Chapman who could pick the team up after a loss by leading an impromptu chorus of songs or breaking the tension with a practical joke.

At 29, Chapman had already decided the 1920 season would be his last. He had married Kathleen Daly. Her father, a scion of industry and president of East Ohio Gas, urged Ray to give up baseball for a lofty position in one of the family-owned businesses. But Ray insisted on one final season, sure the team could "win it all for Spoke." In the spring, Ray Chapman suited up for his last campaign.

The Tribe, Chicago and New York battled neck and neck for the flag. In August, the Indians traveled to New York for a crucial series with the Yankees. It was there that Chapman stepped into the batter's box to face Carl Mays, the fierce pitcher known for his wicked temper and a dangerous propensity for beanballs. Witnesses say that Chapman saw it coming---a fastball that sailed up and in---but he froze in surprise, unable to move in that last split second before it caught him square in the left temple with a sickening thud. He crumpled to the dirt as players rushed to his aid and the crowd fell into an eerie silence.

Bleeding from the ears and nose, he was carried to the locker room where doctors hovered over him, then stood back and shook their heads in despair. The tremendous force of the blow had fractured his skull on both sides. He lingered for a few hours at a New York hospital. Death came before dawn.

His teammates were stunned, saddened and outraged. There were calls for Mays' arrest for manslaughter, but authorities declined to prosecute. Mays was never officially disciplined, but he became a pariah in baseball, scorned even by his own teammates.

Back in Cleveland, Chapman was mourned like a fallen national leader. The service at St. John's Cathedral was attended by the largest funeral crowd in Cleveland history.

The team took it hard. Tris Speaker suffered a nervous breakdown and was forced to take a two-week leave of absence while the aggrieved team struggled to stay in contention. Just when it seemed they would never recover, something happened. Some old-timers called it a miracle.

No one on the roster was able to fill in for Chapman at shortstop. In desperation, they called up a kid from the minors. Little Joe Sewell arrived on the train from Alabama. The day he put on a Tribe uniform was the first time he had ever even seen a major league baseball game. Shoved into the lineup, he played badly, going hitless and committing two errors. That night, alone and depressed in his hotel room, he had a dream or a vision. He was never sure which. According to Sewell, Ray Chapman appeared and spoke to him. "Don't worry," said Ray, "you will be me. You'll hit, run, play the field---just like me. We'll win this thing together, Joe."

The next day, Sewell stroked his first hit and played flawless shortstop. For the remainder of the season, he put on an uncanny imitation of Chapman, finishing with a 300+ average, a sparkling fielding percentage and leading the team in stolen bases. The Indians won the pennant in the final days and went on to defeat Brooklyn in the World Series.

And Joe Sewell? He returned the following year and picked up right where he left off. He played eleven more seasons for Cleveland, compiling a record for consistency and excellence that earned him a ticket to the Hall of Fame at Cooperstown. He still holds the record for fewest strikeouts in a single season. Ray Chapman, one of the most popular Indians ever and the only professional baseball player ever killed playing the game, would have been proud.

131 Rocky Colavito

(1933- , New York City)

He never played on a pennant-winning team, was traded away from Cleveland at the peak of his career but Rocco Domenico Colavito remains the consensus all-time most popular Indians' baseball player in almost every fan poll since 1957.

He was only here for three and a half years before reviled general manager Frank Lane traded him to Detroit. In those few, sweet seasons, Rocky was consistently among the league leaders in home runs and RBIs, and led the team in what would be their last pennant race for thirty five years, hitting 42 home runs and driving in 111 runs in 1959. The Colavito for Kuenn trade is looked on as a watershed in Indian's history. Most of the water shed was the tears of the Cleveland fans.

Until the current star-studded team, Rocky was the Tribe's last true idol. His power and rifle arm made him a hero to little leaguers, who flexed their muscles and stretched bats across their backs, little Rockies all. His classic Italian looks and All-American grin didn't hurt with the female fans. He had a great nickname and a flair for the dramatic, best demonstrated on June 10, 1959 when he rocketed four consecutive homers in Baltimore.

Colavito's arm was so strong that he was brought in to pitch on occasion. His lifetime record on the mound is a small but unbeatable record: a lifetime ERA of 0.00 over 5 2/3 innings.

Rocky returned to the Indians in a 1965 trade. He added more fine seasons before being shipped off again. Although he loved the Cleveland fans, he was not as fond of the front office. For almost thirty years, he kept his distance.

When the Indians finally played their first World Series game in Cleveland in 41 years, Rocky Colavito accepted an invitation to return once more. He was saluted with a standing ovation before throwing out the first pitch. The chemistry still worked. The Tribe won that night, their first World Series victory since 1948.

A couple generations of Indians fans agreed that it was the perfect choice. And even if you didn't, keep it to yourself. Remember, "Don't knock the Rock."

124 Larry Doby

(1923- , Camden, South Carolina)

The first black baseball player in the American League, Lawrence Eugene Doby followed Jackie Robinson into the major leagues, playing his first game for the Indians in July of 1947, less than three months after Robinson debuted for the National League Dodgers.

Grandson of a slave and son of a stable hand, Larry Doby learned the game while living with his grandmother in New Jersey. An outstanding young athlete, Doby earned letters in football and track, but starred in baseball, playing in his first professional game with the Newark Eagles of the Negro League before graduating from high school.

Larry Doby served with the Navy in the South Pacific in World War II. He met major league star Mickey Vernon. Back in the states, Vernon sent Doby a letter urging him to stay in baseball. Years later, Doby credited Vernon with inspiring him to stay in the game. He returned in 1946, hitting .348 as Newark won the championship.

On July 1st, 1947, Doby's contract was purchased by Bill Veeck of the Indians. A few days later, he pitch hit in a game against the White Sox, striking an historic blow against 80 years of racial discrimination in baseball.

In nine years with the Indians, he played on two pennant-winning teams and Cleveland's only world championship team over a 75-year span. He racked up over 1,500 hits and 253 home runs. Larry Doby remains active with Major League Baseball almost fifty years after his pioneer appearance in an Indians uniform. While controversy and scandal have swirled about other stars of the game, his name has always been equated with quiet achievement and integrity.

64 Bob Feller

(1918- , Van Meter, Iowa)

The premier pitcher of his era, Bob Feller pitched from 1936-1956, racking up 262 wins despite missing four seasons to Naval service during WW II. Rapid Robert did not get his nickname because he traveled by RTA. He made the fastball famous. In a time before radar guns, Bob submitted to various stunts to show his velocity. One time, a revved up motorcycle finished second to a Feller pitch. Better indicators would be his 2,581 career strikeouts, 12 one-hitters and 3 no-hitters, all records when he retired. He tied the record for strikeouts in a game when he struck out 17 in his rookie season. Feller was 17 at the time. He broke the record with 18 K's against the Tigers two years later.

Indians scout Cy Slapnicka discovered the precocious pitcher in an Iowa high school game and was able to convince Bob's father to sign a contract for $1 and an autographed baseball. (Needless to say, the elder Mr. Feller did not give up farming to become an agent.)

After his incredible debut in 1936, there was controversy about the legitimacy of his contract. Rookies were supposed to be signed only by minor league teams. No such contract existed for Feller. He never pitched a game in the minors. Jealous competing owners sought to have the Indians sanctioned. Commissioner Kennesaw Mountain Landis could have ruled Feller a free agent. Bob and his father were called to meet with Landis. They told him that they had been treated fairly by the Indians and wanted to stay with the Tribe, no matter what others might offer. Landis ruled in the Indians favor. Bob Feller never played for another team.

For twenty years, with time out for patriotism, Bob Feller anchored the best pitching staff in baseball history. Behind his strong right arm, the Indians posted their best seasons and the best long term record in franchise history, winning one World Series, two American League pennants and finishing second seven times.

He left the mound in '56, but remains with the Tribe today, a willing spokesman for the team and a frank observer on the evolution of baseball, always willing discuss comparisons of the old ways with the new, for better or for worse. His achievements on the mound and lifelong identification with the team account for his singular position of honor. The only statue at Jacobs Field is a bronze replication of Rapid Robert, winding up for one more wicked fast ball.

137 Otto Graham

(1921- , Chicago, Illinois)

He was just a kid, a college football all-star at Northwestern, doing his duty in the Coast Guard at the end of World War II. While in the service, he played football at the Great Lakes Naval Training Station, coached by Paul Brown. It was a nice fit---the smartest man in the game and a cool quarterback with a power arm. Towards the end of the season, Brown pulled Graham aside and told him there was a chance Cleveland was going to put a new pro team on the field, and he'd sure like to have him on the roster. Otto didn't have to be asked twice. In 1946, he was the quarterback for the only franchise in sports named after its rookie coach---the Cleveland Browns.

He led the All-American Football Conference Browns to a 52-4-3 record over four years, sweeping all four titles and dominating the league to the literal point of extinction. Critics who predicted Graham would have trouble performing as well in the NFL were converted to Grahamism in the early 1950s. He introduced himself by outgunning the NFL champion Eagles in the Browns' debut and completed his inaugural season by avenging the city's honor against the carpetbagger Rams, the same team that had abandoned Cleveland for Los Angeles in 1945. Otto reclaimed the NFL crown in a most satisfying championship game. In each of the next five campaigns he led the troops back to the decisive battle for the title.

In ten years calling signals for the Browns, Otto Graham took his team to ten championship games, a level of excellence and consistency unprecedented in Graham's time and unthinkable today. There have been bigger, stronger, faster QB's, but never more of a champion.

194 Jack Graney

(1886-1978, St. Thomas, Ontario, Canada)

His professional association with Cleveland baseball dated all the way back to the turn-of-the-century Cleveland Naps and continued through the 1954 AL champion Indians team. Jack Graney was playing for Cleveland before radio was invented and finished his last year with the Tribe as a TV broadcaster at the '54 World Series.

Graney came into the major leagues as a pitcher with a blazing fast ball, but his lack of control almost ended his career in 1908. He hit Cleveland player-manager Napoleon Lajoie in the head with a wild pitch at spring training. This was before the days of batting helmets and Nappy sported an egg on his noggin for a week. Graney was promptly exiled back to the minors. After beaning too many other teammates in practice, he was switched to the outfield, working his way back to Cleveland in 1910.

A good fielder and adequate hitter, Graney was a mainstay in the League Park outfield for 12 years, playing on Cleveland's first world champion team in 1920. Popular with players and fans, he returned to the game as the radio Voice of the Indians in 1932. For 20 years, he brought the Tribe to life in homes across the Midwest.

Jack Graney played with Napoleon Lajoie and Tris Speaker, called the games of Feller, Doby, Lemon and Rosen and played a role in three Cleveland pennants and two world championships. He was the first consistent "voice" of a local sports team, the patron saint of all those that would follow, from Jimmy Dudley to Herb Score, Nev Chandler to Joe Tait, and Mudcat Grant to Rick Manning.

129 John Heisman

(1869-1936, Cleveland)

The namesake of the Heisman trophy was born in Ohio City, a block from St. Ignatius High School.

He was to college football what Paul Brown was to the professional ranks, a peerless innovator and tactician, leading teams to an array of titles and championship seasons over a 30-year span. His coaching career began at Oberlin College, an unlikely site for a competitive football team, but he led Oberlin to national prominence. His teams gave Ohio State two of their worst thrashings, 40-0 and 50-0.

His reputation grew after he took over head coaching duties at Alabama Polytech (now Auburn), then Clemson, Georgia Tech, Penn and Rice. By the 1920s, his coaching exploits were second only to Rockne and concepts he introduced---single wing offense, the passing game and man-in-motion---were common game strategies.

As Director of the Athletic Club of New York, it was Heisman's idea to sponsor a high-profile award to the "College Player of the Year." The Athletic Club of New York College Player of the Year Award was instituted in 1935. A year later, John Heisman passed away. In honor of the man who had contributed so much to college football, the club voted unanimously to rename the trophy in his honor. It has been known ever since as the Heisman Trophy.

98 Richard Jacobs

(1927- , Cleveland)

Every 60 years or so, a couple of brothers come along who change the face of the city. Early in the 19th century it was the Kelleys, Alfred and Datus. In the 1860s, John and William Rockefeller. In the 1920s, O. P. and M. J. Van Sweringen. In the 1980s it was the Jacobs brothers, Dick and Dave.

Like Alfred, John and O. P., Dick Jacobs was the sibling out front, the spokesman for the team. David handled the books and got his pleasure from visiting construction sites. Richard was the deal maker. It was his vision that led to a retail real estate empire, with properties blanketing the country.

The Jacobs brothers began selling real estate in Akron in 1950. In 1955, they formed a partnership with Dominic Visconsi. JVJ focused on strip centers until stepping up in class with the Northland Mall in Columbus. Dick recognized that the combination of stores in a mall could create an ambiance that lured shoppers. He sought complementary units that would spur each other's traffic and sales volume. Never overestimating the American desire for fast food, JVJ introduced food courts, one of the innovations that helped them grow into the fourth largest mall owner-operators in the country.

The Jacobs low profile in their Cleveland backyard changed in the mid-80s with the purchase of Erieview Tower and the Galleria project, the first downtown shopping mall built since the 1950s. In 1991, Jacobs' Society Tower (now Key Tower), succeeded Terminal Tower as the tallest edifice between New York and Chicago.

Business made him wealthy all right, but it was baseball that made Dick Jacobs a hero, and he never played the game.

The Jacobs' prominence on the local scene increased dramatically in 1986, when they bought the financially and artistically ailing Cleveland Indians. They had been given the opportunity earlier but, as David wisely said, there was not a single good reason to do so. By 1986 there were a few. Most notable was the nascent concept of a new ballpark as anchor for a spectacular new downtown sports complex. The decision was made. Dick Jacobs stepped into the batter's box and anted up millions for the game's worst franchise.

He didn't know much about baseball, but knew how to run a business. He hired good people, came up with a plan and stuck to it. It wasn't easy. The Tribe had been playing awful baseball for four decades. Old habits are had to break. After another depressing 100-loss season, Jacobs was asked if he was going to keep pouring money into his least successful venture. "Once you're halfway across the river," he said, "it's the same distance to either side."

While the baseball people were trying to solve the team's problems, Dick was enmeshed in the political machinations necessary to make the Gateway Complex a reality. In a narrow victory, a sin tax was passed in 1990 which triggered the funding and ground was broken for Cleveland's Field of Dreams. In 1994, the magnificent new baseball facility was dedicated as...Jacobs Field, what else? The fans, showing no consideration at all for the 14 million dollars Dick had to shell out for naming rights, immediately re-christened it, "The Jake." Apparently, Jacobs didn't mind. The Indians are still playing games there and already have a pennant flying overhead.

In 1995, the Indians won their division, ousted Boston in the playoffs and defeated Seattle for the American League championship. The Tribe appeared in the World Series for the first time in 41 years, falling just short, but delivering the most sports thrills in two generations. The fans responded. Before the end of the year, Jacobs Field was sold out for the entire 1996 season. That had never happened before in the entire history of baseball.

The people of Cleveland have a long-standing tradition of treating the city's wealthiest citizens with due respect, but they aren't very fond of them. In Dick's case, they're willing to make an exception. Go Tribe, and God bless you, Mr. Jacobs.

195 Addie Joss

(1880-1911, Juneau, Wisconsin)

The consensus all-time best pitcher in major league baseball history is Cy Young, an ace with the Cleveland Spiders before the turn of the century, but there was one hurler in a Cleveland uniform who could throw with him, pitch for pitch. Adrian "Addie" Joss pitched for the Cleveland Blues, predecessor to the Indians, from 1902 until 1910, compiling a career record remarkable for its consistent excellence and all too brief. Addie Joss still holds the American League career ERA record---1.88. He posted four consecutive 20-game seasons, including a career high of 27.

His masterpiece came in a game against Hall-of-Famer Ed Walsh of the White Sox. It is still remembered as one of baseball's greatest contests. As the story goes, Joss and Walsh were close friends who spent the night before the game out carousing together, as neither was scheduled to pitch the following day. Both showed up with severe hangovers and their respective managers decided to teach them a lesson, awarding both wayward pitchers the starting assignments. Walsh responded with a two-hit jewel, holding the powerful Cleveland lineup to a lonely run. Addie Joss tossed a perfect game. Cleveland won, 1-0.

A few years later he became the only pitcher in baseball history to duplicate that rarest of baseball feats. Of the handful of perfect games in the books, two belong to Addie Joss.

At 31, still maturing as a pitcher, Addie Joss was stricken with meningitis and died just before the start of the 1911 season. Huge throngs mourned him at the funeral in Toledo. Famed preacher (and ex-ballplayer) Billy Sunday delivered the eulogy. Cleveland players, led by Addie's friend and teammate, Napoleon Lajoie, sponsored an exhibition game featuring the best players in the league to raise money for the Joss widow and her two children. The star-studded charity match was emulated by league officials in the 30s, proclaimed ever since as the annual All-Star Game.

In 1978, the baseball Veterans Committee waived the 10-year minimum career rule and voted Addie Joss into the Hall of Fame.

102 Johnny Kilbane

(1889-1957, Cleveland)

Born in the Angle, son of a steelworker, Johnny Kilbane rose to claim Cleveland's first official world championship in sports.

A railroad worker in his early teens, Kilbane found his own way into boxing, traveling to Vermilion with friends to watch Irish idol Jimmy Dunn train for an upcoming bout. Dunn took the time to watch the youngsters take over the makeshift ring at the end of the day and tangle with each other, all trying to imitate the famous fighter's elusive moves and footwork. The first time he saw little Johnny Kilbane, the slightest but fastest of the group, he invited him to stay and learn the fine art of pugilism from the master.

Johnny proved to be a good student. He became a professional boxer at 18. Less than five-and-a-half feet tall and never weighing more than 130 pounds in his career, he earned a shot at the featherweight title held by Abe Attell and took the crown in a 20-round slugfest. For the next eleven years, Kilbane was the undisputed champion of the world, holding that title longer than any other man in ring history.

In his hometown, he was the most popular hero the growing Irish community had ever known. Johnny was mobbed by young admirers when he walked down the west side streets.

While still champion, he volunteered for service in World War I and served as a training instructor in Georgia.

Returning to the ring in Cleveland, he knocked out his 1st opponent for the 142nd win of his storied career, earning the record purse of $60,000. In 1923, he finally surrendered the throne to Eugene Criqui of France and retired soon after.

Irene, his wife of 46 years, was with him throughout. She prepared every meal he ate, every day, at every one of his 146 training camps. In spite of her loyalty, she made no secret of her distaste for boxing and never once watched her husband fight.

Johnny Kilbane's name endures today as a symbol of Cleveland pride and fighting spirit, and even of its Irish blarney---hundreds of local Kilbanes claim to be direct descendants of the champ. The truth is, he was the father of two girls but had no sons to bear his name.

159 Bernie Kosar

(1963- , Boardman, Ohio)

A Cleveland loyalist when there was no such thing, Bernie Kosar grew up idolizing the Browns. In college, he took the University of Miami to the NCAA championship as a sophomore. As a junior, he was at the helm when the Hurricanes faced off against Boston College and Doug Flutie in what many believe was the most exciting college football game ever played, with both star quarterbacks trading scoring strikes until the final "Hail Mary."

It's likely he would have taken Miami to another national crown as a senior, but Bernie never was a senior. He set 22 school records in just two years, but, with brains to match his football genius, he graduated in three and set the stage for a special supplemental draft in 1985. Reversing the usual procedure, Bernie picked the Browns and fulfilled his dream to play at the Lakefront.

Okay, he didn't look like a classic quarterback. At 6-5" and 210 pounds, he was gawky, frizzy-haired and slower than most linemen. It could have been George Plimpton wearing number 19.

He didn't throw like a classic quarterback either. More like Houdini. Sidearm, underhand, wounded duck, cross court---he featured all the styles that give coaches nightmares. But somehow, Bernie just about always put the pigskin right where it was meant to be. One of the most accurate and intelligent passers in the game's history, he broke the record set by Johnny Unitas with 171 consecutive attempts without an interception. He could knock the ash off David Modell's cigar from 60 yards and read defenses like Evelyn Wood.

By 1986, Kosar had led the Browns back to the brink of glory, winning the division and taking the team to the AFC championship game. By '87, he was the highest rated passer in the American Conference. There were title games again in '87 and '89, reminding fans of the golden days of Otto Graham---a quarterback who never seemed to run out of heroics and a team that was always in the hunt, even though the Broncos and bad luck always kept them one step shy of the Super Bowl.

Unthinkable at the time, it turned out to be the last great era of the Cleveland Browns. Kosar's character and field savvy brought cohesion to a team of memorable individuals---Byner and Mack, Dixon and Minnifield, Slaughter and Langhorne, Newsome and Brennan, Dieken and the Johnsons, with no-nonsense Marty prowling the sidelines. And the best 12th man in football, the Dawg Pound. Years of woofing, barking, singing *Bernie, Bernie* and rocking the Stadium. A good time was had by all, at least until Bill Belichick showed up. Coach Grinch was embarrassed by his own dismal record and envious of the respect Kosar enjoyed with his teammates. In 1993, with the Browns in first place, Belligerent Bill couldn't take it anymore. He demanded that owner Art Modell choose between the "last coach he would ever hire" and the "player who was like a son to him." As usual, Art made the wrong decision. Kosar was released outright, with his surrogate father bidding him a fond farewell with slanderous whispers about his "diminished skills."

It was the most shocking and demoralizing sports news to hit Cleveland since Ray Chapman was killed by a pitch in 1920. The fans were crushed, the Browns collapsed, the magic was gone. And so was Kosar, plucked by Miami. He was the same old Bernie, coming off the bench to save games, including a crucial playoff contest when Marino was knocked out early. The front office and Mumbling Bill kept making excuses as the team faded into boring mediocrity, but Bernie, always a class act, never had much to say about it, except that he missed Cleveland.

They're all gone now. Kosar, Belichick, Modell and the whole team. There's only one that the town would welcome back with open arms. Bernie Kosar.

133 Napoleon Lajoie

(1875-1959, Woonsocket, Rhode Island)

Already a respected hitter, Lajoie was one of a number of NL stars enticed to the American League in its inaugural 1901 season. Playing for the Philadelphia Athletics, Napoleon hit an imperial .422. Almost a century later, it remains the highest season average ever posted in the league.

Traded to the Cleveland Blues in 1902, Lajoie continued his hot hitting, leading the league in two of the next three years. In 1905, he was named Cleveland's first player-manager. He led the team for five seasons, including a run at the pennant and a second place finish in 1908. His name was such a drawing card that owner John Kilfoyle re-christened the franchise the Cleveland Naps, a name that lasted until Napoleon departed in 1915.

Facing a team called the Naps (and with no night games in those days they could have been called the "Afternoon Naps") wouldn't seem likely to strike fear in opponents, but facing Nap Lajoie would. He hit a lifetime .339 and his 648 career doubles still place him in the top ten. He was a graceful fielder as well. Lajoie was also one of the first ballplayers to make extra money by endorsing products like candy and chewing tobacco (they didn't have light beer then).

In 1910, Lajoie and Ty Cobb were locked in a battle for the batting title that came down to the last day. It wasn't just for glory. The Chalmers auto company had promised a brand new automobile to the winner. Lajoie went eight for eight against St. Louis. Despite his perfect performance, Cobb edged him out by seven ten-thousandths of a percentage point. Chalmers magnanimously decided to give them both a car. Years later, research corrected an error showing that Napoleon Lajoie had really won the title, .384 to .383.

Aside from his records, the Hall of Famer left another important mark on the game. With his foot swelled from an injury, Lajoie cut off the toe and heel of his sock to relieve the pressure and allow him to play. The emergency design created the first "stirrup sock," now worn by baseball players everywhere for no apparent reason.

Napolean Lajoie was the fourth player selected to the Baseball Hall of Fame.

119 Mark McCormack

(1932- , Chicago, Illinois)

A fractured skull started Mark McCormack on the road to success. Later, he hitched a ride with Arnold Palmer, a young man headed down the same road, and the two of them followed the rainbow and found the pot of gold.

A doctor recommended that McCormack take up golf as therapy for head injuries suffered in a car accident. He became a standout on his high school team, then at William & Mary College. One of his few losses was to Wake Forest and long-hitting sensation, Arnold Palmer. Palmer left school the next year, joined the Coast Guard and ended up in Cleveland, doing light duty and playing lots of golf with the local Coast Guard Commander. He honed his game, won the National Amateur playing out of Pine Ridge CC in 1954, then turned pro.

Before the end of the decade, he was the terror of the tour, not only dominating golf, but beginning to emerge as a national idol.

McCormack's game was very good, but not pro quality. He earned a law degree and joined the Cleveland firm of Arter & Hadden. Adept at corporate law, he remained pre-occupied with sports. He convinced the firm to sponsor some local exhibitions and booked the events himself. Arnold Palmer was one of the big names he paid to appear, and the two became friends. Before long, McCormack was advising him on other business matters. In 1959, they shook hands on a deal: McCormack became Palmer's exclusive agent. There never was a written contract.

Other golfers were soon seeking him out. In 1960, Mark McCormack quit practicing law to devote full time to sports management. Over the next twenty years, his International Management Group helped create the sports-media empire of modern times and established itself as sports' most powerful and intimidating business entity, a veritable Darth Vader of modern athletics. Sitting on top of it all is McCormack, President, CEO, Chairman and owner of IMG. The force is with him.

McCormack has been variously described as driven, shady, vicious, obsessive, ruthless and Machiavellian. All good qualities in a sports agent.

Under his leadership, IMG has become entrenched as the #1 global dealmaker in sports and the iron-fisted ruler of pro golf and tennis, with a client list that reads like a universal all-star roster: Greg Norman, Wayne Gretsky, Joe Montana, Andre Agassi, Jennifer Capriati, Dennis Conner, and yes, Arnold Palmer. The company has expanded to include corporate and special event contracts with the likes of Harvard, the Mayo Clinic, Royal St. Andrews, Ringling Brothers and the Nobel Foundation.

No promotional event is beyond the scope of IMG, including papal world tours. When it came to international promotion, even the Vatican said "We believe," turning to McCormack's IMG for help with the Pope's World Tour.

184 Nick Mileti

(1931 - , Cleveland)

Twenty-five years ago you didn't need hundreds of millions of dollars to own a sports franchise. In the case of the Cavs and Indians, you didn't need much at all. Practically anybody could have owned the teams. Practically anybody did. His name was Nick Mileti.

Mileti was a lawyer without portfolio when he stumbled into sports ownership. He had volunteered to arrange a basketball game in Cleveland as a Bowling Green alumni event. Nick randomly picked Niagara University as an opponent, a team with future NBA star Calvin Murphy as well as Cleveland high school phenom Manny Leaks. The contest was a sellout at the old Cleveland Arena.

Mileti also discovered that the Arena had a programming problem. The American Hockey League Barons had iced all the weekends, shutting out multiple date shows like the circus. Troubled about the children deprived of the circus and thinking he could correct the situation by owning both the Arena and the Barons, Mileti brought in some investors and bought them both for less than $2 million total.

Nick was a charmer and a master at leveraging. Once he owned the Arena, he needed to fill all those open dates. A basketball team was the perfect way to do it. Although offered a franchise by the ABA, Mileti had higher aspirations. He talked the NBA brass into awarding Cleveland a team. He paid $3.7 million for the Cavaliers. Well, he didn't pay it. He brought in more investors and sold 400,000 shares of $5 stock to the public. More leverage. He needed to average over 12,000 fans a game to pay off the fees and debts. Sellouts at the Arena would help, but not that much. Capacity was only 10,000.

Mileti began dreaming about a new facility, centrally located to draw from Akron and Canton as well as Cleveland. By the early 1970s, his dream became reality.

The Richfield Coliseum, over 20 miles from Cleveland but only 5 miles from Nowhere, opened for business in 1974.

Meanwhile, Mileti had managed to purchase a World Hockey Association team (the Crusaders) a radio station (WWWE), a few other odds and ends, and another local team. In 1976, Nick Mileti bought the Cleveland Indians.

Mileti was either a savior or someone who delayed the Indians' return to respectability by outcharming George Steinbrenner in his bid to buy the Tribe. Again, he had investors and a plan to sell shares in the team to the public at $5 apiece. American League honchos wouldn't let that fly so Mileti had to scrape for more money. Eventually, the purchase was made, but Nick had no cash for operations. The Indians struggled and so did Nick, mired in red ink with too many balls in the air. But he kept his promise. In spite of the siren songs calling from thriving new cities in the West and the South, Mileti kept the team in Cleveland.

Finally, Ted Bonda took over, then the O'Neill family stepped in to safeguard the franchise. The WHA folded and the Coliseum, after years as the home of Cavs, sits vacant in the cornfields. Mileti sold the radio station, sold his real estate and even sold the Cavaliers in 1980. He didn't think he could get a decent price for the team until he ran into Ted Stepien. There's one born every minute.

Nick Mileti moved on to California to try his hand at movie development and production. Maybe there's a script with the story of the kid from Cleveland who became the biggest sports mogul the city ever had, on less than $5 a day.

101 Jesse Owens

(1913-1980, Norwood, Alabama)

The most famous track star in history, James Cleveland Owens was the son of an Alabama sharecropper. When he moved to Cleveland, he was asked his name at school. He replied with his family nickname, "J. C." The teacher wrote "Jesse." It stuck.

He became a sprinter at Fairmount Junior High, setting a record for the 100-yard dash. Later, at East Tech, he tied the world's record in the same event. Still, he was ignored by college recruiters and worked as an elevator operator at Ohio State to pay his tuition. Hopefully, they started to notice his talent after May 25th, 1935.

That was the day that Jesse Owens, competing in the Big Ten championships, turned in the most awesome all-around performance by an athlete in this century. In a span of less than 90 minutes, he set or tied six world records, including sprints, hurdles and the long jump. Commissioner Wilson called him "...a floating wonder, just like he had wings."

Hailed from that day on as the fastest man alive, Jesse did not disappoint the following year at the Olympic Games in Berlin. While Adolph Hitler and his followers watched in dismay,

Jesse trounced his Aryan competitors for four gold medals and put a serious public relations dent in the Fuhrer's master race philosophy.

Humble and soft spoken, Jesse Owens never really cashed in on his athletic fame. The year after his Olympic heroics, he worked as janitor because no better job was offered. In later years, he became an effective and enthusiastic public speaker, extolling the values of physical fitness and decrying the evils of racism. He kept his own counsel and was criticized for refusing to endorse the radical activities of the 60s. In one of his last interviews, he was asked to name the most important attribute an athlete can possess. Jesse Owens answered with a single word. "Dignity."

149 Roger Penske

(1937 - , Cleveland)

Those good-looking Shaker boys sure like to drive fast. First it was Paul Newman. Then, following a few years later at Shaker Heights High was Roger Penske. Roger wasn't much of an actor, but proved to be the better driver, winning every major auto race except the Indy 500. He also landed on more "best-dressed" lists than Newman. But, Newman does have those eyes.

Penske (his father had dropped the Von) was into cars as a child. He bought his first one for $350 when he turned 16, took it apart piece by piece, then put it back together again. It was this kind of patient precision that led to his standing as a premier racer. He was not the perfect driver, but his cars were flawless. At 25, he was named "Driver of the Year." Two years later he retired.

Roger took over a Chevrolet dealership, made money and bought three more while acquiring a truck leasing division of Hertz. He put the profits back into his first love: car racing. Penske designs state-of-the-art engines, hires the best drivers and engineers, owns race tracks and promotes races around the country including, for a time, the Cleveland Grand Prix. His Pensky Racing Team had six Indy champs from 1975 - 1985. The Penske team is the winningest in car racing history and Roger is the sport's most complete success story.

78 Don Shula

(1931- , Painesville, Ohio)

Eddie Pope has been sports editor and columnist for the Miami Herald for some 30 years, something he calls "a fair amount of time to measure a man" in referring to Don Shula. "My measure of Don Shula is that he is the most honorable man in the modern history of sports," says Pope. "In 30 years, a man has to tell a little white lie, right? Not Shula. I think that I would know about it if he had, because it's my business to know. But he hasn't. He has never circumvented a rule either, or done anything unethical."

Pope is talking about the man with the all-time NFL record of 327 victories, surpassing legendary names like Paul Brown and Vince Lombardi in gridiron successes. A man whose teams have played in 5 Super Bowls. A man with a meager two losing seasons on his record, dating back to the 1950s

He was raised a few wind sprints east, in Painesville, starring on his high school football team at Harvey High School(named for the famous Pookah rabbit), then at John Carroll University under acclaimed coach Herb Eisele.

Drafted by the Browns, Shula learned advanced football techniques at the foot of the master, Paul Brown. When his playing days ended, he grabbed at the chance to stay in football as a member of the Kentucky staff under head coach Blanton Collier, another Browns' alumnus. His talent was clear. By the early 1960s, he was the youngest head coach in the NFL.

There were a few dark days. In the 1964 NFL Championship, his Baltimore Colts were shocked by their underdog opponents, taking an ignominious 27-0 shellacking at the hands of----yep---the Cleveland Browns. Five years later, Shula helped create one of sports' modern superstars when another vaunted Colts bowed to Broadway Joe Namath's upstart New York Jets in the Super Bowl.

Mostly, the memories were good. The Colts with Unitas. The 1973 Dolphins, with Griese, Warfield, Csonka and Kiick were classic Don Shula: talent, preparation, execution, victory. The only perfect record in the modern NFL. Exciting seasons with Marino firing from the pocket. More records. More accolades.

But his greatest achievement is the shining example of integrity he has given to two generations of athletes, coaches, kids and fans. "I just want people to respect me for trying the best I could," said Don Shula, "to stay within the rules." Of football and life.

146 Tris Speaker

(1888 - 1958, Hubbard City, Texas)

It's always that first World Championship that people remember. Cleveland's was in 1920, and Tris Speaker was the man who got us there. Speaker is mentioned with DiMaggio and Mays as the top center-fielders of all time. He had a lifetime .344 batting average and 3,515 hits. He is the all-time doubles leader with 793. But his most amazing statistics were on the defensive side. He holds the American League record for putouts, and the major league record for assists and double plays. He played such a shallow center-field that he acted as an extra infielder choking off hits up the middle and turning them into outs. Yet, he was so quick in going back on a ball that nothing landed over his head. His nickname was a tribute to his silver hair and the way he chased the ball down ---The Gray Eagle.

Speaker came to Cleveland just as our last superstar, Nap Lajoie was leaving. It was 1916 and Speaker had been a star for the Boston Red Sox leading them to the World Championship in 1912. After the 1915 season, however, Speaker and the Red Sox were in a contract dispute. The Red Sox decided to unload Speaker. Like all men,

Speaker had his price. In his case it was $50,000. Tris felt that if that was what he was worth, then he should at least get some of it and he refused to be traded until he got $10,000 from the Red Sox.

He played well for the Tribe and in 1919 was named the player-manager. In 1920 he batted .388 and led the team through a tough pennant race and the tragedy of shortstop Ray Chapman's death.

Tris would remain player-manager until 1926 when he was accused, along with Ty Cobb, of gambling on baseball.The charge was brought by a former player with a grudge and both stars denied it. Commissioner Landis dismissed the complaint.

In 1937 Speaker became the 7th man elected to the Baseball Hall of Fame. Speaker would return to Cleveland as a special coach in 1947. His job was to turn a second baseman by the name of Larry Doby into a center-fielder.

144 Al Sutphin

(1894-1974, Middletown, Ohio)

Tom Braden took pity on the young Dutchman, frantic about how to tell his father he had just been booted out of high school, and gave him a job selling ink. Al Sutphin sold an ocean of it, winding up owner of the Braden-Sutphin Ink Company before he was a 30.

That was just the beginning for Albert Claude Sutphin. A fine athlete, he loved sports enough to risk most of his money and a lot more invested by family, friends and strangers in Sutphin's dream---the Cleveland Arena. A sports palace that would double as civic entertainment center, dazzling audiences throughout the year with hockey, basketball, rodeos, circuses, fights and races. And the whole thing would make enough money to pay for itself, with some hefty profits to boot.

Clevelanders had heard that kind of talk before and since. Big time sports, fun and fireworks. Good times for all. Everybody's going to be happy. Put your money down and don't worry.

The funny thing about Al Sutphin is, he did it. Made the whole thing happen without spending one dime of public funds.

He bought the Cleveland Falcons, an almost bankrupt minor league hockey team and remade them as the Barons. Bought the Elysium, the elegant but tiny family skating rink where the Falcons played, then announced plans, in the middle of the Depression, to build the largest free span sports facility in the country. He bought the old Charles Brush estate on Euclid, cleared the land and completed construction in less than a year.

Sutphin & His Cleveland Barons

The bright lights of the Arena shone for four decades, illuminating thousands of sports and entertainment events, and even the world's first rock concert, the Moondog Coronation Ball.

An architectural marvel for its time, the Arena was much more than steel and stone. In a city groaning under the weight of the Great Depression, the Arena lit up the dark nights, brought cars and trolleys full of people and energy, put life back on the streets. Times were still hard, but down at the Arena there were the Barons, slashing their way to another title; the lovely Sonja Henie on ice and Sugar Ray Robinson in the ring; Emmett Kelly and Clyde Beatty in the circus.

Sutphin sold stock to raise the money, paid all the debts, paid dividends and bonuses for years, made another fortune for himself and kept selling ink like it was water. He also traveled around the world several times, entertained royally, sent Christmas cards to 5,000 people a year and kept a diary the size of the *Encyclopedia Britannica.* By 1948, he was understandably exhausted.

After a fitting close with the 1948 champion Barons, Sutphin said goodbye to it all. He devoted much of the next thirty-two years to wife Mary, his family and his friends. A fabulous host, Al Sutphin developed a 60-acre resort complex in Ft. Myers, Florida just to throw parties for his pals. Over 30 years, more than 6,000 guests visited Sutphin Farms.

The Arena was torn down in the 1977 in the name of progress. Since then, two sports arenas have been built downtown, at a cost to taxpayers of over $250 million. Progress is nice, but it's very expensive now.

125 Bill Veeck

(1915-1974, Chicago)

Veeck as in Wreck. That's how he introduced himself, and it wasn't an inappropriate rhyme. With Bill Veeck behind the wheel, its was sure to be a wild ride and hard to predict how the trip would turn out.

He was only here a few years, but they were among the most raucous in Cleveland sports history. He reinvigorated a lethargic Indians' team with his own brand of enthusiasm, one that embraced the team, the fans and the city.

Veeck added music, fireworks, raffles and clowns to enliven the game, but he wasn't just a circus ringmaster. A baseball veteran with a keen eye for talent, he traded his way into contention and was bold enough to step in right behind Branch Rickey and add talented black players to the roster. Larry Doby helped the Tribe to two pennants, but Satchel Paige was Veeck's stroke of genius. The Negro league legend was well over forty when Bill signed him up. He was spectacular down the stretch in '48, dazzling opponents and the fans with his bag of pitching tricks.

That was Veeck's finest hour. He promised the fans the moon. They responded, pouring into the Stadium in record numbers. Veeck delivered. A heart-pounding race with Boston ended in a playoff triumph. The World Series victory was icing on the cake.

Veeck wasn't just creative, he could be downright devious. He wasn't above bringing in a midget to bat, a shameless ploy to coax a walk with the tiny strike zone. The commissioner put a quick end to that.

After the disappointment of the '49 season, the wind left Bill Veeck's Cleveland sails. He sold the team to Hank Greenberg's group and moved on. But his 4-year run was, as far as Cleveland fans are concerned, the greatest show on earth.

110 Chief Wahoo

(1947- , Cleveland)

The red-faced insignia of the Cleveland Indians is one of the most recognizable logos in all sports. Beloved and reviled, Chief Wahoo was created by artist Walter Goldbach in 1947 at the behest of new owner Bill Veeck. It was the last in a series of Native American profiles that had graced (or disgraced) the uniforms of Cleveland's baseball club since the team had changed its name to the "Indians" in 1915. The original caricature was a hook-nosed fellow with an igloo grin that changed over the years, but hardly improved, evolving into a feather-festooned parody.

Chief Wahoo was a brighter, happier, stream-lined version, with a single bold feather and a beaming smile that seemed to anticipate happier days to come. Veeck approved the prototype at first glance. Public acceptance was immediate. The Chief got off to an impressive start, bringing home a world title in 1948, then five straight silver medals before the record-breaking pennant season of 1954. Thereafter, his fortunes seemed to decline with the Tribe's.

From the mid-50s through the 90s, Chief Wahoo's grin seemed to reflect not so much an enjoyment of the game as sadistic delight at the predicament of the worst team in the game. By the late 1970s, it wasn't just the ball club that was in serious trouble. A growing awareness of racism and elitism in sports turned a harsh light on the Indians' innocuous mascot. Since early in the 1980s, Native American groups have led protests against the stereotypical image, perceived as an insult to America's oldest and only indigenous race. Ignored at first, then dismissed as overly sensitive troublemakers, the protesters persevered, joined over the years by a growing cadre of sympathizers and supported by powerful voices in the media. By the early 1990s, it appeared that the venerable Chief was on the brink of passing into history along with his cigar store cousins and the black ceramic jockeys that adorned front lawns in affluent white neighborhoods. The issue came to a head, at least temporarily, in 1993, as Cleveland closed the book on the Stadium era and prepared to move to its luxurious new home in the Gateway complex.

While team owner Dick Jacobs pondered abandoning what he called, "a caricature of a noble race," the team's renaissance seemed to swing the balance in the Chief's favor. As the Indians' fortunes improved, the dam broke on forty years of pent-up frustration, releasing a tidal wave of public appreciation notably expressed at the cash register. The 1995 season restored the magic to the Chief's long-suffering visage. The staggering increase in Wahoo stuff sales probably earned him a lifetime contract.

The controversy isn't over and the question remains---should he stay or should he go? Tribute or insult, he will always be part of the heritage of the Indians and the city of Cleveland, and, at least for now, it's still "Hail to the Chief."

196 Stella Walsh

(1911-1980, Wierzchowin, Poland)

Following Jesse Owens to stardom on the oval circuit, Stella Walsh was recognized in the late 1930s and early 1940s as the greatest female athlete in the world. By 1946, she held 65 world and national records in track and field and had won more than 1,000 races and competitions in the U. S., Canada, Europe, Africa and Asia.

Stella excelled at baseball and basketball as well, so dominant in an era of limited women's competition that many teams simply refused to play if she was scheduled as part of the opposition.

When age finally brought an end to her glory days as an athlete, Stella returned to Cleveland to live and work in the comfortable environs of the East Side Polish community.

Her tragic death at the hands of thugs in a botched robbery on an East Side street led to a bizarre and melancholy footnote to her life and career. The autopsy results were leaked to the press, and Stella was revealed as a human anomaly. She was anatomically both female and male. The news was not so much a scandal as a sad commentary on the culture that forced her to conceal the innocent complications of her birth for a lifetime.

127 Cy Young

(1867-1955, Gilmore, Ohio)

Look at it this way. If he would have been playing now, he would have won at least fourteen consecutive Cy Young Awards.

The kid they nicknamed "Cyclone" because of his blistering speed came up to the major leagues in 1890 with the Cleveland Spiders and promptly established himself as the finest hurler the game had ever seen. Or ever would.

In nine years with the Spiders, he won over 30 games four times and averaged 29 victories a season. He still holds the all-time records for games won (511), games started (818), complete games (751), innings pitched (7,377) and 30-game-winning seasons (5). No other pitcher is close in any category. He never earned more than $5,000 in a single year.

Cy Young was traded after the 1898 season, then returned to the city to play for Cleveland's American League entry from 1909-1911, still a dominant pitcher. The year after his death, baseball established the Cy Young Award, given annually to the outstanding pitcher in each league.

The Cleveland 200

HONORABLE & DISHONORABLE MENTIONS

SAMUEL CLARK AIKEN The first pastor of Old Stone Church.
DUDLEY PETER ALLEN & FAMILY Distinguished surgeons.
SHERLOCK ANDREWS Father of the Cleveland Bar Association.
SIDNEY ANDORN Columnist, society writer, critic.
MAY HILL ARBUTHNOT Celebrated children's author.
ALFRED ARTHUR Founder of Cleveland School of Music.
SAMUEL AUSTIN Created Austin Company "design-build" method.
EARL AVERILL Indians' slugger of the 1930s.
JIM BACKUS Mr. Magoo!
EDWARD MOSE BAKER Founder of the Federation of Jewish Charities.
ELBERT H. BAKER Founder of modern *Cleveland Plain Dealer.*
JOSEPH BARBER First mayor of Ohio City.
OHIO COLUMBUS BARBER The Match King.
GIOVANNI BARICELLI Heart specialist and Italian community leader.
CLAUDE BECK Pioneer heart surgeon.
JOHANN HEINRICH BECK Conductor-composer.
JULES BELKIN Jules rules Cleveland's popular music concert scene.
JESSE GROVER BELL Founder of Bonne Bell cosmetics company.
GEORGE HARRISON BENDER Influential Republican senator.
HALLE BERRY Television and film actress; starred with Eddie Murphy and married to Dave Justice, both briefly.
WILLIAM BINGHAM Oil, finance, industry. Big money. Big family.
MORRIS BLACK Founded Lindner Company, later Sterling-Lindner-Davis; co-founder of the Civic League.
ERNEST BLOCJ Composer/conductor/ music professor.
CHARLES BOEHM Hungarian Catholic monsignor, established St. Elizabeth's, first Hungarian Catholic Church in the United States.
JAMES BOLLES Progressive rector of Trinity Cathedral.
LOU BOUDREAU Player-manager star of '48 Indian champions.
RENA BLUMBERG Cleveland civic activist and media personality.
EDWARD BLYTHIN Noted jurist; Sam Sheppard trial.
ERNEST BOHN First national expert on public housing.
JAMES A. BOHANNON Carling Brewery & Peerless Motor Car owner.
BONE, THUGS & HARMONY Quintuple platinum rap singers.
JOHN BRECK Founder of Brecksville.
JACK BREEN Innovative Sherwin-Williams CEO.
WILLIAM BRETT The nation's foremost librarian.

JOSEPH BRIGGS Conceived and implemented system for free home delivery of mail, first in Cleveland, then nationally.
JACK BUCK National TV sports announcer; Hall of Fame.
FRANK BUNTS Co-founder of Cleveland Clinic.
JESSE BURKETT In 1995, Eddie Murray led one of the finest hitting teams in baseball history with a .323 average. Exactly 100 years earlier, Jesse Burkett led the Cleveland Spiders, hitting exactly a hundred points higher, .423; named to the Hall of Fame in 1946.
EDGAR BYER Liberal activist and defender of taxpayers' rights.
JOSEPH CAHOON Early settler of Dover Township.
ROBERT CALFEE Co-founder of Calfee, Halter & Griswold.
ERIC CARMEN Rock-n-roll star; leader of the Raspberries.
CARNEY BROTHERS James and John; west side business leaders, real estate owners, respected Democrat party leaders and office holders.
AUSTIN CARR Notre Dame All-American was Cavs' 1st star player.
GENE CARROLL Host of wonderfully terrible *Gene Carroll Show.*
JOE CAVOLI Longtime restaurateur.
ALBINA CERMAK Social activist and 1st woman candidate for mayor.
MILDRED CHADSEY First municipal housing commissioner.
TRACI CHAPMAN Popular music singing star.
JOE CHARBONEAU Super Joe was Tribe's one-year wonder.
STANLEY CIEMNOCZOLOWKSI Businessman and community leader.
NETTIE CLAPP First woman elected to Ohio House of Representatives.
CARRIE CLIFFORD Most active woman in the Niagara Movement.
JOSEPH COLE Good businessman, bad newspaperman.
CONWAY FAMILY Successful in multiple business ventures over several generations; pioneer micro-brewmeisters.
TIM CONWAY Ubiquitous funny man on film and TV.
JOHN T. CORRIGAN Untouchable chief prosecutor for over 20 years.
DAN COUGHLIN Popular columnist, sports commentator & humorist.
THOMAS COUGHLIN Vista Communications founder; philanthropist.
JACOB COX President of Cleveland Twist Drill; set national standards with innovative employee relations policies.
LILLIAN CRAIG Co-founder of National Welfare Rights Organization.
CLARENCE CRANE Candy mogul invented the Life Saver.
JEDEDIAH CROCKER Early settler of Rockport area.
ROBERT CROSSER Populist congressman for 38 years.
GLENN CURTIS Pioneer aviator: historic Cleveland to Put-In-Bay flight.
PAT DAILEY Cleveland's leading troubadour for decades.
BYRON DALTON Architect; founder of Dalton & Dalton
HARRY E. DAVIS Crusading black political activist.
HARRY L. DAVIS Four term mayor; Governor of Ohio (1920-1922).
RUSSELL H. DAVIS Leading black historian.
EDWARD DEBARTOLO Youngstown retail titan; gave Ed, Jr. the San Francisco 49'ers as birthday present. Billionaire businessman. Nice dad.

GARY DEE The bad boy founder of modern Shock Talk Radio.
ALEXANDER DEMAIORIBUS Longtime Republican party leader.
JAMES DEMPSEY Co-founder of Squires, Sanders & Dempsey law firm.
LOUIS DePAOLO "Mayor of Little Italy."
H. K. DEVEREUX Champion harness racer.
E. MANDEL DE WINDT Eaton Corp. CEO led business community's civic efforts for 2 decades; Cleveland Tomorrow prime mover.
HARRISON DILLARD Four-time Olympic gold medalist.
HENRY EATON Founder/chairman of Dix & Eaton PR firm.
JOSEPH ORIEL EATON, JR. Founder of Eaton Corp.
LUKE EASTER Indian slugger hit Cleveland's longest home run (478 ft.).
HARRY EASTMAN Judge created nation's model juvenile system.
HARLAN ELLISON Best-selling science fiction writer, author of 62 books; co-creator of TV shows *Twilight Zone* and *Star Trek.*
RUTH EINSTEIN Jewish Community Leader.
ERNST BROTHERS Alvan and Theodore became Ernst & Ernst. If you don't know who these guys are, you don't have any money.
JOE ESZTERHAUS The highest paid Hollywood screenwriter ever; as *Plain Dealer* reporter in 1969, broke My Lai massacre story.
DINA REES EVANS Longtime director of Cain Park Theater.
CHARLES FARRAN Led Griswold-Eshelman ad firm to prominence.
THOMAS FAWICK Prolific automotive inventor.
THE FEIGHANS Francis and Ed: both popular Democratic congressman.
SERENO PECK FENN Sherwin-Williams co-founder: YMCA patron.
HARRY FIGGIE Feisty founder and leader of A-T-O conglomerate.
RUTH FINLEY Clairvoyant author and ouija boarder early in 20th century.
BILL FITCH Cav's first successful coach.
SYLVESTER FLESHEIM Founded Master Builders.
LENNY FORD Browns' Hall-of-Fame defensive end in 50s.
CLAUD FOSTER Inventor of auto shock absorber and Gabriel horn.
GERDA K. FREEDHEIM Civic activist and philanthropist.
CLAIRE FREEMAN Led CMHA recovery.
JAMES R. GARFIELD Distinguished lawyer was 15 when his father was assassinated, carried on nobly in local, state and federal service.
CHARLES GARVIN First black doctor in the U. S. Army (World War I).
JOHN GILL Contractor built Terminal Tower, Hanna Building, theaters.
HENRY J. GERSTENBERGER Eminent pediatrician built foundation for the modern Rainbow Babies and Children's Hospital.
CHESTER GILLESPIE Leading civil rights attorney; NAACP leader.
FRANK GINN Partner in Blandin, Rice & Ginn (later Jones, Day); Cleveland's most accomplished corporate lawyer.
THOMAS GIRDLER President of Republic Steel: staunch labor opponent.
FRED GLOVER Cleveland Baron's star and fan favorite.
SOLOMON GOLDMAN Internationally known Zionist leader.
ZOLTAN GOMBOS Hungarian community leader, editor and publisher.

BILL GORDON Smoochie legend in local radio.
JOSEPH T. GORMAN CEO of TRW; international business VIP; advisor to Presidents. Very big mover. Very big shaker.
FREDERICK GOTTWALD Artist; co-founder of the Art Club.
JOEL GREY Stage and screen star; Cleveland Playhouse alumnus.
MOSES GRIES Temple leader and proponent of Reform Judaism.
FRED GRIFFITH Endearing and enduring host of *Morning Exchange*.
LOU GROZA Football Hall of Famer Lou the Toe.
VIRGINIA DARLINGTON GREEN Champion of children and schools.
DANNY GREENE Maverick gangster was legendary for narrow escapes---all except last car bomb attempt in 1977.
BELL GREVE Pioneer social worker.
LINDA THAYER GUILFORD Founder of Miss Guilford's School; among most respected educators in city's history.
TIM HAGAN Longtime county commissioner and populist spokesman.
EDGAR HAHN Hahn, Loeser & Parks ancestor; expert in financial law.
T. P. HANDY Leading 19th century financier and philanthropist.
TOM HANKS Playhouse graduate; winner of 2 Academy Awards.
STEPHEN HARKNESS The original big money behind Standard Oil (can you imagine a time when John D. Rockefeller needed a loan?)
LUTE HARMON Founder, publisher of *Cleveland Magazine*.
COBURN HASKELL Invented the modern golf ball.
ELIZABETH HAUSER Women's activist, author and leading suffragette.
JAMES HAWKEN Educator; founder of Hawken School in 1915.
JOHN HAY Distinguished statesman; Secretary of State.
HIRAM HAYDN Pastor of Old Stone Church for over 25 years.
MAX S. HAYES Leading American socialist. *Citizen* editor.
WILLIAM HAYWARD Co-founder of Cleveland Grays in 1837.
CHARLES HEARD Noted architect: Central HS, Old Stone Church.
MICHAEL HEATON Widely quoted Minister of Culture.
JOSEPH HEINEN Store clerk founded the Heinen's supermarket chain.
HERMAN HELLERSTEIN Renowned cardiologist. Was among first liberators of Nazi concentration camps; Holocaust scholar and activist intentionally raised six children, one for each million Jews lost.
EDWARD HENNIG First Cleveland Olympian, Hennig starred in the 1904 games in St. Louis, winning two gymnastic gold medals.
SISTER HENRIETTA Tireless social worker for the Sisters of Charity.
THOMAS HERBERT World War I aviation hero; governor of Ohio.
MARIA SMITH HERRICK One of Cleveland's earliest women activists, writer/editor; co-founded Female Moral Reform Society.
IRENE HICKOX Founder, principal at Cleveland's 1st girls' school.
EDWIN HIGBEE Co-founder of Higbee's.
ALBERT M. HIGLEY Leading local building contractor.
EDWARD F. HOBAN Longtime Archbishop of Cleveland.
WILLIAM HOCKING Famous Cleveland resident artist.

JOSEPH HODGE "Black Joe" guided the Cleaveland's 1796 expedition.
HAL HOLBROOK Stage, screen and TV actor; *Mark Twain Tonight!*
ALLEN C. HOLMES Managing partner at Jones, Day; presided over vast expansion of firm. Civic leader.
ERIE HOPWOOD Co-founder American Society of Newspaper Editors.
KAREN HORN Bank One, Cleveland CEO. Leading area businesswoman.
NATHANIEL HOWARD *Cleveland News* editor and city historian.
JAMES HOYT 19th century developer helped create 1st neighborhoods.
FRABK HRUBY Patriarch of leading family of musicians.
JOSEPH HRUDKA Mr. Gasket.
WILLIAM HUNKIN Founder of Hunkin-Conkey Construction.
JANE EDNA HUNTER Founder of the Phyllis Wheatley Society.
ROBERT HUGHES Longtime county Republican party chairman.
GUSTAVUS HYDE Cleveland's first weatherman (1850s).
CHRISSY HYNDE Lead rock singer with the Pretenders.
JOSEPHINE SAXTON IRVIN Spokeswoman for women's rights.
PERRY JACKSON Honored legislator, prosecutor, councilman, judge.
VIC JANOWICZ Star athlete; Heisman Trophy winner.
SHOELESS JOE JACKSON Only rookie in baseball history to hit over .400 (Cleveland, 1911); traded; banned after 1919 Black Sox scandal.
ELIZA JENNINGS Friend to the elderly, children, indigent and infirm, endowed the Eliza Jennings Home and the Children's Aid Society.
LEVI JOHNSON Pioneer Great Lakes shipbuilder.
THOMAS JONES Distinguished lawyer; co-founder of modern Jones, Day.
MORITZ JOSEPH Patriarch of Joseph & Feiss clothing manufacturer.
PAT JOYCE Tavern owner extraordinaire.
JAMIL KAIM Lebanese community leader; founded Aitaneet Brotherhood.
ISADOR KALISCH First Cleveland rabbi; co-editor of *Minhag America.*
MAX KALISH Internationally renown sculptor.
SAMMY KAYE "Swing and sway with Sammy Kay," big band leader.
HENRY GEORGE KELLER Famous naturalist artist.
CLARK KELLOGG St. Joseph's HS star, NBA player, TV sports analyst.
FRANK H. KELLY Founder of Sterling Plate Glass, glazed landmarks.
MARIETTA KELLY Co-founder of HELP, model children's organization.
WOODS KING World War II hero and patron of Mounted Police.
JOSIAH KIRBY Yacht Club commodore became famous stock swindler.
STANLEY KLONOWSKI Polish American banker and philanthropist.
TIHAMER KOHANJI National Hungarian American leader; editor and publisher of *Szabadsag*, largest Hungarian newspaper in the U. S.
LAZAR KRIVOKAPIC First Clevelander of Serbian descent (@1891).
THEODORE KUNDTZ Furniture maker and community leader.
CHICO KYLE St. Ignatius HS football coach's teams hold six state championships and two national titles.
HENRY LaCONTI Founder of the Agora.
FRANK LANE Reviled Indians' GM dismantled team in late 1950s.

JOHN LANIGAN Most listened to radio personality over two decades.
FRANK LAUSCHE Cleveland mayor, governor and senator respected for integrity and programs encouraging racial and ethnic harmony.
DANTE LAVELLI Legendary "Gluefingers, " Browns' Hall of Famer.
ROBERT LEACH Cleveland's first black physician.
CARL LENHART Leading Cleveland surgeon and medical researcher.
FANNIE LEWIS Outspoken council member and neighborhood activist.
FRANKLIN "WHITEY" LEWIS Sports editor of the *Cleveland Press.*
MIKE LEWIS Fabled local toastmaster and humorist.
ISAAC LEISY Founder of largest family-owned brewery.
AL LERNER Self-made billionaire businessman and wily deal broker.
EDDIE LEVERT Member of the O'Jays, leading Motown singers.
PETER LEWIS Progressive insurance mogul.
NATHAN LOESER Hahn, Loeser founder; patron of Mt. Sinai Hospital.
ANGELO LONARDO Mafia leader Big Ange traded gangland secrets for leniency; his testimony dismantled Cleveland mob.
DAVID LONG Cleveland's first practicing physician, leading early citizen.
TONY LOPARDO Accomplished CEO of Fineline Printing.
AL LOPEZ Hall-of-Fame Cleveland Indians manager in early 1950s.
GEORGE "JIGGS" LOSTEINER Trigger-happy crook and bank robber brought down in wild Bedford shootout (1918).
JOE LOVANO Grammy winning sax player; 1995 Jazzman of the Year.
ROELIF LOVELAND Award-winning columnist and war correspondent.
MIKE MALLEY Founded Malley's Chocolates. Mmmmm.
MILTON MALTZ The Big Buzzard at Malrite Communications.
MANDEL BROTHERS Joseph, Jack and Morton founded Premier company in 1940; noted for spectacular business success and extraordinary philanthropy. They should be in the *Cleveland 200*, but they are so private, we couldn't find out enough about them.
RED MANNING The radio voice of the Indians and Ohio State football.
ROBERT MANRY First solo sailor across Atlantic in *Tinkerbelle.*
WARD MARSH *Plain Dealer* film critic for over 50 years.
GLENN MARTIN Aviation pioneer and founder of Martin-Marietta.
MARY BROWN MARTIN First black School Board member.
JOSEPH MARTINEK Czech-American socialist author, poet and activist.
JOHN MacLEOD Nobel Prize winner in 1922 for insulin.
ERIC MATTOON Progressive educator; honored friend to needy.
MICKEY McBRIDE Colorful original owner of the Cleveland Browns.
NORMAN McGHEE Cleveland's first black stockbroker.
JIM McGINTY Popular Haymarket district councilman
IGGY McINTYRE Popular restaurateur, tavern owner.
JOHN T. McMYLER McMyler Company led world in heavy handling equipment; George Hulett was an employee.
GENERAL JOHN R. McQUIGG Spanish-American War hero; mayor.
BURGESS MEREDITH Leading character actor in film and TV.

HOWARD METZENBAUM Parking lot magnate; liberal U. S. senator.
RAY T. MILLER Powerful Democratic party boss for over 20 years.
WILLIAM MILLIKEN Masterful Cleveland Art Museum director.
NORMAN MINOR Celebrated criminal trial lawyer.
WILLIAM MINSHALL Longtime U. S. Congressman.
A. MALACHI MIXON III Big wheel at Invacare.
JACOB MOESSMER Founder of Paramount, city's only distillery.
ALAN MORITZ Father of modern forensic pathology.
MARION MOTLEY Hall of Fame fullback for Cleveland Browns.
JACOB MUELLER Noted German community leader.
EDWARD MURPHY Teamster labor boss.
M. E. MURPHY Founder of Murphy's Oil Soap.
GEORGE MYERS Hollenden Hotel barber parlayed friendship with VIP clients into political influence. By his own admission, Myers bribed a state legislator to insure Marc Hanna's election to the U. S. Senate.
JASON NASSAU Leading astronomer.
ROBERT NAVIN President of St. John College.
OZZIE NEWSOME The Wizard of Oz, Browns' star receiver.
LAURENCE NORTON Oglebay Norton executive; noted philanthropist.
MARY ROSE OAKAR Street-smart West Side congresswoman.
CHARLES OAKLEY Star forward for the New York Knicks.
FREDERICK ODENBACH Physics professor at John Carroll, Odenbach was the leading developer of the modern science of seismology.
JUNIOR O'MALLEY Colorful race track patron and raconteur.
PATRICK O'MALLEY Respected leader of the UAW and the AFL-CIO.
STEVE O'NEILL Co-founder of Leaseway Transport and Indians owner from 1961-73, helped keep franchise in Cleveland.
FRANK OSBORN Founder of Osborn Engineering.
SATCHEL PAIGE Legendary pitcher dazzled Indian fans in 1948.
SETH PAINE The founder of Painesville.
ARNOLD PALMER Golf's all-time favorite won Ohio Amateur titles, then National Amateur in 1954, playing out of Pine Ridge CC here.
ARTHUR LaRUE PARKER Founded Parker Appliance (Parker Hannifin).
SETH PEASE Surveyor provided the first map of the Western Reserve.
ELIHU PECK 19th century shipbuilder.
HARVEY PEKAR The Dark Man of comic books.
JOHN PENTON Founder of Penton Publishing in 1904.
BERYL PEPPERCORN Labor leader helped establish the Cleveland CIO.
RALPH PERK Fiery-haired 1970s Cleveland mayor.
ROGER PERKINS Oversaw the creation of Cleveland's water system.
GAYLORD PERRY Hall-of-Fame spitballer; Cy Young Award winner.
JAMES PICKANDS Co-founded Pickands, Mather & Company.
JIMMY PIERSALL Volatile Indians' 60s outfielder and fan favorite.
LIONEL PILE Founder of Hough Bakery. We miss you, Lionel.
RICHARD POGUE Jones, Day managing partner and community VIP.

ALBERT POLIZZI Powerful mob leader.
ISRAEL PORATH Leading Cleveland rabbi for over 40 years.
ALBERT S. PORTER County engineer and Democrat force for 30 years.
PHILIP PORTER *Plain Dealer* columnist helped start City Club Forum.
SALLY PREISAND First woman ordained as a rabbi in the United States.
FRANCIS PRENTISS Founder of Cleveland Twist Drill.
ORVILLE PRESCOTT Nation's leading literary critic for 25 years.
NEWBELL PUCKETT Pioneer in black history and folklore.
BERNICE PYKE First woman to serve as a Cleveland city administrator.
CHARLES RAMMELKAMP Renown physician and researcher, medical director at City Hospital (Metro Health Center) for 20 years.
RUFUS RANNEY Ohio Supreme Court jurist and 1st president of Ohio Bar.
JACK RAPER *Cleveland Press* columnist and political commentator.
JACOB REED Self-made millionaire; co-founder of Cleveland Associated of Colored Men. Leading citizen of early Cleveland black community.
RUTH REED Reputed turn-of-the-century clairvoyant.
THE REGO FAMILY Supermarket moguls: Stop-N-Shop 'til you drop.
TRENT RESNOR The hammer that drives Nine Inch Nails rock group.
JAMES FORD RHODES Leading national history scholar and author.
HARVEY RICE Co-founder of the firm that would become Jones, Day; victim of a mysterious murder that has never been solved.
EMIL RING Prominent Czech-born conductor and composer.
FRANK ROBINSON First black manager in major leagues.
LARRY ROBINSON The Diamond Man.
MOISHE ROCKMAN Financial wizard of Jewish crime syndicate.
WILLIAM GANSON ROSE Eminent Cleveland historian.
AL ROSEN Indians' all-star third baseman; last Tribe MVP in 1953.
MAX ROSENBLUM Founded 1st pro basketball team: Rosenblum Celtics.
BENJAMIN ROUSE Builder and philanthropist.
ELIJAH RUSSELL He founded Russell Township.
FRANK RYAN Math doctor was QB of Browns' 1964 NFL champions.
LUCIE SALHANY First female CEO of national TV network (FOX).
WILLIAM B. SANDERS Co-founder of Squire, Sanders & Dempsey.
JACOB SAPIRSTEIN Founder of American Greetings in 1906.
JOHN SCALISH HM Godfather of Cleveland mob for decades.
LEVI SCOFIELD Leading 19th century architect.
HERB SCORE Voice of the Indians for over quarter century.
LESTER SEARS Founder of Towmotor.
ROCCO SCOTTI Patriotic local tenor identified with national anthem.
EZRA SHAPIRO Jewish educational leader.
BRIAN SIPE QB and heart of Kardiac Kids, Browns' 1980 overachievers.
ARTHUR SKEEL Nationally recognized pediatrician.
ANTANAS SMETONA Former President of Lithuania, lived in Cleveland after Soviet takeover in 1940.

THE SMITH BROTHERS Not the cough drop guys: Albert, Kent and Vincent Smith founded Lubrizol.
ALLAN SMITH, JR. Famous portrait artist.
CURTIS LEE SMITH Dedicated civic leader in 50s and 60s.
HARRY C. SMITH Leading black political activist and crusader.
JOSEPH SMITH Mormon founder stopped here long enough to oversee construction of Kirtland Church, plans supposedly provided by God.
ANSON SMYTHE Co-founder of Cleveland Library system.
NIKOLAI SOKOLOFF First conductor of Cleveland Orchestra.
TORALD HERMAN SOLLMAN Father of modern pharmacology (not counting amateur Timothy Leary) authored *Laboratory Experiments in Pharmacology*. Revered Dean of Western Reserve Medical School.
WILLIAM SOMMER One of Cleveland's most esteemed artists.
AMOS"MAJOR" SPAFFORD produced 1st detailed map of Cleveland
RUFUS SPALDING Abolitionist lawyer and congressman.
ANSON STAGER Telegraphy pioneer with Jeptha Wade; his Millionaire's Row mansion is one of few survivors, serving as University Club site.
MICHAEL STANLEY Cleveland's favorite rock music performer.
ROBERT STEELE Judge convicted in murder-for-hire plot against wife.
TABITHA STILES The first girl born in the Western Reserve.
IRVING STONE Started creative division at American Greetings and spurred spectacular growth. Internationally appreciated philanthropist.
MARTIN STREIBLER Civil War hero.
BENJAMIN STRICKLAND Cleveland's first dentist (1835).
THE SULLIVAN FAMILY Frank founded RPM; Thomas guided coatings company to record growth and profit run to billion dollar plateau.
AMBROSE SWASEY Optic innovator; partner in Warner & Swasey.
JACK TANKERSLEY The pilot light at East Ohio Gas.
ART TATUM All-time jazz legend lived and worked here for a decade.
WILLIAM O. TAYLOR Champion chair-maker.
JOHN MICHAEL TEBELAK Composer of *Godspell.*
MANLY TELLO Crusading editor of the *Catholic Universe Bulletin.*
NATE THURMOND Leader of Cavaliers' Miracle at Richfield season.
CHARLES F. THWING "Prexy" was longtime president of Western Reserve University, honored author and educator.
MADISON TILLEY One of the area's 1st successful black entrepreneurs.
DANIEL R. TILDEN Anti-slavery crusader.
CLAYTON TOWNES First Cleveland City Manager in 1920s.
HELEN DEKAY TOWNSEND Editor of *Cleveland Town Topic*: 1st gossip rag for social set.
WILLIAM TREUHAFT Founder of Tremco.
HAL TROSKY Indians' star of the 1930s.
LOUIS TUCKERMAN Patriarch of family of physicians and activists.
WILLIAM VAN AKEN First mayor of Shaker Heights.
WILLIAM VIXSEBOXSE Established Cleveland's first art gallery.

HARRY VOLK Founder of Sun Newspapers.
THELMA VOTIPKA Acclaimed opera singer with the Met.
MARS WAGAR Member of one of Rockcliff's pioneer families.
NORMAN WAIN WIXY 1260 radio mastermind.
MAUDE WAITE First woman elected to Ohio Senate.
FRANK WALKER Eminent architect, co-founder of Walker & Weeks.
HAZEL WALKER First black school principal and black woman attorney.
WILLIAM O. WALKER Lifelong editor and publisher of the *Call & Post.*
GEORGE WALLACE Fire chief molded modern Fire Department.
JOE WALSH Rock star on his own and with the Eagles.
WORCESTER WARNER Co-founder of Warner & Swasey.
ABEL WARSHAWSKY "Buck" was noted impressionist artist.
THE WASMER FAMILY Lake Erie Screw; noted philanthropists.
LOU WASSERMAN Founder of MCA entertainment conglomerate.
BOB WATERFIELD Led Cleveland Rams to NFL title as a rookie QB in 1945; married for 25 years to screen siren Jane Russell.
ROBERT WEAVER Founder of Ferro Enameling Company
GUSTAV WEBER Eminent surgeon; co-founder of St. Luke's Hospital.
DON WEBSTER Perennial weatherman hosted syndicated *Big 5 Show.*
LENNY WEISS Car wash mogul and sole Jewish delegate to West Side.
ROBERT WELSH Respected president of St. Ignatius High School.
MOISHE WEXLER Lovable proprietor of Theatrical Grille.
CARL WEYGANDT Chief Justice of Ohio Supreme Court for 30 years.
SCOTT WEILAND Lead singer of Stone Temple Pilots.
THE WESTROPP SISTERS Founded Women's Federal Savings & Loan.
JOSH WHITE Folk singer/songwriter was mainstay of country-folk era; murdered by racist thugs.
SIDNEY WICK Business and society standout of noted local family.
AQUILA WILEY Civil War hero and decorated wartime administrator.
LENNY WILKENS Longtime Cavs' coach; NBA's all-time winner.
JOHN S. WILLEY Mayor during "Battle of the Bridge" dispute.
WALTER WILLS Funeral home founder, community leader.
MARIE WING Pioneer feminist; 1st female attorney, council member.
DEBRA WINGER Famed film actress; Academy Award nominee.
SAMUEL WISE President of ARCO and respected philanthropist.
PETER WITT Tom Johnson disciple and mass transit expert.
ROBERT WOODS Co-founder of Telarc, respected production studio.
CONSTANCE WOOLSON 19th century novelist.
LOIS WYSE Wyse Advertising president and best-selling author.
FRANKIE YANKOVIC World's most famous accordion player.
SEAN YOUNG Film actress and tabloid personality.
STEPHEN YOUNG U. S. Senator.
CHARLES ZIMMERMAN Decorated Civil War commander.

THE CLEVELAND 200
Alphabetical Index

NAME - RANK (CATEGORY - PAGE)